YOUR MONEY MATTERS

OTHER BOOKS BY JONATHAN D. POND

YOUR MONEY MATTERS

21 Tips for

Achieving

Financial

Security

in the

21st Century

JONATHAN D. POND

G. P. PUTNAM'S SONS · NEW YORK

This publication is designed to provide accurate and authoritative
information in regard to the subject matter covered. In publishing this
book, neither the author nor the publisher is engaged in rendering legal,
accounting, or other professional service. If legal advice or other expert
assistance is required, the services of a competent professional
should be sought.

G. P. Putnam's Sons
Publishers Since 1838
a member of
Penguin Putnam Inc.
375 Hudson Street
New York, NY 10014

Library of Congress Cataloging-in-Publication Data

Pond, Jonathan D.
Your Money Matters: 21 tips for achieving financial security in the 21st
century / by Jonathan D. Pond.
p.   cm.
Includes index.
ISBN 0-399-14569-9
1. Finance, Personal.   2. Investments.   I. Title.   II. Title:
Your Money Matters.
HG179.P5559   1999   99-39267 CIP
332.024'01—dc21

Printed in the United States of America

1   3   5   7   9   10   8   6   4   2

This book is printed on acid-free paper. ∞

Book design by Tanya Maiboroda

To my wife, Lois,

and our three puddles,

Elizabeth, Laura, and Emily

ACKNOWLEDGMENTS

The people who are most responsible for this book are the many individuals and families whom I have had the pleasure of meeting over the past decade—in person and on television and radio. They have been eager to share with me their financial concerns and know-how. These discussions have enabled me to prepare a book that I think reflects the pressing financial concerns and hopes that we all share as we embark on the 21st century. I thank each and every one of you.

The insights of Jeremy Katz, my editor at Putnam, were always helpful. I'm lucky to have an editor who agrees that money can be funny. Fortunately for Jeremy (not me), his personal finances are in much better condition than his handwriting. The advice of Peter Ginsberg, my agent, is also gratefully acknowledged. I just wish he would follow my advice and quit leasing cars.

Much appreciation also to Richard Merrill, our webmaster, who, I'm sure you will agree, has built a web site that will enhance immensely the value of *Your Money Matters*.

This book would not exist without the support and contributions of my assistant, Pauline Kelly. If you think writing a book might be trying for an adult ADD author, that's nothing compared to the demands on she who makes sure the book is up to her uncompromisingly high standards.

Authors' families suffer immensely. The spouses inevitably think they've made an error in matrimonial judgment. Their children must feel it's an accident of birth. I'll leave it to other authors to chronicle the travails that inevitably befall their loved ones. I'll just thank my family yet again for their patience.

■ Contents

■ Introduction

The New Century holds a lot of promise—for working-age people striving to achieve financial security, for retirees wanting to make their golden years truly golden, and for younger generations who are entering an era of unprecedented economic opportunity.

Your Money Matters focuses on the most important financial matters that you'll need to attend to in the 21st century. Each of the 21 chapters that follow provides you with suggestions for meeting the challenges and taking advantage of the opportunities of the 21st century. Along the way, I hope you'll be entertained as well as informed. Who says money has to be serious? If you look back on some of the things you've done with money in the past, you've got to be amused.

No matter what your age, income, wealth (or lack of wealth), and financial know-how might be, *Your Money Matters* contains a lot of useful guidance. It doesn't waste your time with boring technical details. Rather, it gives you sound advice that you can understand and, more important, put into action to improve your financial future. It also offers a healthy dose of humor, because money—particularly our relationship with money—really is quite amusing.

The New Century offers unprecedented opportunities for you to enhance your life. Medical advances will improve the quality of life and begin to slow the rise in medical-care costs that have become such a large item in the family budget. Technology will make our lives easier and more productive. The Internet will make information readily available for virtually limitless pursuits, including information that will help you improve your financial future.

Speaking of the Internet, you'll notice many references to my web site throughout *Your Money Matters*. Any time you would like more information or the latest guidance on any subject that has a web site cross-reference, just follow the instructions to go directly to the topic

FINANCIAL GUIDANCE JUST FOR YOU, NO MATTER WHERE YOU ARE IN YOUR FINANCIAL LIFE

Age
- If you're just starting out in your career, which retirement plans are best for you? (See page 199.)
- If you're in the middle of your career, are you on the right track to achieving financial security? (See page 188.)
- If you're focusing on retirement, you'll need to address some crucial matters before you retire. (See page 193.)
- If you're retired, are you withdrawing too much money from your retirement nest egg? (See page 220.)

Income
- If you're like most people and are on the low end or middle of the income totem pole, you may need some advice on building up your savings. (See page 11.)
- If you've got so much income that you're in one of the top brackets, there are a lot of ways to whittle down your tax bill. (See page 177.)
- If you earn enough income by mid-January each year to put you up in the top tax bracket, Uncle Sam loves you, and will love you even more when you die if you don't do something now to reduce estate taxes. (See page 249.)

that interests you. For example, if you want to buy a house, my web site will provide you with extensive guidance. If you want the latest information on the Roth IRA (Congress has been altering or clarifying the rules almost monthly), you'll find it on my web site. While *Your Money Matters* itself provides all the information you need to thrive in the New Century, the combination of the book and my continually updated web site can become your essential and up-to-date resource for personal financial information.

Wealth
- If you've got more loans than investments, make it a temporary affliction by devising a plan to put your loans on a diet. (See page 73.)
- If you're just beginning to accumulate some savings, there are ways to invest a small amount of money just like the big pension funds invest their billions. (See page 131.)
- If you're on the road to building up a good-sized portfolio, tax-efficient investing can put more money in your pocket. (See page 171.)
- If you've got so much money that your calculator doesn't have enough digits to record it, you're going want to take advantage of some great estate-planning techniques that can reduce taxes and benefit you, your heirs, and your favorite charities. (See page 247.)

Financial knowledge
- If you don't know a stock from a bond, you can still become a smart mutual fund investor. (See page 96.)
- If you want to become more savvy about financial matters, find out about the best investments for the New Century. (See page 163.)
- If you fancy yourself a pretty knowledgeable financial person, I'll bet you can still benefit from some investment strategies that many Wall Street pros don't understand. (See page 166.)

21 QUESTIONS

No matter what your current financial situation (or predicament) might be, you will find a lot of useful, sensible guidance in this book. To give you an idea of the areas that it covers, I have included below 21 questions that I am frequently asked by audiences across the country.

If you need help on any of them right away, simply go to the page indicated.

1. Technology stocks, particularly Internet stocks, have taken off. Is it too late to invest in this area? (See page 149.)
2. We're saving for our children's education. I've been hearing about a new tuition savings program that sounds like a great way to invest for college and save on taxes at the same time. What is it? (See page 142.)
3. A lot of people are saying that there will be no Social Security when baby boomers retire. What's your opinion? (See page 188.)
4. The Roth IRA sounds like a great thing, but I don't understand it. (See page 201.)
5. I love to trade stocks on the Internet, and I save a lot of money to boot. I'm almost afraid to ask your opinion about trading on the Internet. (See page 271.)
6. Why should I make extra payments against my mortgage when I can earn more by investing the money instead? (See page 80.)
7. Index funds have been doing very well lately. Should I invest in them even though they never beat the indexes? (See page 168.)
8. There are so many different retirement plans. Which are best? (See Chapter 16.)
9. One of my mutual funds lost money last year when the stock market was up. Should I sell it? (See page 148.)
10. Do deferred annuities make sense for a retiree? (See page 126.)
11. I've heard that investment allocation doesn't matter anymore. Should I just put all my money into big-cap U.S. growth stocks? (See page 110.)

12. How can I teach my children to be more responsible about money? (See page 31.)

13. My stocks and stock funds are way up. It can't go on like this forever. Should I get out of stocks before they drop? (See page 153.)

14. I'm about to retire. How much can I safely withdraw from my retirement funds and not have to worry about running out of money? (See page 217.)

15. What are "tax-efficient" investments, and should I be investing in them? (See page 171.)

16. How much can I transfer to my children without having to pay any estate taxes? Is there anything I should be doing now to reduce my estate? (See Chapter 20.)

17. In planning my future, is it safe to assume that stocks will continue to grow at a 12 to 15 percent annual rate? (See page 189.)

18. Should I get long-term care insurance? (See page 57.)

19. How can I give cash gifts to my children (to whittle down my estate) without spoiling them? (See page 254.)

20. Some of my friends are either borrowing on margin or taking out home equity loans to increase their investments. Is this a sensible thing to do? (See page 67.)

21. Which industries are likely to do best over the next decade? (See Chapter 13.)

I wrote *Your Money Matters* because your money does matter a great deal. By following the suggestions in this book, I hope you will begin the New Century with the confidence of knowing that you're always making progress in your financial life and that you'll be able to achieve your financial dreams.

EXCLUSIVE READER WEB SITE

In addition to my web site cross-references throughout this book, you can take advantage of my private web site to receive my up-to-date commentary on economic and investment conditions as well as timely mutual fund information. To access my private site, just click on:

http://jonathanpond.com/YMM2000.html

Chapter 1

THE DIFFERENCE BETWEEN A RICH PERSON AND A POOR PERSON IS JUST TWO CENTS

> Earn a little, spend a
> little—less.
>
> *John Stevenson*

The difference between a rich person and a poor person is just two cents. This wonderful expression migrated to our shores along with the flood of Eastern European immigrants: "The poor person earns a dollar and spends $1.01 while the rich person earns a dollar and spends 99 cents." That two-cent difference may not be the difference between wealth and just getting by, but the sentiment is right on target.

WHAT DO YOU WANT YOUR MONEY TO DO FOR YOU?

All of us share some common financial goals in life. Keep them in mind as you plan your financial future, because they are the "carrots" that motivate you do the right things with your money throughout your adult life. For most everyone, financial security means being able to meet life's big expenses such as:

➤ Buying a home
➤ Educating the kids or ourselves
➤ Being able to retire with enough money to be comfortable and not run low on money during our retirement years

➤ Surviving whatever curveballs life throws our way, like unemployment and disability

It's obvious that all these goals have one thing in common: they require money—a lot of it.

For more guidance on deciding what financial goals are most important to you and how to develop strategies to achieve them, click on:

http://jonathanpond.com/general.financialgoals.htm

Good record keeping will help you plan your financial future as well as avoid a lot of record keeping hassles along the way. Tips and work sheets on personal record keeping can be found by clicking on:

http://jonathanpond.com/general.recordkeeping.htm

The Four Legal Ways to Achieve Financial Security

There are four legal ways to accumulate the kind of money that's necessary to achieve financial security. Unfortunately, this is not the kind of buffet lunch or smorgasbord that allows you to select anything that meets your fancy. Alas, most of us will have to pick number four.

1. **Marry it.** This has considerable appeal since it permits you to become wealthy at a relatively young age (although you can never be too old to marry a few million dollars). There are some impediments to this strategy, however. First, you might be married already. If so, and you didn't strike it rich at the altar, following this strategy could be messy. Second, if you're eligible, albeit impecunious, finding someone with big bucks who will marry you is an uphill battle. It's been my experience that people with lots of money usually like to hang out with others who are similarly encumbered with great wealth, but maybe that's just my bad luck. It never hurts to try. As your mother or father undoubtedly once told you, it's just as easy to love a rich person as a

poor person. (Perhaps you should some day ask Mom [or Dad] why she didn't follow her own advice. If either of your parents had followed that advice, you might benefit from the next wealth-creation strategy.)

2. **Inherit it.** Several trillion dollars will be inherited over the first two decades of the New Century. Too bad a good-sized portion of that money isn't going to find its way into your coffers. As luck would have it, the ones who are going to receive most of the inherited money are already pretty well off through gifts, trusts, and other wealth-transfer techniques. (See Chapter 20.) Nevertheless, you might be on the receiving end of a more modest inheritance. Don't get too excited. First, you've got to wait to receive it, and sometimes it can be a long, long wait. Your benefactor could well live into his or her 90s or later. You might get that inheritance just in time to help pay *your* nursing home bills. Second, and you have me to blame for this, I've been telling every retired person I can find (except my parents and my in-laws) to spend it all before they die. I regret to report that your parents and everyone else's are very receptive to that idea.

3. **Win the lottery.** This is a strategy that all too many people are staking their financial futures on. (In my home state of Massachusetts, the average lottery spending per person—man, woman, and child—is over $500 a year. What a waste.) True, you can achieve lifetime financial security if you hit the big one, but you might want to devise a backup plan just in case.

POND'S LAWS OF LOTTERIES

1. Your chances of winning the lottery are less than the chances that you'll be struck by lightning at the precise moment you're being kidnapped by foreign terrorists.

2. Anyone with a winning scratch ticket will use said winnings to purchase additional scratch tickets until such time as he or she is in possession of only losing tickets.

3. The quickest way to determine how many of your relatives and acquaintances are in need of immediate financial assistance is to win the lottery.

4. **Spend less than you earn.** Last, if you aren't going to marry it, you're not going to inherit it, and you have a sneaking suspicion that you're not going to win the lottery, the only other legal way I can conjure up to achieve financial security is by spending less than you earn. Sadly, this takes work and sacrifice, indeed decades of work and sacrifice. I could candy coat it by saying that this is the noblest way to achieve financial security. But that hardly takes the sting out of it. The facts are clear. People who don't get into the habit of living beneath their means—saving regularly—will probably never achieve financial security. Of course, once the money is saved it needs to be invested wisely. And, if you've set a financial target that exceeds mere financial security, then you need to create wealth. It isn't as mysterious as it may seem.

How Wealth Is Created

Perhaps you aspire to exceed the goal of achieving lifetime financial security. Perhaps you want to create wealth that will benefit future generations, be they heirs or charities. Or, perhaps you just want to be rich, stinking rich. If so, here's a short lesson on how wealth has been created in the past and how it will undoubtedly be created in the future.

If you truly want to create wealth, you need to have a partner in your financial endeavors. Your partner will provide you with the financial backing that has been utilized by generations of multimillionaires. You'll be surprised to learn that your partner is Uncle Sam. The tax laws provide big breaks to certain kinds of investments—not oil wells or luxury hotels; these breaks are bestowed on the garden-variety investments you already understand. All of them take advantage of one or both of these tax incentives:

> **POND'S LAW OF FINANCIAL SUCCESS**
>
> Financial success is less dependent on how much you earn than it is on how much you save.

1. The ability to have investment profits taxed as capital gains. Capital gains tax rates are at least 30 percent lower, and can be as much as 50 percent lower, than the rate at which other types of investment income are taxed, including interest and dividends.
2. The ability to permanently postpone capital gains taxes. There are ways for assets to be transferred at death to heirs (or to charity) with no capital gains taxes due.

Keeping your generous uncle's tax incentives in mind, here are the ways that wealth is created:

➤ **Owning individual stocks.** Most rich families got that way by buying individual stocks and holding onto them for the rest of their lives. So long as they hold onto the stock, they never pay capital gains taxes, even though the stock probably rises in value a great deal over the decades. Then, when they die, their heirs receive the stock with a "stepped up basis," which means that they generally inherit the stock at a tax value computed at the date of the dearly departed's death. So, for example, Great-aunt Annie paid $2 per share for her IBM stock several decades ago, but her heirs inherit it with a stock value of $150. If they turn around and sell it right away for $150, they won't owe any capital gains taxes. If they hold onto the IBM stock and pass it on to the next generation, they, like their forebears, will never pay capital gains on the stock.

➤ **Owning investment real estate.** Investment real estate—like apartments and small office or industrial buildings—works a lot like stock. You enjoy rising income through increased rents and don't pay any capital gains taxes as long as you hold onto the property. If you eventually pay off the mortgage, you could end up with a lot of income from the property. Investment real estate is without doubt one of the best ways for average people to create a lot of wealth.

➤ **Starting a business.** This is the long shot, but being your own boss is the American dream. If you're successful, you can earn a lot of money along the way and, if you're lucky as well as successful, you'll be able to sell the business for a lot more money. Like individual stocks and real estate, your business can grow in value free of tax until you sell it.

Another advantage of stocks, real estate, and a family business— if you do sell, the capital gains taxes are usually only 20 percent of the profit.

FOOD FOR THOUGHT: THE THREE BASIC MONEY GROUPS

The fundamental money challenge we face throughout our adult lives is balancing the three basic money needs and desires. Just as good nutritional health requires spreading your food intake among the basic food groups, good financial health requires distributing your money outgo among the three basic spending groups.

1. **Necessities.** The need to provide for the health and welfare of yourself and the others who are dependent on you.
2. **Luxuries.** The desire to reward yourself by acquiring various creature comforts.
3. **Saving for the future.** The need to set aside a portion of your current income for supporting yourself in retirement as well as coping with any financial disruptions that may occur before you retire or during those golden years.

While these three spending groups, like the food groups, seem to be pretty straightforward, they're easy to confuse. For instance, I like to think I can meet my daily requirement for dairy products by eating ice cream, but my nutritionist friend disagrees. With the money groups, it's easy to confuse basic needs (necessities) with creature comforts (luxuries). We all do that. Some of my car-hound friends have come to believe that a $45,000

POND'S LAW OF YARD SALES
Everything that's bought at a yard sale eventually ends up in the purchasers' yard sales.

car falls under category #1, necessities that provide for basic family needs. But, since $15,000 to $20,000 will buy a perfectly decent new car, wouldn't it be better for them to view the excess they spend on their high-priced wheels as part of category #2, luxuries?

Distinguishing between Needs and Wants

We all struggle to distinguish between needs (necessities) and wants (luxuries), and this confusion risks shortchanging category #3, saving for the future. Persuading yourself that you really need something is often the end result of convincing yourself that some luxury has become a necessity. The more you think about acquiring something, the more you'll realize that you've got to have it. If the item goes on sale during your deliberations, forget it. For example, if that $250 cashmere sweater (it should come as no surprise that the first syllable of cashmere is cash) that was a luxury last month is marked down to $199.99, you're sunk. That sweater, which has preoccupied your thoughts, has become an absolute necessity, right up there with food and shelter.

We also deceive ourselves in category #3, saving for the future. We all like to believe we are saving for the future, but most of us aren't saving enough. For example, maximizing the amount you contribute to your employee savings plan, like a 401(k) plan or a 403(b) plan, will probably not provide enough money, when combined with Social Security, to retire in the style you'd like. If you also contribute to an IRA every year, you'll come a lot closer to realizing your retirement dreams assuming you start early enough. So don't delude yourself into thinking that your

> **Pond's Law of Markdowns**
>
> The more an item is marked down, the more someone will shift their feelings from wanting the item to needing the item. (At 60 percent off, you will not be able to sleep until you've bought it.)

> **Pond's Law of Profligacy**
>
> The longer you think about some nonessential luxury item, the more you will convince yourself that you absolutely, positively need to have it. Now.

5 percent annual 401(k) contribution along with a 2 percent employer match is going to put you on the road to financial nirvana. It won't.

IF YOU'RE JUST STARTING OUT OR YOU'RE A LATE STARTER

Do you recall seeing any of these headlines?

Recent Public Stock Offering Makes Multimillionaires out of Two Local Entrepreneurs

Microsoft Millionaires Are Driving up Local Home Prices

Twenty-Nine-Year-Old Whiz Kid Now Worth $300,000,000

Stock Market Gains Swell the Ranks of Millionaires

Neighbors Irked at Planned 40,000-Square-Foot Home

Depressing, aren't they? And these headlines are particularly depressing if you're just beginning to get your financial act together. The facts belie the headlines. While many people who have been saving and investing in the 1980s and 1990s have benefited greatly from the great bull market, a large proportion of Americans haven't made much headway in their financial lives. There are a lot of reasons why this is the case, but that's beside the point. If you're one of the many millions who have not yet made much, if any, progress toward a secure financial future, don't dwell on the past. Don't fret about your current financial situation. And above all don't be depressed by all the wealth that seems to be everywhere. Actually, the vast majority of "wealth" that you observe is not real wealth; it's conspicuous consumption. As was so aptly pointed out in the book *The Millionaire Next Door*, the wealthy don't tend to flaunt their wealth. It's the wannabe wealthy who like to show off what they *don't* have.

> ### POND'S LAW OF POCKET CASH
>
> Cash in your wallet will be spent twice as fast as you intend. For example, if you withdraw enough money from the ATM on Monday to last a week, it will be spent by Wednesday.

Saving what's required to achieve your financial dreams is daunting if you're just starting out in the work world and even more so if you're a late starter. But it's never too early or too late to start getting on track for financial security. Here are some pointers.

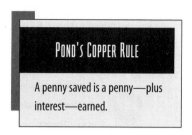

Pond's Copper Rule

A penny saved is a penny—plus interest—earned.

1. **Begin to save regularly.** Even if it's only $5 or $10 a week, begin to save on a regular basis. The best way to save is to never get your hands on the money in the first place. Have money deducted at regular intervals from your paycheck or bank account and invested in a retirement or investment account. Once you begin saving even a little bit, you'll find you like the feeling. By the way, don't convince yourself that there is no way you can save any money. You can, and you must. (See Chapter 2.)

2. **Invest your savings wisely.** While beginning a modest savings program is a big step, you should also learn about investing, because even small amounts of money can be invested: Don't convince yourself that because you only have a small amount of money, you can't invest it. You can. (See Chapter 9.)

3. **Pay down your debt.** Whether it's credit cards or student loans, you need to reduce your debt if you're going to make real headway in preparing for a secure financial future. If debt has been a problem in the past, for heaven's sake don't add to it. Devise a plan to get out of debt over the next few years. But don't use all of the money that you have left over to pay down debt. Save some of it, even if it will take you longer to pay off your loans. Paying off loans is a drag, but saving money regularly is good for the soul. Starting to accumulate even a small amount of savings will spur you on to great financial progress in the future. (See Chapter 7.)

4. **Obtain necessary insurance coverage.** If you haven't already, be sure to obtain sufficient insurance coverage to protect you and your family from the unexpected. As you begin to progress in your personal fi-

nances, there's nothing worse than losing years of hard-earned savings from some uninsured loss. (See Chapter 6.)

*No matter what your age, you can obtain more information on important first steps to
achieving financial security by clicking on:*

http://jonathanpond.com/general.startingout.htm

Chapter 2

LIVE BENEATH YOUR MEANS (WITHOUT DEPRIVING YOURSELF)

> A budget tells us what we can't afford, but it doesn't keep us from buying it.
>
> *William Feather*

Cutting expenses is never as difficult as one thinks. Like dieting, it's the thought of having to cut back that keeps us hungering for more — even when we aren't hungry. But just a cursory look at where your money goes will probably reveal several items that could be eliminated or reduced. If you're not saving enough, do you really have any choice? Try out a few simple and painless ways to cut back. Be sure to reward yourself by putting the savings somewhere where you can watch them grow.

DEVELOP A COST-CUTTING PLAN

Carl and Carla Cantsave, like many other couples in their 30s, haven't saved very much. But they're starting to worry. Instead of uttering the same old line, "There's no way we can afford to save," they've taken a closer look at where they're spending their money. They've come up with the following money-saving ideas:

Here are five areas where they think they can cut back.

	Weekly Savings
Take muffin and coffee to work rather than buying en route	$12
Bring lunch to work rather than go to a restaurant or deli	$22
Reduce lottery ticket purchases from $15 to $3 per week	$12
Quit using the cellular telephone to make unnecessary phone calls	$3
Reduce restaurant dining from three to two times per week	$26
Expected weekly savings	$75

If they can stick to their plan, the Cantsaves can begin saving without a great deal of personal deprivation. While $75 a week in savings may not sound like a lot, it adds up. Here's how much $75 per week amounts to over the years at an annual investment return of 8 percent:

1 Year	$4,000
3 Years	$13,000
5 Years	$24,000
10 Years	$60,000
20 Years	$192,000
30 Years	$488,000

Not bad, considering the small sacrifices Carl and Carla will have to endure. These savings accumulations assume that they'll maintain the $75 weekly savings level throughout. But they should be able to increase that amount over time as their incomes grow and their living expenses start to level out.

POND'S LAW OF MADISON AVENUE

Our culture teaches us that spending is good and living beneath your means is a crime against society.

SAVE YOUR RAISE

Here's an idea that used to be pretty commonplace but is now considered revolutionary: Save all or most of your annual raises. Saving a raise is a relatively painless way to add to your investments. For example, you'd like to increase the amount you contribute to your retirement savings plan at work, but you can't seem to come up with the extra money. However, the next time you get a raise, you will have extra money. So at the same time you get the raise, increase the percentage of your income that you put into your retirement savings plans.

> ### Pond's Law of Sales
>
> Nothing ever goes on sale because too many people want to buy the product.

Raise-Saver Par Excellence

A couple whom my parents had known since before I was born had just retired and were about to embark on a round-the-world cruise aboard the *QE2*. I was then a fledgling financial writer, and when they announced their trip I became concerned that these long-time family friends were going to blow their retirement nest egg on this trip. The husband was a teacher and the wife hadn't worked outside the home for decades, and a round-the-world cruise on the *QE2* costs about 10 buckets of money. I asked them point blank how they had come up with the money to pay for the trip. The husband said that a cruise like this had been something they had long wanted to do, so about 15 years before retirement he began saving his raises. Inflation was pretty high then; it was a struggle to keep the family spending in check. But they had their eyes on the prize. I was still concerned, because it seemed that they were spending all those savings on the cruise—savings that might be necessary later in life. He then told me how much he had accumulated just from saving his raises. "Accumulated" is the wrong word. He had "amassed" so much money that the tab for the *QE2* cruise was a drop in the bucket.

> ### Pond's Law of Raises
>
> Spending increases in anticipation of a raise at a rate that exceeds the amount of the raise eventually received.

21ˢᵗ CENTURY HALL OF SHAME

The Biggest Wastes of Money in the New Century

1. SUVs (they ought to call them SAVs, suburban assault vehicles)
2. Any TV set that costs more than $500
3. Day trading
4. Granite kitchens
5. Borrowing to invest
6. Designer label clothing for children
7. Courses that teach you how to get rich with no money
8. Credit card loans
9. Internet stocks
10. Lotteries

If you want to get serious about living beneath your means, help and ideas are just a click away:

http://jonathanpond.com/general.costcutting.htm

BIG TICKET ITEMS TELL A LOT

In counseling individuals and families over the years, I've found that how they handle big ticket items, particularly the home, is a reliable indicator of saving habits. I've talked with numerous singles and couples up and down the income ladder who, by middle age (middle age: *n.*, "anyone who is ten years older than you"), have accumulated a lot of retirement money, have even more money saved outside of their retirement plans, and have no debt. The vast majority of them have one thing in common: the value of their homes—or the amount of their rent—is way below what they could afford. One couple whom I met with recently had always had a modest income. But by careful saving and smart investing, they had accumulated $700,000 in retirement plan investments and another $200,000 in non-retirement investments. But their mortgage-free house was worth only a bit more than their annual income.

> ### POND'S LAW OF AIR FARE INSANITY
>
> No matter how hard you try to obtain the absolute lowest air-fare, the person sitting next to you on the plane paid less.

Another couple had enjoyed many years of six figure incomes, had paid off all their debt, had about $2,000,000 in investments—and a $175,000 house. If you applied the usual lending rules of thumb to this couple based on their income, they could afford a $700,000 house. A third example, a single person getting ready for retirement, was earning $50,000 per year, but was paying only $400 a month in rent—less than 10 percent of his income. He was 53 years old and had saved enough to be able to retire right then and there. It's hardly a coincidence that these people lived in housing that was way below what they could afford. Their modest housing expenses allowed them to accumulate large amounts of money. None of them had the slightest desire to trade up. By the way, none of them lived in shabby circumstances. They all had lovely homes in nice neighborhoods far from toxic waste dumps.

DREAM HOUSE DREAMERS

Let me contrast the above people with some others I've met. One couple in their late 40s had just bought their fourth house—their "dream house," they told me, although I suspect the first three houses were dream houses as well. Every time they traded up, they increased their mortgage. I know that trading up on your home is one of the American dreams. However, after almost 20 years of home "ownership," this couple had a higher mortgage than they did when they first bought. After 20 years of mortgage payments, they still had 30 years to go on their new mortgage. Their high spending ways were also reflected in other areas of their financial lives, notably two late model cars with fat car loans. This couple's two kids were about to enter college and financing those costs was going to be

---

> **POND'S LAW OF SPENDING RESTRAINT**
>
> You know you've got your financial act together if you spend the same percentage of your income between Thanksgiving and New Year's as you do between New Year's and Thanksgiving.

a challenge. But worse, their combined savings—retirement and otherwise—were less than their annual income. This family is leading the good life, but they're sacrificing their financial future in the process.

Why is it that some singles and families have made so much financial progress while others have not? It isn't just being a victim of circumstances. Certainly, some people are dealt tough cards in life and end up suffering financially as a result. But among people who have otherwise similar financial circumstances, who have the same income history and the same number of mouths to feed, the reason is as simple as how well—or how poorly—they have learned to distinguish among the three basic money groups described in Chapter 1: necessities, luxuries, and saving for the future. Those who have succeeded financially have, more than anything else, been able to distinguish between necessities and luxuries and have spent accordingly. Despite a growing income, the notion of buying trophy homes doesn't even enter their minds.

LESSONS FROM OUR PARENTS

Speaking of housing, why is it that our parents seemed so content that, once they bought a home, they wanted to stay in it? The notion of trading up to a more expensive, more expansive home is a relatively recent phenomenon. Within a few weeks of moving in to a new home, you're already planning to buy a bigger and more expensive home. It's this attitude of always wanting more and more and more that has caused a widespread financial malaise. We have so much to learn from our parents and grandparents, because, by and large, they were happy with what they had, even though they probably had a lot less than we do right now.

> **POND'S LAW OF THE DIVINE LIFE**
>
> To spend is human, but to save is divine.

THE POWER OF COMPOUNDING

There's nothing more powerful to your financial future than the power of compounding. You'll see in Chart #1 how much you can accumulate by investing $1,000 over various time periods, but an increasing savings rate is often more realistic than a level one. After all, over the years your income should increase and, hopefully, your living expenses will eventually settle down. So this chart also shows how much more you can accumulate by increasing your year-to-year savings rate by 5 or 10 percent. The amounts assume an annual investment return rate of 7½ percent.

- Rodney Roth is 25 years old and, for the first time, he can afford to put $2,000 away into an IRA. If he continues this for 35 years, how much will he have available for retirement from his IRA contributions? The answer, assuming that Rodney averages 7½ percent per year on his IRA investments, is $332,000. (According to the chart, he would have

		CHART #1	
	The Eighth Wonder of the World: Compound Growth		
		Starting with $1,000 and Increasing Year-to-Year Savings Rate by	
Number of Years	**Saving $1,000 Each Year**	**5%**	**10%**
5	$6,000	$7,000	$8,000
10	15,000	18,000	23,000
15	28,000	37,000	52,000
20	47,000	66,000	108,000
25	73,000	114,000	204,000
30	111,000	185,000	371,000
35	166,000	294,000	668,000
40	244,000	455,000	1,170,200

$166,000 had he invested $1,000 per year, but since he's planning to invest twice that, or $2,000, he will amass $332,000.)

- Peter and Penny Prince are 25 years from retirement and they're now at a stage when they can afford to start putting some serious money away. They figure they can save $5,000 this year and increase that savings rate by 5 percent each year thereafter. If they stick to the plan, in 25 years the Princes will have the princely sum of $570,000 (5 x $114,000).

- Laura and Larry Latestarter really feel like they're behind the eight ball. They're 15 years from retiring and, while they have some money set aside, they realize that they're going to have to save aggressively for retirement. They'd like to put away $6,000 this year and feel confident that they can increase that amount quite a bit—by 10 percent—each year thereafter until they retire. If they do, this could make a big difference in their retirement lifestyle because, assuming a 7½ percent annual return, they'll accumulate $312,000 (6 x $52,000) by the time they retire. A tidy sum.

Nothing in Your Financial Life Is "Either/Or"

> **I've been rich and I've been poor. Rich is better.**
>
> *Sophie Tucker*

A lot of people think that most of their financial decisions are "either/or" decisions. In other words, when confronted with a financial decision, you must either take one course of action or the other. But most financial decisions don't require you to do *either* one thing *or* the other. Often, a combination is more appropriate. Examples abound:

➤ If you can't decide whether to sell an investment you own, you can always sell half.

➤ If you're trying to decide between using a full-service broker or a discount broker since you make some of your own investment decisions, why not use a discounter for your own investment decisions and the full-service broker for investment guidance and recommendations. (See Chapter 3.)

➤ Here's a common problem (actually it's not such a bad problem to have): "I can manage to save an extra $200 a month. Should I put the $200 against the mortgage or invest it?" A good solution might be to split the money in half and do both. (See Chapter 8.)

➤ If you're trying to decide whether term insurance or cash value insurance is better, many people are best served with part cash value and part term insurance. (See Chapter 6.)

➤ Owners of traditional IRAs who qualify are often in a quandary as to whether or not they should convert them to a Roth IRA. But again, this isn't necessarily an either/or decision. Perhaps converting part of the IRA money to the Roth is the answer. You could always convert the rest later. (See Chapter 16.)

➤ Some people think that when they retire they must either take a lump sum payout from their company retirement plans or take an annuity. But again, perhaps a combination of a lump sum and an annuity is the better course of action. (See Chapter 15.)

So always keep in mind that nothing in your financial life involves an "either/or" decision. Realizing this will help you take control of your financial future; one absolute certainty is that *you* are your own best financial planner. Nevertheless, we all can benefit from the services of at least some financial professionals.

YOU ARE YOUR OWN BEST FINANCIAL ADVISER

You probably already know a lot more about personal finance than you give yourself credit for. If you're like most Americans, you manage your day-to-day finances, control your spending, insure against the unforeseen, borrow judiciously, work at minimizing your taxes, and invest your resources carefully. You may not always know the answers and you may sometimes even feel financially illiterate, but in fact you probably already have the basic skills. They just need honing.

In fact, each and every aspect of your personal financial life is simply too important to either ignore or to pass on lock, stock, and barrel to someone else to handle. It doesn't matter how professional an accountant, broker, or financial planner may be and how little you may think you know. The first and most important thing to keep in mind is to never give up control of your own money! Information on managing your personal finances, in addition to this book, is available in daily newspapers, magazines, radio, and television. The Internet is becoming a major source of good personal financial advice. Most of the information that you receive from these sources is trustworthy, so long as you don't feel compelled to act on every recommendation.

For a bibliography of good resources to help you make the most of your finances, including the best Internet sites, click on:

http://jonathanpond.com/general.personalfinanceresources.htm

IT'S TIME WELL SPENT

You may think you don't have the time to attend to all your money matters, let alone read about matters of finance. Good personal financial planning doesn't require a lot of time. Rather, it requires discipline, patience, and an interest in achieving financial security. Most of the important areas—insurance, retirement planning, and estate-planning—need consideration only once or twice a year.

You will be well rewarded for paying closer attention to the most dynamic area, investments. On the other hand, if you spend too much time studying the investment markets and reviewing your investments, you probably will be prone to making the wrong decisions. The more you fret about your investments, the more you will feel compelled to do something. One of the eternal truths of investing declares that more often than not the best thing to do is nothing.

SELECTING THE RIGHT PROFESSIONALS TO HELP YOU ACHIEVE FINANCIAL SECURITY

It's helpful to be able to get some objective professional advice on financial matters from time to time. However, some of the people who work in the financial services industry aren't inclined to provide unbiased recommendations. Rather, they would prefer that you buy whatever it is that they have to sell. Lack of objectivity doesn't make them pariahs, however. In fact, these professionals can be very helpful in providing guidance in their areas of expertise, so long as you understand that their interests may not be entirely in sync with yours. They can be a valuable resource in resolving many of those "either/or" financial decisions.

Many people fail to select appropriate financial advisers or neglect to work with them effectively. You probably need to take a more active role in making sure your advisers (or the advisers you are thinking of hiring) are providing you the best possible advice and service.

Finding the right advisers is well worth the effort. There is no single ideal way to identify the cream of the crop, but word-of-mouth recommendation is often the most effective way. Finally, if you're unhappy with one of your advisers, it may be because you have not taken an active role in the relationship. First, try to resolve the problem, but if it persists, don't hesitate to make a change. It's amazing how many people dislike or distrust their advisers yet continue to do business with them. A discussion of the four types of advisers appears below, although they probably don't want you to hear some of what I have to say.

INSURANCE AGENT

It's usually, but not always, better to select an independent insurance agent who has the capability and willingness to shop among several insurance companies for the best possible coverage rather than an agent who represents a single company. But independent agents may have a conflict of interest in that certain insurance products pay them much higher commissions than others.

Good Agents Will Go to Bat for You. In the worst instances, mediocre agents may not even suggest essential coverage to you (such as umbrella liability insurance) because it provides them with such a low commission. The better agents will review your coverage with you at least annually, shop around for appropriate policies, and go to bat for you when necessary. If you are having difficulty securing life or disability insurance because of a health problem, for example, a good agent will work hard to find you the necessary insurance at the best possible price. To assure a good relationship, you must keep your agent informed of changes in your circumstances and, if necessary, insist on a periodic review of your coverage.

Should You Go It Alone? It is possible to acquire all or most of your insurance needs without an insurance agent. Some people are comfortable doing that, but many are not. A good agent can provide you with guidance that is very difficult and time consuming to acquire on your own. On the other hand, you may be able to save some money by going direct. One of the trends that you will see in the New Century is that more and more insurance companies will be offering their insurance products directly to the public. Remember also that the decision to use an agent or buy your insurance direct is not an "either/or" decision. You may want to buy some of your coverage—term life insurance, for example—direct and obtain your automobile and homeowners insurance through an agent.

If you want to consider buying insurance on your own, you will find more information and a list of companies that offer insurance directly to the public by clicking on:
http://jonathanpond.com/insurance.directsellers.htm

ATTORNEY

You may not yet have a family attorney. But you'll need one at least to prepare necessary estate-planning documents such as wills and powers of attorney. (See Chapter 19.) You should use an attorney who is roughly your age or younger. You'll probably use the same attorney over the years, and you don't want to be burdened by having to find a new lawyer when your current one retires.

On the other hand, you may outgrow your attorney's expertise if your estate grows to a level that would benefit from more sophisticated estate-planning techniques. (See Chapter 20.) These techniques often require the skills of an attorney who devotes all of his or her time to estate-planning. Whatever attorney you select, he or she should be responsive to your needs and should conduct his or her work in a timely manner.

STOCKBROKER

It's certainly no secret that stockbrokers have an inherent conflict of interest in advising you on your investments. You are usually better off holding onto your investments, while a broker is under pressure to generate transactions (and hence commissions). In addition, a broker is often given incentive to promote certain products whether they are right for you or not. Nevertheless, there are many excellent stockbrokers who can deal with these conflicts and still act in your best interest. On the other hand, if you make your own investment decisions, why do you need a "full-service" stockbroker at all? Use a discount broker.

A final note on full-service stockbrokers: Don't do business with a stockbroker who cold-calls you and is unwilling to meet face-to-face with you. These cold-call jockeys who disturb your dinner hour are usually calling from hundreds of miles away, and the last thing they want to do is meet with you or engage in helpful conversation.

FINANCIAL PLANNER

If you are your own best financial planner, does that mean you don't need a professional one? That depends. While financial planning sounds like a service everyone could use, many people don't benefit significantly from the services of a financial planner. You may do quite well on your own. First, too many people think that a planner can turn their finances around. But financial planners aren't miracle workers. Second, many financial planners are actually insurance agents or stockbrokers who may not be capable of or interested in dealing with the multiplicity of matters that affect a person's financial well-being, including credit management, pensions, retirement planning, and estate-planning. They may understand a lot about investments or insurance, but they're not well versed in other important financial planning areas.

Some people—typically those who have a major matter that needs evaluation (setting up an education fund or planning for retirement) or those who have a lot of money and too little time available to manage it—may well benefit from an evaluation of their financial situation. If you feel you need a financial planner, you have many to choose from, since all sorts of people call themselves financial planners. In fact, anyone can call himself or herself a financial planner.

How Financial Planners Earn Their Pay. Financial planners are compensated for their efforts through fees, commissions, or a combination of the two. A *fee-only planner* is paid on an hourly or retainer basis. If one of these planners spends ten hours devising a portfolio strategy for you, a bill for ten hours of work will come to your door. Whether you buy a single bond or a million dollars worth of bonds makes no difference to this type of planner, for he or she has no monetary stake in the investment you purchase. In fact, a fee-only planner may well steer you to lower-cost ways to buy investment and insurance products. But is it worth the fee? Perhaps—and perhaps not.

A *commissioned planner,* on the other hand, doesn't get paid on the basis of the time he or she spends working on your behalf. A commissioned planner's income is generated purely by what—and how much— he or she sells you. The more transactions you make and the more products you purchase, the more money the planner takes in. Do these obvious conflicts of interest mean that you should avoid commissioned financial planners? Not necessarily. Many excellent and well-qualified financial planners earn commissions. But if you take this route, beyond the obvious matter of finding a good one, you must keep in mind the inherent conflict of interest.

Some planners combine these two means of compensation, earning their keep through both fees and commissions. Fees are earned by providing a review of your overall financial situation together with recommendations. If you accept their recommendations, then the planner will earn commissions.

Certification. The fact that a planner is a certified member of a financial planning organization does not necessarily prove that he or she is going to be competent. One planner, as a joke, actually got his schnauzer certified as a financial planner (that organization has since tightened up its requirements). Nonetheless, certification is a starting point, and at least it shows that the planner has taken the initiative to learn about the diverse fields of financial planning. Most certified planners are stockbrokers and insurance agents who have taken the accreditation course. There are three main "degrees" financial planners can earn: Certified Financial Planner (CFP), Chartered Financial Consultant (ChFC), and Personal Financial Specialist (PFS). The last certification, PFS, is available only to certified public accountants.

Some planners boast of being "registered investment advisers." This merely means that the planner is registered with the U.S. Securities and Exchange Commission (SEC) or with their state securities departments. The law requires everyone giving investment advice to register with either the SEC or their state securities departments, and often the only skill required is being able to complete an application form.

Finding a Good Planner. What constitutes the right kind of planner for you depends on your needs. If you want to be assured of getting objective advice, use a fee-only planner—but be prepared to pay for the service. If you don't want to pay what can amount to a large fee, consider a commission-only planner—but be sure to select one that would put your interests first, not the opportunity to earn a fat commission. Look around; there are many excellent financial planners in your community.

Whomever you choose, be sure he or she is truly qualified to be a financial planner. While anyone can call himself or herself a financial planner, *you* need to find one who is truly qualified to provide good analysis and advice in all the areas of financial planning important to you. Accreditation is certainly a plus, but it doesn't guarantee competency. If your situation is particularly complicated—for example, if you have unusual tax problems or estate-planning needs—the best route is probably a CPA or lawyer who is actively involved in financial planning.

> ### POND'S LAW OF FINANCIAL CREDENTIALS
>
> There is no relationship between the number of credentials a financial adviser has earned and his or her level of competence.

Finding a good financial planner is no different from finding a qualified lawyer, insurance agent, stockbroker, or tax preparer: word-of-mouth recommendation. Ask your acquaintances, co-workers, or banker for referrals.

You can find additional information on selecting and managing your financial advisers, including links to the web sites of leading associations of insurance, legal, and financial advisers by clicking on:

http://jonathanpond.com/general.financialadvisers.htm

SENIORS: WHOM ARE YOU INVESTING FOR?

Here's a common "either/or" dilemma that many seniors aren't even aware that they should be considering. Affluent retirees might not realize it, but they may well be investing not only for themselves, but also for their children, grandchildren, nieces, or nephews. If so, the way such a person should invest may be quite different from the standard investment allocation formulas and guidelines that are often recommended to retirees. (See Chapter 10.)

Consider, for example, a couple who has two adult children, four grandchildren, and a sizable investment portfolio in addition to their pensions and Social Security. Whom are they investing their money for? The appropriate answer in this and many other situations may be: for three generations. Therefore, they shouldn't be investing all of their money as if it were all going to be used by the eldest family members.

One approach you may want to take if you're in this fortunate situation is to divide your total investments into two portfolios. The first would be invested to meet your anticipated needs while the second will be the portfolio earmarked for younger generations. In essence, the younger generation's portfolio would be invested more aggressively than would be the "patriarch's and matriarch's" portfolio.

So give some consideration to who will ultimately be receiving your money and what the best way is to invest that money for the intended re-

> ### PONDS'S LAW OF
> ### THE COMPLETE LIFE
>
> Your life isn't complete until
> you've spent all your money.

cipients. In other words, it's fine for a 75-year-old to invest money that he or she is going to use like a 75-year-old. But it doesn't make a lot of sense for a 75-year-old to invest money the same way if it is ultimately going to be enjoyed by, say, a 50-year-old child or a 15-year-old grandchild.

Incidentally, even very affluent retirees can avoid the challenge of managing portfolios for three generations by simply increasing their spending so that they'll have little—or better yet, nothing—to pass on to the ingrates.

For additional guidance on investing for multiple generations, including a case study, click on:

http://jonathanpond.com/investments.seniors.htm

NEVER TAKE FINANCIAL RESPONSIBILITY FOR ANYTHING THAT EATS, BUT IF YOU DO . . .

Certainly there are lots of things in life that money won't buy, but it's very funny—
Have you ever tried to buy them without money?

Ogden Nash

One reason you may be reading this book, rather than relaxing on your 65-foot sailboat somewhere in the Caribbean or Hawaii, is that you've made an expensive financial commitment from which there is little hope of escape: taking financial responsibility for things that eat, notably children, a spouse or partner, and pets. While there's no denying that each of them can bring great joy to your life, the plain fact is that they also change the course of your financial life.

Children, in particular, are enormously expensive. It may take a village to raise a child, but I figure it also costs about the equivalent of two houses to raise a child to adulthood, and that assumes that they eventually leave the home. If you raise two kids, what do you have to show for it? Probably a late start on preparing for your retirement and one house that they didn't quite manage to destroy when they were growing up. If you had had no children, if my math is correct, you'd have a house that's in pretty good shape, plus enough money to buy four more houses. Oh well, I'm darn glad I didn't let such mundane concerns as money get in the way of our having three daughters. I have told them, however, that I can afford to throw only one wedding. So if they want to have a wedding, all three of them will have to settle on the same date.

Kids beget not only big financial responsibilities but also the responsibility to teach them to be financially responsible adults. The way I look at it, by helping our children become financially literate we accomplish two things. First, we're helping them become financial contributors to society rather than financial drains. Second, everything we do to teach our children about sound money habits reduces the possibility that they will become financial drains on us in our old age. It's too much to expect that they would actually be financial contributors to us, but if we can launch them into financial independence, we've accomplished a lot in this day and age.

LEARN HOW TO COMMUNICATE ABOUT MATTERS OF FINANCE

In an age when business, economics, and household budgets dominate the news as well as everyday conversation, it's amazing how little most of us truly know about basic financial planning. While there's no excuse for this, there are a few good reasons for it. We are neither taught nor told about the birds and the bees of finance. In the movie *It's a Wonderful Life*, Jimmy Stewart puts one "Momma dollar" and one "Poppa dollar" into a bank vault in order to raise more cash. Anyone who has a savings account but not a mutual fund account is doing the same, hopeless kind of "money-making." As a first step in the important task of helping every family member become financially literate, you need to open lines of money communication:

➤ **Talk** with your parents to learn about their financial errors and successes.
➤ **Talk** with your children to educate them about what worked and failed for you.

➤ **Use** the Internet's vast resources as a source of information on personal finance.

➤ **Use** your public library's financial planning and investment section.

➤ **Don't make** talking about money taboo.

Finally, don't let money matters interfere with the big job of raising your children. The best way to raise great kids is to spend half as much money and twice as much time on them.

> ### Pond's Law of Grocery Store Design
>
> Grocery stores are designed so that the candy and other child delights are placed on the shelf that is at eye level height to a child sitting in a grocery cart.

Helping Your Kids Learn about Money

I doubt that my kids appreciate it, but the Pond household is a living, breathing laboratory on kids and money. My kids are, for better or for worse, guinea pigs for my experiments on ways that parents can help teach their offspring about money. While there are a lot of people who have written on teaching kids about money, in my opinion, the best is

> ### The Four Magic Words
>
> It's unfortunate that so many parents (often aided and abetted by the grandparents) feel compelled to indulge every material desire of the youngsters in their lives. It's almost as if they feel that they've somehow failed their children if they deny them anything. To the contrary, if they do acquiesce to a child's or grandchild's acquisitiveness (and how acquisitive they can become), then they have failed the child, because that child will probably grow up feeling entitled to everything. So do the kids a favor by setting limits on what they can acquire. Periodically tell them the four magic words: "We can't afford it."

Neale Godfrey, author of several books, including *The Kids Money Book* and *Money Doesn't Grow on Trees*. I've used many of her strategies with my kids, and they work very well.

ALLOWANCES

The weekly allowance can be a powerful tool in teaching younger children about the importance of developing sound spending and saving habits. As well, it can teach them to distinguish between "needs" and "wants"—something that many adults are not particularly adept at.

Neale Godfrey urges parents to divide the weekly allowance into three equal parts:

1. **Spend as you wish.** The child can spend one-third of the allowance on anything he or she wishes. This helps your daughter or son understand that total income is always much greater than the amount that may be spent. The remaining money must be put aside for later. Also, the amount that can be spent immediately must last a whole week (an eternity for most kids). If the child chooses to spend it all within ten minutes of receiving the allowance, so be it. She'll have to wait another week—unless she chooses to tap into her short-term savings.

2. **Short-term savings.** The second part of the allowance is put into a short-term savings fund that is kept handy. The purpose of this fund is to gradually save up for something "big" that the child wants and couldn't otherwise afford with the weekly allowance. Once the child catches on, you'll probably see the short-term savings account mounting up in anticipation of some large purchase. This helps the child learn about the importance of setting money aside for future use, just as adults need to do to be able to pay for large expenditures—either expected or unexpected—without having to wreak havoc on the family finances. It also helps Junior realize that you have to be patient and wait awhile to accumulate sufficient money to afford the good (i.e., expensive) things in life.

3. **Long-term savings.** The final third of the weekly allowance should be earmarked for long-term savings. Therefore, it should be invested in some type of account that lets the youngster see that money set aside for a long time will grow in value. While the easiest way to do this is to put the money into savings-type accounts, you might want to consider opening up an investment account so that money is invested in stocks or mutual funds that will allow the child to really begin to learn about investing. Stocks and mutual funds will also help youngsters learn about risk because, once they start following their investments in the newspaper, they will learn a crucial lesson that every successful long-term investor must learn sooner or later: All worthwhile long-term investments will periodically decline in value, but over the long term, gains should handily outweigh losses. Savings accounts and U.S. savings bonds simply don't impart that lesson, since they never lose value (and, as a result, barely keep up with inflation).

LEARNING TO DISTINGUISH BETWEEN NEEDS AND WANTS

I guess it should come as no surprise that children so quickly learn how to conjure up all manner of reasons why they absolutely, positively have to have something. They have lots of willing teachers: their parents, their spoiled playmates, and Madison Avenue advertising. Sadly, kids soon learn the joy of acquiring things and the sheer misery of being denied material pleasures.

If any youngster is going to become a financially responsible adult, he or she needs to be able to distinguish between "needs" and "wants." If you look at those friends (or, perhaps, yourself) who never seem to be able to get their financial acts together, the root cause is often a consuming desire to consume. The best way to indulge and ra-

POND'S LAW OF ALLOWANCES

No matter how high the allowance bestowed on a child, he or she will be able to find another kid whose allowance is higher.

HOW MUCH ALLOWANCE IS ENOUGH?

There are some questions that you never ask someone who might be on the receiving end of your financial largesse, because you're almost assuredly not going to receive an objective answer. For instance, it's a waste of time asking your youngsters how much allowance they should receive. While they may not understand the concept of infinity, the amount they suggest as an appropriate allowance will approach it.

But parents are usually concerned about whether they are giving their children the right amount. You may want to consider community standards by asking the parents of your kid's peers. But that effort may not yield a suitable amount because, if you use the allowance to teach financial responsibility in the manner I described above, the child will receive only one-third of the allowance for current spending. The other two-thirds will be put away for the future. My friend and fellow author Neale Godfrey suggests that a level of one dollar per week per year of age might be a useful benchmark. Thus, a nine-year-old would receive a $9 weekly allowance, of which one-third, or $3 could be used for immediate spending, while putting away another $3 to save up for something more expensive than the $3 allowance will buy. The final $3 is invested for the long term.

tionalize consumptive behavior is to mentally transform something that they want into something that they need.

So, it stands to reason that the sooner one learns to distinguish between things needed and things wanted, the better able one will be to restrain one's spending and, hence, live beneath one's means. There's no reason why you, as a parent, can't help your child learn this crucial money lesson. Here's how it works in the Pond household:

The short-term savings that our daughters accumulate out of their weekly allowances (see above) are the basis for teaching them, and it works almost every time. Whenever one of my three daughters starts pestering my wife or me about needing some nonessential item (doll, toy, software, whatever), we listen patiently. Of course, over a period of a few days the frequency of the entreaties accelerates as do the reasons why the item in question is an absolute necessity. Eventually, we offer a compromise of sorts. The most recent occurrence involved my oldest daughter who pestered us for several days about something (I can't even recall what it was). It got to the point where she opined that her life would be forever shortchanged if we didn't buy this thing for her. Finally, I asked her how much she had in her short-term savings account. She informed me that she had an amount that was approaching three figures (she's actually a pretty good saver). As I had often done in the past under similar duress, I then offered a compromise by agreeing to pay half. By the way, her half would only have used up about one-tenth of her short-term savings. What was her response? She wouldn't do it; she didn't want to use any of her money. What's more, we never heard her mention the item again. This scenario has been repeated in my household countless times, and while my kids don't realize it, they're getting a firsthand lesson in being able to differentiate between things they need and things they want. Now, if only we adults could learn the same thing.

HELPING OLDER KIDS LEARN A CRUCIAL MONEY LESSON

Here's a super way to provide a lot of vital money lessons to an older child or grandchild if you can spare the money. Once a child begins to earn money from a job, say from babysitting, mowing lawns, a part-time job or a summer job in high school or college, you might want to give them some money above and beyond their hard-earned wages to invest in an IRA—probably the wonderful Roth IRA (page 201). Many bro-

> ### PexD'S LAW OF "HOW DID MY CHILD TURN OUT LIKE THAT?"
>
> If you have two or more children, no matter how diligent you are in teaching them about financial responsibility, one will end up with appalling financial habits.

kerage firms, banks, and mutual fund companies will let you do this even if the child is a minor.

You're sending an important message to them that says: "Even though retirement is many decades away, this gift of an IRA is my way of showing you how important I feel it is for you to start putting money away as early in your life as possible." (If only we had learned such a lesson when we were in our teens or early 20s.)

But the gift of an IRA provides other benefits as well. The youngster will sooner or later learn about the value of tax-deferred investing since the gains from the IRA will not be taxable so long as the money stays in the account. Also, since even a small IRA can be invested in mutual funds, it will provide your child or grandchild with an opportunity to learn there, too. Finally, it will provide an appreciation of the power of compounding since this money is intended to be kept intact for decades.

You might want to show the child or grandchild the following chart, which illustrates the benefits of starting to save early in life. It compares three different IRA contribution scenarios, each of which results in accumulating $250,000 at age 65. First, someone who starts contributing at age 36 and contributes for the next 30 years will accumulate about

CHART #2	
The Benefits of Starting to Save Early in Life	
Contribute $2,000 to an IRA at These Ages	Approximate Value at Age 65
Ages 36 through 65 (total contributions of $60,000)	$250,000
Ages 27 through 36 (total contributions of $20,000)	$250,000
Ages 17 through 20 (total contributions of $8,000)	$250,000

They Ought to Put Empty Nesters on the Endangered Species List

In the old days, life went something like this: A child was born, and the parents raised the child until he or she became financially self-sufficient. In their old age, parents moved in with child who dutifully supported the parents for the rest of their days. Life had some balance back then. You paid to raise your kids and they paid for your retirement.

Alas, here's how it works today: A child is born and the parents raise the child until he or she has enough education to be financially self-sufficient. But, for any number of reasons, adult child isn't very good at earning an adequate living. So adult child moves back home (if he or she ever left in the first place) and continues to enjoy the financial benefits of being a dependent. And, just as the child rebelled at doing family chores at the age of five, the 35-year-old child takes umbrage at having to perform menial household tasks. After all, they reason, someone with a master's degree, albeit unemployed, shouldn't have to do the laundry. Even if and when child leaves the parents' domicile, child continues to rely on parents for at least some financial support. But as surprising as it may seem, child feels guilty. After all, taking money from retired parents is going to cut into child's inheritance. Now there's something to feel guilty about!

$250,000, assuming, as in each scenario, an average annual investment return of 7½ percent. The second scenario involves someone who starts contributing $2,000 at age 27, continues doing so for 10 years, and then stops. He or she will also accumulate about $250,000. Finally, someone who starts contributing at age 17, does so for just four years, and then stops, will also accumulate $250,000. Of course, no one should stop contributing to their retirement until they're retired. But Chart #2 clearly demonstrates the enormous benefit of starting to save early in life. If you can afford to help the younger generation members in your life get

HOW GRANDPARENTS CAN HELP

Grandparents can help grandchildren learn about money, even if the parents (your children) aren't doing such a hot job. Grandparents who can afford it are probably already giving the child some periodic cash gifts—or U.S. savings bonds. If you can afford to give a little more, either all at once or on a regular basis, you can give the child stock or a mutual fund. With discount brokers and direct investment programs (DIPs, page 234), you can buy even a small amount of stock at a low commission. Some mutual fund companies still welcome small investments of $1,000 or less. Many fund companies that don't have low minimum initial investment requirements still allow investments in their funds if the investor (or, in this case, a willing grandparent) authorizes the fund company to make small (typically $50 or $100) monthly withdrawals.

Also, tell the grandchildren about your experiences with money in the "olden days." My first lesson about inflation came from my grandmother who used to captivate us with tales about how far money would go when she was a child—and how little money people earned.

into the retirement savings habit, you'll be providing a lifelong financial lesson.

Kids are experts at separating their parents from their money through outrageous manipulation. If you feel like putty in your kids' hands when it comes to money, you can find a compendium of common kids money ploys and how to respond to each by clicking on:
http://jonathanpond.com/children.moneyploys.htm

Teaching Kids about the Importance of Charity

The allowance is a powerful tool for helping youngsters learn to become financially responsible. Supporting charities is an important matter in most families, and you can teach even very young children about the importance of giving money to worthy causes. If the kids receive an allowance, encourage them (which usually means force them at first) to set aside a percentage of their allowance for charity. Once they've saved a few dollars for charity, help them donate the money to a charity of their choice. The parents may want to make some suggestions at first. That way, the child can experience firsthand the good feelings that come from helping. This is a lesson that can last a lifetime.

Pond's Laws of Grandparents and Grandchildren

1. Grandparents will spend more money on a grandchild in one weekend than they ever spent on their children in one year.
2. The first economic lesson that a child learns is that it's a lot easier extracting money and other goodies from grandparents than it is from parents.

Chapter 5

■ LEARN HOW TO TOLERATE YOUR LOVED ONE'S ANNOYING FINANCIAL HABITS

> A miser is proof that not every fool and his money are soon parted.
>
> *Anonymous*

here's nothing like money to get in the way of a good relationship. How many times has your spouse or partner committed some financial act that just about drove you nuts? If only you could train him or her to have excellent financial deportment just like you do. Good luck. And by the way, are you really some paragon of financial virtue? I'd be interested in the opinion of your spouse or partner.

There are some things that just can't be changed, and I believe the way we view money, particularly in our day-to-day financial activities, is cast in concrete early in adult life. But there is undoubtedly some room for improvement in the way you communicate as a couple about family finances. You'll also benefit from understanding that no couple will see eye-to-eye on all money matters.

GET USED TO IT

Let me first state the obvious. Arguing periodically with your spouse or significant other about money is inevitable. The reason is simple:

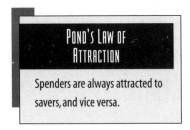

POND'S LAW OF ATTRACTION

Spenders are always attracted to savers, and vice versa.

Spenders are attracted to savers. In fact, all enduring relationships consist of one saver and one spender. The challenge is to learn how to become tolerant of your spouse's or partner's annoying financial habits.

HITCHED TO A SPENDER?

If your spouse or partner is the spender in the family, you know how tough it is to bite your tongue when he or she claims to have saved money by buying something that's on sale. You worry that your loved one will begin to believe that the more things bought on sale, the more money the family will save. You fully understand that no one in the history of the world has ever "saved" money by buying something on sale.

HITCHED TO A SAVER?

On the other hand, it's no picnic when your spouse or partner is the saver in the family. You probably think that he or she has been put on this earth for one primary reason: to deny you any material pleasures. About the only hope you have is to outlive the cheapskate. Then you'll be able to spend some money without recriminations. That reminds me of the old ditty: "Misers may be tough to live with, but they make wonderful ancestors."

Whatever your situation, please try to tolerate your loved one's financial foibles. You're not going to change them, so learn to cope with their strange money habits.

POND'S LAWS OF SAVERS AND SPENDERS

1. Savers are put on this earth to deny their loved ones any material pleasures.
2. Spenders actually think they save money when they buy something on sale.

CONFIDENTIAL NOTE TO SAVERS

It's easy to be feel holier than thou if you're the saver. But keep in mind that your future financial success depends heavily on spenders. Spending is the fuel that propels our economy, produces jobs, and elevates the stock market. In fact, in the best of all worlds, everyone (except you and me) would be spenders.

Minimizing Marital Money Squabbles

When was the last time you argued with your spouse or significant other about money? If you ever want to have an argument, money matters are an omnipresent and very convenient catalyst. While the vast majority of couples tends to agree on important, long-term family financial matters, they often differ over smaller, day-to-day financial matters. There are a few things you can do to minimize interspousal money tensions.

1. Set aside an annual date for the two of you to review your financial status and make some plans for the next year. The date you select shouldn't be around tax-return preparation time, however. That's already stressful enough on couples. Good record keeping throughout the year will make this "day of reckoning" much easier.

For some suggestions on setting up a personal record keeping system and sample forms, click on:

http://jonathanpond.com/recordkeeping.htm

2. Work with your spouse to achieve the financial goals that you've both agreed upon. They don't take care of themselves. To accomplish your goals, you will have to know what they are and work toward them together. Try to come to an agreement, defining what both of you will do over the next year toward the goals. For example, you could agree how much each partner will contribute to your respective retirement plans at work or set weekly cash budgets for each other.

3. If you haven't already, try to come to some agreement about managing the family's day-to-day finances. If you can work out a way to do that smoothly, you will have eliminated a big stumbling block to

ARE YOU A SPENDER OR A SAVER? TAKE THE QUIZ

If you're not sure whether you're a spender or a saver, or if you're just interested in finding out how hopeless your financial habits are, take the following quiz. (There are no right or wrong answers to this quiz. But it should help you better understand your financial inclinations.)

1 You've been known to drive ten miles to:
   a. Spend ten cents
   b. Save ten cents

2 You define "stock" as:
   a. Department store inventory
   b. An investment

3 If you go shopping with ten items on your shopping list, you'll come home with:
   a. five items
   b. 15 items

4 Which of these statements do you agree with?
   a. It only costs a nickel more to go first class.
   b. Anything that's first class is a waste of money.

family financial felicity. One of the earliest tests in a relationship involves the family checking account. You may discover that the old, lovely dovey joint checking account doesn't work very well. It's a lot for some couples to expect that both partners have enough discipline to write checks out of the same account and assiduously enter them into the same check register. There's a fair chance that it won't work. If so, separate checking accounts will probably lead to a cozier financial relationship. Common family expenses have to be paid out of one account, but it's a lot easier to agree on that than argue over who's spending what out of the same joint account. Some couples

5 You've just been told you're going to get a raise. The first thing that comes to mind is:

a. Saks

b. Saks stock

6 A car has 60,000 miles on it. You think it should be:

a. Sold

b. Bought

7 Which best describes your holiday season spirit:

a. "It's better to give than to receive."

b. "It's better to receive than to give."

8 Which of these four-word expressions brings you more joy?

a. "Dow reaches new high."

b. "Attention all K-Mart customers."

9 When you're handed a restaurant check, you:

a. Double check the addition

b. Wonder if you've got enough credit left on your credit card to pay it

10 You've been smitten by Cupid's arrow, and your love's birthday is next week. Your idea of the perfect gift is:

a. An expensive present and a romantic night on the town

b. This book

successfully use a joint account for joint family expenses and separate accounts for individual expenses, but that can add up to a lot of monthly checking account fees.

BOTH PARTNERS NEED TO BE INVOLVED

Both partners need to understand the family finances. While it's not uncommon for one partner to take charge—to be the family

POND'S LAW OF MARITAL BLISS

The sooner a newlywed couple abandons their joint checking account in favor of separate checking accounts, the longer the marriage will last.

THE DILEMMA OF DUAL CAREER PARENTS

Most parents of young children confront the dilemma of whether both parents must work outside the home during their children's early years. Many are greatly conflicted by the choice that involves one partner interrupting a career, not to mention the financial sacrifice, and a great number of parents conclude that they simply cannot afford to live off one paycheck. But a closer inspection of the amount of money that the second paycheck adds to the family coffers may be revealing. Consider the following example.

Patrick and Patty Parente have two preschoolers. Patrick and Patty gross $52,000 each from work for a total family income of $104,000. With their expenses they can't foresee any way that one of them could leave the work force. But before making a final decision, they did some number crunching to determine how much the second paycheck earner brings home given day care expenses and the other costs of having both Patrick and Patty working. Here's their analysis:

Weekly gross income from second paycheck	$1,000.
Less income taxes:	
Federal @ 28 percent (all of the second paycheck will, in effect, incur federal income taxes since the first paycheck causes all of the second paycheck to be taxed at 28 percent)	(280.)

"Chancellor of the Exchequer"—the other partner shouldn't stay or be left in the dark. Life is unpredictable, and there may come a time when the less-involved partner has to take over quickly. Even if that never happens, the more aware both partners are of the family finances, the better. It's a very uncomfortable feeling when you don't know what's going on.

Social Security @ eight percent	(80.)
State @ four percent	(40.)
Total income taxes	(400.)
Weekly after-tax income	600.
Less expenses associated with both parents working outside the home:	
Day care for two children (less tax credit)	(325.)
Other work-related expenses that could be avoided if one parent leaves work force (work clothes, commuting, meals at work, etc.)	(75.)
Total expenses	(400.)
Weekly income provided by $1,000 second paycheck	$200.

Depending on Patrick's and Patty's financial circumstances, the second paycheck may still be a financial necessity. But this couple, like many others who have performed a similar analysis, are startled by how little the second paycheck actually brings home. In this example, only one-fifth of the income ends up with the family.

So there may be a lot of compelling reasons why both parents of young children want to work outside the home, but for many, the additional money that the second paycheck brings home is not as great as it may seem at first glance.

Preparing Financially for the Unexpected

Life is full of unexpected and unpleasant financial surprises. They can range from minor annoyances, such as car repairs or an unanticipated large tax bill (are they ever unexpectedly small?) to a major disruption in your finances such as a fire in the family home or the disability or death of a breadwinner. The following chart summarizes these major life events. One of the most essential things you can do to stay on course to achieving financial security is to prepare for these unpleasantries because you will almost certainly experience some of them if you haven't already. Here are the two basic rules of thumb:

➤ Use savings and investments to pay for minor financial disruptions
➤ Use insurance for protection against most major financial disruptions

Coping with Minor Financial Disruptions

Chances are that one piece of financial advice your parents gave you when you started your first real job went something like this: "Now *(fill in your name)*, the first thing you need to do is to save about six months'

CHART #3

Life Events That Could Affect Your Financial Security

Family
- Family members with special financial needs
- Aging parents
- Separation and divorce
- Death of a spouse or other close family member
- Major losses from fire, accident, or theft
- Lawsuits

Occupation
- Decline in income
- Unemployment
- Forced early retirement

Health
- Disability
- Old age
- Chronic illness
- Terminal illness

worth of salary as an emergency fund. Keep the money safe in a savings account or checking account so that you'll be able to get at it quickly." If you were an obedient child, you probably spent the next 14 years or so setting money aside for your emergency fund. With all due respect to our parents, that advice wasn't so hot. Letting a lot of money, even emergency money, languish in accounts that pay very low interest doesn't make a lot of sense. True, in the old days it was tougher to get money quickly out of an investment account. But today you can get access to your money in most investment accounts in a day or two or, in many instances, in a matter of hours. (In deference to our parents, please turn to page 73 to learn about the best financial advice our parents ever gave us.)

I'd prefer that you invest most of your emergency money primarily in stock mutual funds and/or individual stocks so that it will have a chance to grow as opposed to letting it sit in a savings account or money market fund. The main disadvantage of investing the money is that when and if you need to draw some of it, you may have to pay commissions or capital gains taxes for the privilege. But that's a small price to pay for the growth you should be able to enjoy with the money over the years. After all, a financial emergency is not a common event (we hope). A final reminder: A sale doesn't constitute a financial emergency.

GETTING YOUR HANDS ON MONEY QUICKLY

There may come a time when you need to raise a lot of cash fast to meet an unexpected expense—a big April 15th tax bill or home repairs, for example. Before you take out a cash advance on your high-interest credit cards, however, consider other ways to get your hands on money posthaste.

- **Borrow from your IRA.** You can borrow from your IRA without penalty or interest as long as you replace all of the money borrowed within 60 days. This privilege is available only once a year.
- **Borrow from your 401(k) plan.** Depending on your employer's rules, you may be able to take out a loan from your 401(k) plan at work.
- **Take out a home equity loan.** If you have enough equity in your home and you otherwise qualify, a home equity loan can also raise needed cash. Another advantage of home equity loan borrowing is that the interest you pay on the loan is usually tax deductible. But beware of large home equity lines of credit. With a home equity loan, previously unrecognized ways to spend prodigious amounts of money suddenly become apparent. So a word to the wise is: Don't hock the family home for frivolous purposes.
- **Borrow on margin through your brokerage account.** If you have a brokerage account, you may be able to borrow against investments that are in the account. The investments are collateral for your loan.
- **Cash in CDs.** While you'll incur an interest penalty, if push comes to shove, you could cash in a CD early to get your hands on quick cash.

DEALING WITH MAJOR FINANCIAL DISRUPTIONS

If you think about the various types of major financial disruptions that can befall us (as uncomfortable as it is to contemplate such unpleasantries), they fall under two categories:

➤ **Major financial disruptions that cannot be insured against, in the traditional sense, at least,** such as a job loss or divorce. The ability to survive these events financially basically depends on the amount of money you have available to cushion such financial blows.

➤ **Major financial disruptions that can be insured against,** such as a fire, car accident, illness, disability, or death of a breadwinner. Insurance is, of course, an essential defense against most major financial disruptions, and there are important matters to consider for the various categories of insurance that you should carry, or at least consider carrying.

A MENU OF INSURANCE COVERAGE

Insurance is one of those necessary evils in life. You'd just as soon not have to pay for it, but there may come a time when you're awfully glad you did. While most people understand the importance of carrying adequate insurance, many still leave gaps in their coverage. Just one gap in insurance coverage can result in an uninsured loss that could wipe out years, if not decades, of hard-earned savings. Don't jeopardize your financial future by leaving a hole in your insurance umbrella. Moreover, take care to understand each of your policy's limitations and exclusions. Your agent should ex-

POND'S LAW OF INSURANCE

The more insurance you carry for a particular risk, the less chance that the calamity will arise. And vice versa.

plain the coverage although it doesn't hurt to read the policies yourself. Remember, the big print giveth, and the small print taketh away.

Life Insurance

Life insurance replaces part or most of your wage income in the event of your death and may also cover other expenses of your dependents during a readjustment period after death. By the way, why do they call it "life" insurance when you have to die to collect on the policy?

Important Matters to Consider

1. Determine how much insurance coverage you need. Your insurance agent will be happy to assist, but that estimate should generally be considered a maximum amount to meet all foreseeable needs. A minimum amount of coverage, if you have dependents, might be enough coverage to replace five years of job income plus, perhaps, an added amount to pay off the home mortgage and provide a college fund for the kiddies.

2. Examine whether term and/or cash value insurance will best meet your needs. If you have significant insurance requirements over a relatively limited period of time (for example, until the children are out of college), then term insurance will probably best fit the bill. If your insurance needs are more permanent, cash value insurance may be preferable. There are several different kinds of cash value coverage available, but the one that's being most vigorously promoted by your agent may not be the right one for you. So, do some independent investigation. Variable life insurance, a relatively new flavor of cash value insurance, is going to be a very popular type of insurance in the New Century. It allows you to invest the cash value of your coverage in mutual

> ### Pond's Law of Insurance Gaps
>
> The next calamity to befall you will be in the one area where you lack insurance coverage.

POND'S LAW OF LIFE (INSURANCE) STAGES

Your life insurance needs are greatest when you're at a stage in life where you can least afford to pay the premiums. And vice versa.

funds. If you can afford to accept some risk with your insurance coverage, consider variable life insurance. The life insurance industry is very competitive, and comparison shopping could save you money on the one category of insurance that you never want to collect on. An increasing number of financially solid life insurance companies are offering policies direct to the public.

3. Buy life insurance when you're healthy. If you wait until some major health problem arises, a life insurance policy will cost much more — if you can get it at all. Life insurance companies aren't enthusiastic about issuing policies to people who have one foot in the grave and the other on a banana peel.

4. Review your life insurance needs periodically, because changes in your financial or family circumstances may result in a change in coverage. Remember also that life insurance needs typically diminish as you age.

5. A relatively new life insurance policy feature worth considering is the accelerated death benefit, also called the living benefit. If a policy offers this benefit, it will pay the life insurance proceeds while the insured is still alive but is terminally ill.

6. If you're considering purchasing life insurance to help pay estate taxes (second-to-die life insurance, for example), be sure to speak with an estate-planning attorney first to see if there are other ways to reduce your estate tax bill without having to resort to expensive life insurance. Many people who buy life insurance for estate-planning purposes really don't need it. (See page 256.)

For more information on choosing the right kind and right amount of life insurance, click on:
http://jonathanpond.com/insurance.life.htm

HEALTH INSURANCE

Health insurance protects you from both the smaller out-of-pocket costs of health care and large medical bills that major illness can bring.

IMPORTANT MATTERS TO CONSIDER

1. If your employer offers a range of coverage, carefully evaluate the alternatives so that you select the policy that best fits your and your family's needs.
2. If you are self-employed, check with local business associations or trade associations that offer health insurance to their members.
3. Make sure that children who are in college or recently out of the nest have adequate health insurance coverage.
4. If you're retired, select the category of Medicare Gap insurance that will best meet your needs. You may not need the most extensive policy coverage.
5. Examine any medical bills you receive for accuracy. Even though you may not be paying the bill, it is incumbent upon all of us to make sure we're not being overcharged.

For more information on choosing the right kind and right amount of health insurance, click on:

http://jonathanpond.com/insurance.health.htm

DISABILITY INSURANCE

Disability insurance replaces part or most of your job income in the event of disability.

IMPORTANT MATTERS TO CONSIDER

1. All working individuals should have enough disability insurance to replace 60 to 70 percent of their job income. Examine policy provisions carefully to determine the types of disabilities that the policy will and will not cover. Employer-provided disability policies may be unduly restrictive. If so, you may need to supplement it with other group or individual disability insurance.

2. If you need to obtain your own disability coverage, first determine if it is available through any professional groups or associations that you can join. Individually purchased disability insurance policies, while the most comprehensive, are also very expensive. Moreover, the insurance companies that offer individual coverage often restrict the extent and availability of this coverage for members of certain occupations, notably doctors.

3. If your employer provides disability insurance coverage, consider reimbursing the employer for the premium that is paid on your behalf. By doing so, you will be able to receive disability benefits tax-free if you ever need to collect. If the employer has been paying the premium, the disability checks will be taxable.

For more information on choosing the right kind and right amount of disability insurance, click on:

http://jonathanpond.com/insurance.disability.htm

LONG-TERM CARE INSURANCE

Long-term care (LTC) insurance, also referred to as nursing home insurance, will be the biggest insurance topic in the New Century as the baby boomers near retirement age, life expectancies increase, and insurance companies and their agents vigorously promote the coverage.

While some people can benefit from LTC insurance, I believe a lot of people are being sold LTC insurance without understanding its limitations. Long-term care insurance covers part or most of the cost of nursing home care as well as, in many instances, home health care.

Important Matters to Consider

1. Understand the policy limitations and features. Long-term care insurance is aggressively sold, and many purchasers don't really understand what they're getting—or not getting. Become an expert on long-term care insurance before signing up for a policy.

2. Favor policies that provide comprehensive home health care coverage as well as nursing home coverage. Inflation protection is also an important feature unless you're quite old when you acquire the policy. Consider long-term care coverage in the context of your overall financial resources. Experts suggest that the ideal candidate for LTC insurance is one whose estate is in the range of $500,000 to $1 million. Those with smaller estates probably can't easily afford an adequate policy and those with larger estates may be better off self-insuring.

Should You Purchase a Long-Term Care Policy?

Insuring against nursing home and home health care costs may help you sleep better at night, but you pay a heavy price for this reassurance. Moreover, if and when you eventually receive policy benefits, you may be surprised to learn that your policy may cover far less of your daily nursing home costs than you had expected. While the insurance industry has made great strides in improving these policies over the years, there are still some problems associated with LTC insurance. A report by the General Accounting Office (the congressional watchdog agency) noted many deficiencies in the long-term care insurance field: widespread questionable sales practices and confusing or deceptive policy language, for example.

One alternative to long-term care insurance that you may want to consider is to invest the money you would pay in LTC premiums.

Chances are that you could accumulate a significant amount of money by the time you enter a nursing home (if you ever do). If you're worried about a nursing home confinement impoverishing you and your spouse, consider investing some of your retirement savings in an annuity, which will at least assure you a lifetime source of income. On the other hand, many people, particularly couples, have done their homework and have made the right decision for them in acquiring LTC insurance.

If you're single and have enough money to enter a private nursing home, your need for LTC coverage is not as great as it is for couples or others with financial dependents. Singles who want this coverage so they can pass on some of their estate to their children rather than risk having it go to a nursing home should have their kids pay the premium. Don't sacrifice your income on the LTC insurance altar just to give them an inheritance.

If you are considering the purchase of a long-term care policy, do your homework. Examine the various features that LTC policies contain. Review many LTC policies before making a purchase, and don't fall for the first sale pitch you read or hear about. This insurance could be one of your biggest expenses. It requires considerable effort to ensure that you make the most of your hard-earned dollars.

For more information on choosing the right kind and right amount of long-term care insurance, click on:

http://jonathanpond.com/insurance.long-termcare.htm

SPEAKING OF NURSING HOMES

Many seniors are so anxious to protect their money from nursing home costs that they undertake a whole range of elaborate financial maneuvers to reduce the amount of money that has to go toward long-term care. Some use asset-stripping techniques by placing their money in trusts, thereby impoverishing themselves. Others start giving money to their children so that if and when they go into a nursing home, there's less money that has to go to the nursing home. The theory is that the parent will eventually emerge from the nursing home and the children will give the money back to the parents. Who's kidding whom here? Once that money was given to the children, it was gonzo, bye-bye, adios.

Before devising any nursing home cost avoidance scheme, speak with an attorney who is expert in elder care law in your state. Otherwise, your plans could backfire. Ask yourself the following questions: Do you really want to impoverish yourself (or your parents) so that you (they) can go on Medicaid? Do you want to spend your final years as a ward of the state?

HOMEOWNER'S AND RENTER'S INSURANCE

Homeowner's insurance covers property—including the home, other structures, personal property, and general contents of the dwelling—against theft or destruction. Renter's insurance protects the personal possessions of the tenant. These policies also offer limited liability protection.

TAKE A PERSONAL INVENTORY OF YOUR HOUSEHOLD POSSESSIONS

Taking a personal inventory of your household possessions is crucial to assuring that you get back what you deserve should you ever suffer a loss. Record any and all identifying information on your possessions (including serial numbers) as well as a complete description of each item. Photographs of furniture, appliances, and the like will be a big help. Videotapes are even better. Make no mistake about it—taking a household inventory is one of the most boring things you'll ever do! Save it for a rainy Saturday, but don't wait too long to do it. (Don't forget the garage.)

By the way, store your inventory and photographs somewhere away from your house—in your safe-deposit box or in your desk at the office. Also, remember to keep your inventory up-to-date by adding receipts for possessions subsequently acquired to your inventory file.

For a work sheet that will help you record important information for your household inventory, click on:

http://jonathanpond.com/insurance.householdinventory.htm

IMPORTANT MATTERS TO CONSIDER

1. In addition to the basic coverage, consider obtaining replacement cost coverage for your personal possessions and, in the case of homeowner's insurance, the home itself. Construction costs are rising, so be sure your homeowner's insurance coverage keeps pace, whether you have a mortgage or not. With regard to your personal possessions, replacement cost coverage will generally pay to replace lost, stolen, or damaged items rather than giving you their depreciated value.

SAFE-DEPOSIT BOX INSURANCE COVERAGE

If you store valuables such as jewelry in a safe-deposit box, the contents should be insured. Many people don't realize that the contents of safe-deposit boxes are not insured by the bank, and insurance under a regular homeowner's policy is typically limited to $1,000 or less. A rider on your homeowner's or renter's policy can add safe-deposit box insurance at a rate that is usually far less than the cost of insuring valuables that are kept at home. An inventory of the box contents should be stored at home or in the office.

Among the belongings most commonly stored in a safe-deposit box is jewelry, which can be insured for about one-quarter of the cost of insurance for jewelry outside the box. In an effort to find a middle route between cheap in-vault and expensive out-of-the-vault rates, some insurance companies now allow people to switch between the two types of coverage. Typically the owner will notify the agent or company when an item of jewelry is to be taken from and when it's being returned to the safe-deposit box. During the time the jewelry is outside the box, the higher rate will be charged.

2. Strict policy limits apply to valuable possessions. Any valuables should be appraised so that a floater policy can be added. Valuables stored in a safe-deposit box should be insured as well. If you're in an area that is prone to such calamities, obtain flood and/or earthquake insurance.

3. If you're a renter, don't go without renter's insurance. Consider the impact on your financial situation of losing all of your personal possessions. It happens to people every day.

For more information on choosing the right kind and right amount of homeowner's or renter's insurance, click on:

http://jonathanpond.com/insurance.homeownersandrenters.htm

AUTOMOBILE INSURANCE

Automobile insurance protects automobile owners from the potentially large bills an accident could bring. Automobile insurance also protects the car owner from theft and provides some liability protection.

IMPORTANT MATTERS TO CONSIDER

1. Buy sufficient coverage in essential areas such as bodily injury and personal liability, but reduce or eliminate coverage in other areas such as collision and comprehensive if you own an old clunker.

2. Don't buy cars that cost a lot to insure and invite the attention of auto thieves.

3. Don't waste money on car rental insurance if you don't need to. If you're going to rent a car, find out in advance if your automobile insurance policy will cover it (most do).

For more information on choosing the right kind and right amount of automobile insurance, click on:

http://jonathanpond.com/insurance.auto.htm

PERSONAL (UMBRELLA) LIABILITY INSURANCE

Personal liability insurance protects you from losing your assets or future earnings as the result of a liability suit. It provides additional protection on top of homeowner's or renter's and automobile liability coverage.

IMPORTANT MATTERS TO CONSIDER

1. Most adults need at least $1 million umbrella liability insurance. If your estate is growing or you have a high income, you should probably have at least $2 million in coverage.
2. Your umbrella liability insurance policy will need to be coordinated with the liability coverage provided on your auto and homeowner's or renter's policies. Therefore, it's usually advisable to buy the umbrella policy from the same company.
3. If you perform volunteer work, find out from the organization or your attorney if you are indemnified against personal liability.

For more information on choosing the right kind and right amount of personal liability insurance, click on:

http://jonathanpond.com/insurance.personalliability.htm

PROFESSIONAL LIABILITY INSURANCE

Professional liability insurance protects you from lawsuits arising out of job-related activities. Not all professions require liability insurance, but if you are in a business that could leave you open to a lawsuit, that is coverage you need to have.

IMPORTANT MATTERS TO CONSIDER

1. If you're an employee, find out if your employer covers you for professional liability.

2. Self-employed professionals or small business owners should probably acquire professional or business liability insurance. If you need to acquire professional liability coverage, check with your professional association. If they don't offer the coverage, they can probably advise you on insurance companies that do.

For more information on choosing the right kind and right amount of professional liability coverage, click on:

http://jonathanpond.com/insurance.professionalliability.htm

REDUCING YOUR INSURANCE COSTS

Many people spend more than they should to secure adequate insurance coverage. Here are some of the many simple ways to reduce insurance costs and avoid costly mistakes.

1. **Raise deductibles.** You can save as much as hundreds of dollars each year by raising the deductibles on your automobile and homeowner's or renter's insurance policies.

2. **Don't underinsure.** While you should certainly be encouraged to pare down unnecessary insurance costs, don't go without necessary coverage merely to save premium dollars. Eliminating needed coverage can be a costly mistake.

3. **Earn discounts by purchasing all insurance coverage from one company.** Many carriers offer discounts to customers who purchase all their policies, such as automobile, homeowner's, and umbrella liability insurance, from them.

4. **Don't buy insurance through the mail without comparison shopping.** You may periodically receive direct-mail offers for life insurance from a credit card company, association, or famous TV personality. While most of these offers should be rejected, some, particularly those offered by professional associations, may be worth considering. Do some comparison shopping to determine if the mail order deal is a good one.

5. **Reduce life insurance coverage when children leave home.** For most people, life insurance needs decrease when their children are no longer financially dependent on them. In addition, as you age, the role of life insurance changes. While working parents with dependents have considerable life insurance needs, retirees may only need life insurance for estate-planning purposes. (See page 256.) You should periodically reevaluate your life insurance needs to see if your coverage should be reduced or adjusted.

6. **Avoid credit life insurance.** Credit life insurance (and credit accident and disability insurance) is almost always grossly overpriced and entirely unnecessary. If you need a policy to ensure that your loans can be paid off in the event of death or disability, you should buy death or disability insurance—not this overpriced waste.

7. **Inquire about discounts.** Many insurers offer discounts for homeowners who take protective measures against fire and burglary. The cost of installing these systems may be recouped fairly quickly through insurance premium savings. You may also qualify for special discounts on your automobile insurance policies without even realizing it. Check with your insurance agent to find out about various discounts that may be available to you—such as those for driver training courses, theft-deterrent systems, and automobile safety features.

8. **Self-insure.** You may have sufficient capital to assume certain risks, either by raising deductibles or by canceling coverage altogether. The decision to self-insure is a serious one, however, and should only be made after careful analysis.

9. **Avoid "dread disease" or other narrowly defined insurance coverage.** Stay away from cancer insurance, air travel insurance, and other types of insurance that protect against very specific risks. Senior citizens are particularly susceptible to buying narrowly defined insurance policies in that these policies exploit fear and protect against risks that regular insurance already covers. A good medical policy, for instance, renders any disease-specific insurance unnecessary.

10. **Pay insurance premiums annually rather than monthly or quarterly.** Paying insurance premiums annually is usually cheaper than paying monthly or quarterly.

Chapter 7

NEVER BORROW TO BUY A DEPRECIATING ASSET

> If you would like to
> know the value of
> money, go and try to
> borrow some.
>
> *Benjamin Franklin*

The late 20th century may have seen one of the great economic booms of all time, but that didn't stop a lot of people from borrowing themselves into personal bankruptcy. In fact, over the last two years of the century, one out of every 40 families in the U.S. declared personal bankruptcy. While many think that most bankruptcies flow from unemployment or disability, the most common cause is borrowing for the wrong reasons. So let the following be your guide: Never borrow to buy a depreciating asset. In other words, don't borrow for something that isn't going to provide you with ever-increasing benefits in later years. That pretty much leaves out most of things that people borrow money for. Most people borrow to finance either current spending or to buy something that loses value over the years, like, dare I say, a car. I can think of only three things that qualify as *appreciating* assets and are therefore worth going into hock for: a home, sensible home improvements, and a college education. Incidentally, I didn't mention borrowing to buy stock, although a lot of people seem to think that makes a lot of sense. But borrowing to invest only makes sense if you can be sure that your investments will appreciate in value—and no one can be sure of that. So the next time your investment adviser or broker recommends that you either borrow on margin against your current investments or, worse, take out a home equity loan to invest the money, don't do it.

I HATE CARS

I fully realize that, in our culture, cars assume almost godlike qualities. Just look at how much we adore a new car. The owner gets out of the car, looks at it, walks a few steps, looks at it again. . . . A fancy car supposedly bestows upon its driver (note that I say "driver" rather than "owner" since most people never really "own" their cars) a certain level of respect in the community. I've never been very high on cars. I've yet to understand why Americans have such a love affair with their mobile phallic symbols. They're expensive to purchase and maintain and, while you're pouring money into car payments and repairs, the darn thing is depreciating in value. My cars are a source of considerable personal embarrassment to my children. They prefer to be left off a block away from school so that their classmates won't have to see the car. My neighbors apparently aren't very pleased with my car, either. Shortly after we moved into our house, I found a piece of paper on my windshield one morning that said: "Your car violates this neighborhood's standards of good taste." Too bad you feel that way, neighbors. It's because I didn't waste money on cars that I can afford to live in your neighborhood.

I find it so unfortunate that so many people sacrifice their financial future in order to drive around in cars that they really can't afford to own. Or even if they can afford them, they trade their cars so frequently that they're putting a dent in the family budget that could otherwise go toward more important things in life.

POND'S LAW OF CREDIT CARD DEBT

It takes ten times longer to pay off credit card debt than it took to run up the debt in the first place.

Quiz: Question: What's the quickest way to lose $2,000?

A. Bet $2,000 on a horse that finishes out of the money.

B. Drive a new car off the dealer's lot.
Answer: B. You've lost $2,000 in a matter of seconds. (It takes over a minute for your horse to finish out of the money.)

MY CAR STUDY

A few years ago I prepared a study on the cost of car ownership. I compared the cost of buying a new car and trading it every three years with the cost of buying a new car and then holding on to it for ten years. (Yes, Virginia, cars will last ten years.) I then calculated the cost difference between those two approaches over a person's entire working life, about 40 years. The results were astonishing. Based on a car that now costs $18,000, a person who trades his or her car every ten years saves $385,000. That's enough to retire five years earlier than the person who trades or leases a car every three years. By the way, my calculations included enough money to pay for some expensive repairs for the car owned for ten years. The savings are based on one car. If you're a two-car family and trade the machines frequently, your savings could be double the $385,000 amount if you would only come to your senses.

POND'S LAW OF CARS IN THE 'HOOD

The neighbor who has the most expensive car in the neighborhood has the smallest retirement account in the neighborhood.

FINANCING THE BEAST

Financing the total purchase price of your car—or part of it—is the shortcut to ownership that most of us take. But, unless you shop for the lowest rate, it can be a very costly "shortcut."

Of course, paying cash for your car is the least expensive and best way to go, and if you've been going from car loan to car loan, start thinking up a strategy to make this your last car loan.

Car loans come in many different forms—your bank, credit union, and auto

POND'S LAW OF OLD HEAPS

Anyone who owns a car more than eight years will give it a cute name.

dealership are likely to have at least half a dozen different types with differing terms and interest rates. New car loan rates should always be lower than used car loan rates. But just because new car loan rates are lower doesn't mean you should buy a new car. It will cost you a lot less to buy a $7,000 used car at 12 percent interest than a $20,000 new car at 9 percent interest. Often, credit unions beat the best bank rates and the dealer. If you can take advantage of such a deal, why go to a bank?

While the average new car loan is well over four years, I think it's a waste of money to finance a car over more than three years, and two years is better. After two or three years, the car is going to start to need some repairs and it's both financially and psychologically depressing to be paying big car repair bills while you've still got a bunch of monthly loan payments left. Also, if you borrow for three, four, or five years, you're probably one of those unfortunates who just goes from car loan to car loan—forever. If you pay off the car over a couple of years and have the good sense to hold onto the car for many more years, you've got a good chance of paying cash for your next car. If you think about it, once you manage to pay cash for a car, you should be in a position to pay cash for all subsequent car purchases.

Now, if you're really hung up on nice cars, you're probably saying to yourself: "But I can't afford a car if I have to finance it over only two or three years." True, you probably can't afford the car you'd dearly like to have, but you can afford a car that better fits your financial situation.

Home Equity Loans

The tax benefit of paying for your car with a home equity loan is worth considering if you're one of the few borrowers who will pay off the loan in a year or two. There is no deduction for interest paid on consumer loans, but by using a home equity loan—the interest of which *is* generally deductible—you can pay for your car in a more cost-effective manner. Be sure to repay the loan as you would a regular car loan! Don't dig yourself into a financial hole by taking ten or 15 years to pay off a car purchased with a home equity loan long after the vehicle has been replaced.

LEASING

Leasing is an increasingly popular way to acquire a new car—especially one you really can't afford. Many manufacturers offer leasing as an alternative to purchasing, and for good reason. The cars are too bloody expensive to pay for by other means.

There are numerous types of leases, and rest assured that each is more complex, troublesome, and financially disadvantageous than ownership. Leasing lets you take the financial rap for the fact that a car's value declines more in its first two years than it does for the remainder of its life. When your lease is up, the dealer is left with a prime preowned car to sell. Leasing can reduce the hassle of buying and selling, but leasing is more expensive than buying a car, even with borrowed money. It also encourages people to trade in their cars too soon. However, the big advantage of leasing is that it allows you to drive around in a car that you couldn't afford to buy. How much sense does that make?

WHEN TO SELL

Most car owners trade in their iron and plastic master far too soon. Unless you've got tons of money, trading a car every three or four years is truly a waste. Don't tell me that car repairs on an older car make it more expensive to run than a new car. Unless your old clunker has a truly catastrophic problem, no amount of repairs will come close to the real cost of financing a new car. So think twice before getting rid of your middle-aged car. How would you like it if your spouse got rid of you when you became middle-aged?

You can obtain some additional tips on making sensible decisions regarding the purchase and ownership of your iron and plastic master by clicking on:
http://jonathanpond.com/general.cars.htm

PUBLIC ENEMY NUMBER ONE: CREDIT CARDS

Once there were no credit cards. I know that is hard to believe, but trust me. These days they're pretty close to a necessity. If your credit is anywhere near acceptable, you're undoubtedly bombarded with credit card solicitations, but don't be too flattered. Within the last year, my three daughters, ages 12, nine, and five, all received applications for an American Express card—twice.

PONDS LAW OF CREDIT CARD OVERLOAD

If you have a good credit history and you accept every credit card offer you receive in the mail, within two years you will build up enough credit to pay off the entire federal debt.

THE BENEFITS OF CREDIT CARDS

Credit cards are a great convenience and, for those who properly manage them, they can be an effective way to manage daily expenses without having to carry large amounts of cash. Those who make most effective use of their credit cards understand what each type of card can and cannot do. Furthermore, they understand the nuances of credit card repayment terms. If you don't have this level of understanding, get it! It can keep you off financial life-support.

THE BENEFIT OF CREDIT CARD LOANS

None.

If you're interested in finding out about the pros and cons of the various types of credit cards and additional information on managing your credit cards, click on:

http://jonathanpond.com/borrowing.creditcards.htm

Getting Out of Debt Problems

There is no easy way out of debt problems, but you should first try to dig out from under your hill of bills yourself before taking more drastic action such as seeing a credit counselor or filing for personal bankruptcy. One way or another, you can and will emerge from your debt problem. It's not the end of the world. In fact, many who have trod the well-worn path of overindebtedness emerge with much-improved money habits and a bright financial future. The best financial lessons are often those hardest learned, I'm afraid.

First Try to Solve the Problem Yourself

Here are six steps you can take to try to resolve your financial problems. There are no quick fixes; expect to endure some psychological and financial pain. But working through these problems yourself is preferable to the alternatives discussed later.

> ### Pond's Law of Student Credit Card Limits
>
> A college student's credit card borrowing limit will be maxed out in a number of days equal to the cube root of the dollar limit. For example, a $1,000 credit limit will be reached in 10 days.

> ### The Best Financial Advice Your Parents Ever Gave You
>
> When you were an adolescent, chances are your parents gave you the best financial advice you'll ever receive. In a private conversation with you, one or both of your concerned parents probably uttered this sage admonition: "For one moment's pleasure, you could end up paying for the rest of your life." Now as a teenager, you may have thought your parents were talking about something else, but truth be told, they were talking about credit card loans.

1. **Find out where you stand.** Summarize all of your debts, including the total amount due now, the amount due later, the amount overdue, and the minimum payment requirements.

2. **Prepare a bare-bones budget.** You must prepare a budget that cuts your living expenses to the bone so that you can meet your monthly loan-payment obligations. After housing payments and food, debt payments should be the third item on your emergency budget. If, like most people in your predicament, credit cards caused the problem, take the scissors to all but one credit card.

3. **Prioritize.** If you have many debts from different sources and you aren't sure that you'll be able to pay them all on time, prioritize. Work out a plan for paying the most important bills and for avoiding late charges. Missing an important bill might lead to your car being repossessed or to the shutting off of your electricity. Beyond meeting minimum payments for all your bills, pay off the bills with the highest interest rates (like credit cards) first.

4. **Speak with your creditors.** If you're unable to make a loan payment on time, contact the lender (before they contact you) to explain your circumstances and work out a payment plan. They may agree to grant you a temporary reduction or delay in payments, or they may waive your late charges. Don't expect them to work miracles, but if you keep the lender informed of your circumstances, many will be accommodating. Also, don't avoid calls or letters from creditors under any circumstances. Creditors would rather know that you are trying to work things out than fear that you are trying to evade your debt.

5. **Don't be easily seduced by debt consolidation loans.** The idea behind debt consolidation is that you take out one loan to cover all your debts. Paying only one loan in low monthly installments sounds like just what the debt doctor ordered—but this may well be the kind of thinking that got you into credit trouble in the first place. Lower monthly payments usually extend the loan over a longer period of time. Moreover, consolidating loans often frees up your credit cards, leading to even more debt.

6. Don't become a debt recidivist. If you're able to repair your credit yourself, the time will come (it may seem like an eternity) when you will return to a firmer financial footing. Many people, armed with generous credit card balances once again, lapse back into their old free-spending ways. It's the equivalent of successful dieters subsequently regaining all their lost weight. But keeping good financial habits will pay off—and pay off big.

It's a lot easier to save when you know you'll get to keep the money, instead of feeling that it's all going toward paying off last year's binge. (If the cause of your debt problems was something beyond your control, you already know how important it is to save and will welcome the opportunity to resume saving.) It feels good to accumulate some savings, and if your finances catch the flu again, you'll be able to recover a lot faster. Remember, until you get into the habit of spending less than you earn—*living beneath your means*—you won't save a penny.

If you find that you are over your head in debt—beyond your ability to work out of it with your current income—speak with your creditors again. Contact each creditor and explain why you are overextended. They may be able to arrange an easier repayment plan. Many creditors will go along with a reasonable plan under which they will receive their money slowly, if you show that you are *trying* to pay your debts, not avoiding them. Most creditors prefer doing this to repossessing the goods or taking you to court, which is time-consuming and costs them more in the long run.

NEXT, TRY CREDIT COUNSELING

If you have financial problems that you can't resolve on your own, the next step is to consult a credit counselor. Various institutions offer such counseling, including many banks and credit unions, family service agencies, and nonprofit consumer credit counseling organizations. If you are slightly overextended, the agency will usually help you develop a repayment plan for a nominal monthly fee. The agency may take monthly payments from you and distribute them to your creditors. The agency also talks to the creditors and may get them to agree to a delayed or reduced payment. Because these groups are often backed by local merchants or banks, they will do everything possible to help you and to get you to repay your debts.

By the way, make sure that you are dealing with a credit counselor who is affiliated with a *nonprofit* consumer credit counseling service. There are a variety of charlatans out there who hold themselves out as credit counselors but will do nothing more than wreak further havoc on your predicament.

One important thing to remember: If you use a consumer credit counseling organization, it will be reported to the credit bureaus and noted on your credit record. That fact should not deter you from using a credit counseling service, particularly if your only other alternative is filing for bankruptcy. While you may ultimately resort to bankruptcy, give credit counseling a try first.

PERSONAL BANKRUPTCY, WHEN ALL ELSE FAILS

If you find that neither your own good efforts nor those of a credit counselor can salvage your situation, personal bankruptcy may be your only alternative. Some attorneys make it sound easy, but you should consider it only as a last resort.

For additional guidance on getting out of debt and other financial problems, click on:
http://jonathanpond.com/borrowing.problems.htm

Nevertheless, if your situation is hopeless, bankruptcy will allow you to get a fresh start. Bankruptcy is not the end of your financial life, but it will severely impair your credit record for as long as a decade.

WHY BORROWING FROM YOUR OWN 401(K) PLAN ISN'T AS GREAT AS YOU THINK

How would you like to be your own banker? Think how easy it would be to get your loan request approved if it were your money that you're borrowing! Even better, you pay interest to yourself. Life doesn't get much better than that! Employers are usually pretty lenient. Sure the notion of borrowing from yourself and repaying the loan to your retirement account with interest is appealing, but borrowing from your own retirement account is not as great as you might think. Aside from the fact that you sacrifice tax-advantaged growth from that portion of your retirement stash that you've borrowed, you also pay taxes *twice* on the interest you pay. How so, you ask? The following example will show why.

> Debbie Debtor decided to borrow $10,000 from her 401(k) plan at work. The loan terms required repayment in one year with interest at 10 percent. Debbie's combined federal, Social Security, and state income tax bracket is 40 percent. While paying $1,000 interest back to her own account is attractive, she has to earn $1,667 in order to have $1,000 left over after taxes to pay the interest, since interest paid on personal loans is not tax deductible. More bad news: She'll have to earn $16,667 in order to have $10,000 left over after taxes to repay the principal. But, getting back to the interest, a second round of taxes will also have to be paid when the interest you paid to yourself is eventually withdrawn when you're retired. If Debbie is in the 30 percent income tax bracket when she's retired, she'll have to pay another $300 in taxes when she takes out the $1,000 of interest that she paid to her retirement account many years prior. So the grand total taxes she'll pay for the privilege of borrowing from her 401(k) plan and paying herself $1,000 of interest will be $967.

So borrowing from a retirement savings plan at work isn't as great as it appears. Nevertheless, it still beats borrowing from a bank, because at least you end up with some money in your pocket, rather than your banker's.

When does this kind of borrowing make sense? Rarely. Just like home equity loans (see page 87), borrowing from your retirement savings plan should not be taken lightly. With a home equity loan, you're placing your house at risk. With a 401(k) plan loan, your placing your retirement nest egg at risk.

Most people who borrow from their 401(k) plans do so for the wrong reasons. I could justify borrowing for only two reasons. First, to buy a first home if you absolutely, positively need to tap into the money to close the deal and you know you'll be able to pay back the loan. Second, if you're in deep financial trouble and the only way out is to hock your retirement funds. But remember, if the financial trouble was the result of events within (not beyond) your control, borrowing from your retirement plans isn't going to solve your problem. In fact, if you don't mend your ways, it will simply make your financial situation that much worse.

Home, Sweet (Unmortgaged) Home

A h, the American dream. A home will probably be the second best investment you'll ever make (education is first). It will certainly be the most expensive investment you'll ever make, and I'm not talking about the mere $229,000 that the house originally cost (or, if you've been a homeowner for quite a while, the $29,000 you originally paid). I'm talking about what it costs to maintain them. A home is a ceaseless drain on our hard-earned money, but home ownership still beats renting. Aside from the quality-of-life advantages of owning a home, there are two very significant financial benefits of home ownership (beyond the obvious tax deductions for mortgage interest and property taxes):

➤ A home gives you the opportunity to be mortgage-free by the time you retire or shortly thereafter. Owning a mortgage-free home can dramatically improve your odds of enjoying a financially comfortable retirement.

➤ A home is a source of additional income during retirement. Retirees who sell or downsize their homes can put up to hundreds of thousands of dollars of profit in their pockets, free of capital gains taxes. (See page 90.)

Buying and financing a home is no simple task. If you're going to be in that boat anytime
soon, extensive coverage for home buyers is just two clicks away:
http://jonathanpond.com/homes.buying.htm
http://jonathanpond.com/homes.financing.htm

If you're a renter and would like some information on being a financially savvy renter, click on:
http://jonathanpond.com/homes.renting.htm

SHOULD YOU PAY OFF YOUR MORTGAGE EARLY?

I catch a lot of flak whenever I urge people to pay off their mortgages early. So before everyone tells me this is a terrible idea, permit me to spend a moment going over the pros and cons of making extra payments against your mortgage.

ADVANTAGES:

➤ Paying off your mortgage early saves a lot of money because the total amount of money you spend to pay off the mortgage will be less— sometimes far less—than it would if you took the full 30 years. Even though your tax deductions are less if you accelerate the mortgage payments, you're still ahead financially.

➤ If you can pay off your mortgage by the time you retire, you'll need a lot less income to support yourself in retirement than those who are either renting or still making mortgage payments.

DRAWBACKS

➤ If you're in the highest tax brackets, the tax advantages of the mortgage interest deduction may outweigh the advantages of making extra payments.

➤ It reduces the amount of money that you have to invest.

➤ If you can earn an average investment return in excess of the interest rate on the mortgage, making extra payments is not as financially efficacious as investing the money.

"STOCKS DO BETTER"

This is the argument advanced most vehemently by the don't-prepay-your-mortgage crowd. They believe that you'll come out ahead by stretching out the mortgage and investing the money instead. That pretty much assumes that this money will be invested in stocks, and stock returns—even in the go-go years—are far from certain. For example, you know for sure how much "return" you're getting by making a payment against, say, an 8 percent mortgage. But the return on the alternative—stocks—is less clearcut. If you're confident that, over the long term, you'll earn more on stocks than the interest you're paying on your mortgage, then you're better off not making any extra mortgage payments.

But here's another way of looking at the dilemma: If you're investing in a diversified manner—not only in stocks, but also in bonds and short-term investments such as money market funds, CDs, and savings accounts, then you're better off making extra payments against your mortgage, using some of the money that would otherwise be invested in bonds or short-term investments. The interest rate on your mortgage is almost certainly *higher* than the return you'd get on a money market fund or other short-term investment and probably higher than the return on a bond or bond fund.

"I NEED THE TAX DEDUCTION"

Other opponents of prepaying a mortgage aren't stock market fanatics. Rather, they argue that they need the tax deduction on the mortgage interest. Every extra payment reduces the deductible interest on the loan. That argument may have some validity for those in the top tax brackets (although they could have so much income that their mortgage interest deductions may be reduced by other tax rules). But tax theoreticians (Mother, don't let your children become tax theoreticians) say that you have to be in a tax bracket that's higher than 35 percent to make a deduction financially worthwhile. Few of us, however, are in such lofty tax brackets. Most of us are in the 28 percent tax bracket. If so, and you pay $10,000 in mortgage interest this year, you're going to save $2,800 in taxes. Is that such a great deal? Shell out $10,000 to save $2,800 in taxes, and do that year in and year out? Mortgage interest deductions are nice, but they're hardly a reason against prepaying a mortgage, because as Chart 4 (on page 84) shows, making even small extra payments can add up to big total cost savings.

PREPAY YOUR MORTGAGE IF . . .

So, in reckless defiance of the criticism that's been heaped upon me, I still urge you to make extra payments against your mortgage, but if and only if:

➤ You've maximized any and all available retirement plan contributions for the year, including your retirement savings plans at work and an IRA. While there are lots of financial benefits to reducing your mortgage sooner rather than later, tax-advantaged retirement savings plans offer better ones.

➤ You've paid off all other higher interest loans, including credit card loans and car loans. It makes no sense to make extra payments against your, say, 8 percent mortgage while you've got an 11 percent car loan and 18 percent credit card balances.

➤ You've got a stash of non-retirement savings sufficient to pay at least six mortgage payments. This will protect you in the event you lose your job or some other calamity befalls you. Some people get so excited about making extra payments on their mortgage that they use all available money to pay down the loan. That's dangerous, because everyone needs emergency funds (see page 49). The fact that you've been reducing your mortgage payments doesn't enhance your standing with the lender; if you fall behind on your payments, you're not going to receive any special treatment.

How to Prepay

There are numerous ways to prepay a mortgage, and all of them work. They range from the very informal to refinancing your mortgage to a shorter maturity.

1. **Add a few bucks to the monthly payment.** If you've got some money left over at the end of the month, add some of it to your standard mortgage payment. Even a few dollars every month can shorten the time it takes to pay it off. (See Chart #4.) The beauty of this strategy is its flexibility. If you don't have any extra money, simply make the regular payment. If you have a small windfall, include a larger chunk of money with the next payment. Whether it's a few dollars or a few hundred dollars, you can't beat the good feeling of knowing that you'll pay off the mortgage before you become a great grandparent.

2. **Doubling up the principal payment.** This is a great prepayment strategy, particularly for those who have recently taken out a mortgage. You need a mortgage amortization table, but they're commonly available. Check with your lender first. Armed with the table, you simply make the current month's regular mortgage payment (principal and interest) and add the next month's principal payment. Then cross out both months on the mortgage amortization table and do the same thing each subsequent month—make the current month's principal and interest payment and the next month's principal payment. If you do this religiously, you'll pay the mortgage off in half the time. The reason it works so well early in the mortgage is that the principal payments are quite small. The extra monthly principal payment will grow modestly each month, but it still takes several years before they become burdensome. Presumably and hopefully, you'll be better able to make those larger payments as time goes on and your income increases.

   By the way, whenever you make extra payments against your mortgage, either by informally adding some money to your monthly payment or by doubling up, be sure to make it clear on your payment slip and check that you want the money applied against your

CHART #4

The Benefits of Making Extra Payments on Your Mortgage

$100,000, 30-year mortgage with 7½ percent interest. Monthly payment of $700.

Amount of Extra Monthly Payment	Mortgage Will Be Paid Off In	Total Principal and Interest Payments
$0	30 years	$252,000
$50	24 years	$216,000
$100	21 years	$195,000
$150	18 years	$181,000
$200	16 years	$171,000

mortgage. Also, make sure the lender does in fact apply the extra to the mortgage.

3. **Biweekly mortgages.** These mortgages often fit nicely into the family budget, particularly if you're paid biweekly. By paying half of your monthly mortgage every other week, you make the equivalent of 13 months worth of mortgage payments (26 biweekly payments) each year. That extra monthly payment adds up to a considerably shorter mortgage maturity. You generally have to pay a few hundred dollars

CANCEL PRIVATE MORTGAGE INSURANCE AS SOON AS POSSIBLE

Private mortgage insurance (PMI) is expensive, with typical annual premiums of $250 or more for every $100,000 of coverage. Most lenders require private mortgage insurance when you buy a house with less than 20 percent down. But you're not stuck with it forever. Once your equity exceeds 20 percent of the home's value, your lender should be willing to let you drop the coverage. So if you've paid down enough of the principal and/or if real estate has appreciated sufficiently in your neighborhood to increase your equity to more than 20 percent—it may be worth getting a new appraisal of your home and taking it to the bank.

for arranging a biweekly mortgage. You can do it yourself, but if you need the discipline, biweekly mortgages work quite well.

4. **Shorten the mortgage.** If you're contemplating a mortgage refinancing, you could consider a shorter-maturity new mortgage. The advantage of the shorter maturity is that you'll probably get a lower interest rate. For example, it's not uncommon for 15-year mortgages to be available with interest rates of ¼ percent to ⅜ percent lower than equivalent 30-year mortgages. The disadvantage of shortening the maturity is that you absolutely, positively have to come up with the higher mortgage payment each month. The other mortgage prepayment strategies allow you to suspend your extra payments if, for whatever reason, they become unaffordable.

For some illustrations on how much you can benefit by making extra payments against your mortgage, click on:

http://jonathanpond.com/homes.mortgageprepayment.htm

MAKING SURE YOUR HOME IMPROVEMENTS ARE WORTHWHILE

A good home improvement is one that will add value to the home when you resell it. A bad one won't add much, if any, value. Some are so bad that they actually impair the value of the home. A 20-person hot tub, for example, is likely to cause a potential homebuyer to wonder what kind of shenanigans went on in that house (not to mention wonder how much it will cost to remove it). How can you tell the outcome of your investment ahead of time? Fortunately, there have been a number of studies on the value of various home improvements. Kitchen remodeling or an additional bathroom usually pay off handsomely. At the other extreme, swimming pools (particularly in cooler climes) aren't worth the water they're filled with. Here are some home improvement guidelines to help you make the most of your home improvement dollars.

► Avoid extravagant improvements that could make your home harder to sell. Always think about what would appeal to the typical home purchaser when planning improvements.

► Avoid overpersonalizing the improvement to the extent that, while it may appeal to your ego, it would have little or no appeal to the next family that purchases your home.

► Projects that improve energy efficiency are still popular and they may pay for themselves even before you sell the home.

► Don't spend so much on home improvements that you end up owning the most expensive home in the neighborhood. Adding a fifth and sixth bedroom to your home in a neighborhood of three- and four-bedroom houses will just make it harder for you to recoup your investment.

Keep in mind those home improvements that almost always provide good value for your home improvement investment: kitchen remodeling, a second or third bathroom, and decks and patios.

For additional guidance on worthwhile home improvements, financing the project, and surviving the ordeal, click on:

http://jonathanpond.com/homes.improvements.htm

HOME EQUITY LOANS

Lenders are falling all over themselves to grant loans to homeowners who've built up some equity. Don't be flattered by the solicitations, however. Home equity loans are one of the safest loans a lender can grant. You're hocking your house for the privilege of getting your hands on some money. Substantial risks are involved in using your home for credit. The worst case is when you take on too much debt and lose your home to foreclosure. Nevertheless, if you're a homeowner who is facing major expenses—you need to finance a new roof, or your daughter has just been accepted by an expensive private college—taking out a home equity loan (HEL) may be the answer.

A home equity loan is essentially a checking account secured by a second mortgage. Generally, the line of credit is 70 percent to 80 percent of the appraised value of the house, less what's owed on it. For example, a house worth $200,000 with $80,000 still unpaid on the mortgage might qualify for a $70,000 line of credit (75 percent of $200,000 less $80,000). Usually, the amount of credit allowed depends on your income. The length of the loan may range from five to 12 years or longer at some institutions. It's smart to shop among local lenders, because interest rates and fees can vary substantially.

> ## POND'S LAW OF HOME EQUITY CREDIT LINES
>
> Heretofore unrecognized opportunities to spend large sums of money will become immediately apparent after you open a home equity credit line.

There aren't many items that are tax deductible anymore, but interest paid on most HELs (up to a $100,000 loan balance) is one of them. So, for those with Herculean financial discipline, a home equity line of credit is a convenient, flexible, and tax-advantaged way to borrow. Because you are risking your house whenever you draw on your credit line, HELs should be used only for major expenditures and worthwhile purposes, such as home improvements, children's education expenses, major purchases (such as an automobile), and, if you're truly committed to cleaning up your debt act, debt consolidation.

DON'T MAKE YOUR HEL HELL

Home equity loans are a wonderful and comforting source of money needed quickly. On the other hand, it's all too easy to jeopardize your home as a result of abusing this seemingly painless form of credit.

Home equity loan borrowers typically borrow for short-term purposes (vacations, home maintenance and repairs, and payment of estimated income taxes), intermediate-term purposes (automobiles), or longer-term purposes (making major home improvements or paying college tuition bills). Short-term loans should be paid off within a year, intermediate loans should be paid off over a few years at most, and longer-term loans should be paid off over a maximum of 10 to 15 years. Since a common use of HELs is to buy cars, it's crazy not to have paid off the loan on your current car before buying a new car. Yet it happens all the time. Read on.

I spoke with a couple recently who could have been poster children for bad HEL habits. They had just retired and had paid off the mortgage a couple of years prior. But they also had a $150,000 home equity loan outstanding. The loan included five past and present cars and several vacations. In fact, they had done no more than make minimum payments on their ever-increasing home equity loan balance. So this couple, who had worked so assiduously to pay down their mortgage, did nothing more

VACATION HOMES

Most of us dream of some day owning a vacation home—a place for a well-deserved respite from the hectic pace of daily living. They also attract us with their rental and investment potential. It's best, however, to rely more on the former than the latter. If you own the second home exclusively for your enjoyment, any rental income will be icing on the cake. True, rents can sometimes provide some solid income, but rental property may also entail hidden costs. For example, extra maintenance expenses and rental agency commissions put a dent in the rental profit. Moreover, in most areas of the country the period of prime rentability is limited to a few months of the year. And, to make matters more difficult, the competition to rent during these months is often intense. The end result can be disappointing. My parents used to rent a winter home in Florida, and each year the owner lowered the rent to induce them to return. Before long, he was barely covering his property taxes.

than substitute a HEL for their mortgage. They're going to have to take a not-so-small portion of their retirement income over the next decade to retire the HEL.

Obtaining the right home equity loan is a complicated process. For more information and checklists on obtaining a home equity loan and managing the loan appropriately, click on:

http://jonathanpond.com/homes.homeequityloans.htm

For more details and strategies for reducing your property tax bill, click on:
http://jonathanpond.com/homes.propertytaxes.htm

Therefore, if you're thinking of investing in a second home, you need to be painfully aware of how difficult it often is to get a lot of rent off the property. A realistic assessment of rent revenue, free of the often-inflated attestations of the seller or the seller's broker, is essential. There's one other small snag: The prime rental season is often exactly when you want to use the home!

Second homes in vacation areas are particularly susceptible to weakening real estate prices. In fact, a drop in prices can be devastating to vacation homeowners. This happened in many areas of the country in the early 1990s. While soft markets may present a buying opportunity, don't count on a dramatic appreciation in the home's value after you have bought it. So if you're thinking of buying a vacation home, your guiding principle should be to buy it primarily for your enjoyment and that of freeloading relatives and acquaintances. Look at it as an investment in your good health.

HOME SALES ARE LESS TAXING

The tax rules on excluding home-sale capital gains are a real gift to homeowners. In general, for the sale of a principal residence, the amounts of excludable capital gain have been increased to $250,000 for single taxpayers and $500,000 for joint filers. This means that an enormous chunk of profit from your home sale goes into your pocket tax free, and homeowners of any age are eligible. The residency requirement is also pretty lenient. To qualify for it you need only have occupied the home as your principal residence for two out of the five years prior to the sale. Even better, the exclusions are available as frequently as once every two years.

If you fail to qualify for the exclusion under one of the rules (either ownership or use) and you have to sell your principal residence due to certain unforeseen circumstances such as a job change or ill health, you may still qualify for a proportionate exclusion.

For most of us, the new rules make our primary residences an even more compelling investment. And for people who like to renovate old houses, occupy them, and sell them for a hefty profit, the benefits are

CUTTING YOUR PROPERTY TAX BILL

Many homeowners pay too much in property taxes. If you think your home is overassessed, you may be able to lower your tax. Here's how.

- Look for assessment errors. Try to point out specific factors that reduce your home's value compared with others in the town.
- Determine current market value. Find comparable recent sales of similar homes in your neighborhood.
- File an appeal of your property assessment. Nearly half of the people who appeal their property tax assessments end up getting a tax reduction.

great. But perhaps the biggest beneficiaries are retirees. They can down-size their home or relocate to a less expensive locale and plow the profits into their investment accounts.

The tax rules for home sales are (surprise, surprise) rather complicated. But you can profit immensely from understanding them. You can find all of the details presented without all the technical mumbo jumbo by clicking on:

http://jonathanpond.com/taxes.homesales.htm

Chapter 9

There's a Big Difference Between Saving and Investing

> Invest in inflation. It's the only thing that's going up.
> *Will Rogers*

ou don't need to read this chapter if:

1. You're family is so bloody rich that your problem is finding a way to spend all of your income, and

2. You've got someone managing your investments in whom you have complete trust and admiration

Otherwise, join the rest of us who have to do it the old fashioned way, save and invest, save and invest . . . ad nauseum. I hope this chapter and the four that follow will take some of the nausea out of investing. Investing wisely and well isn't very difficult, honest.

The Two Key Ingredients to Achieving Financial Security

Saving regularly and investing those savings wisely are two important ingredients to achieving the financial security that all of us desire. It's important to recognize that these are two separate matters. Unless money mysteriously appears on your doorstep or you have had the good fortune to have relatives who just give you money, you have to save (i.e., spend less money than you take in) in order to be able to invest. But some people who are pretty adept at saving aren't very good at investing. Of course, saving and simply letting those savings sit in low-yield savings accounts is better than not saving at all. However, it's unlikely that you'll be able to achieve your financial dreams if your money doesn't grow at a rate that outpaces inflation—which it probably won't with low-yield savings accounts or CDs.

HOW I GOT HOOKED ON THE STOCK MARKET— LESSONS FOR THE FAMILY

Whether you're a parent or a grandparent, teaching kids about investing can be mutually profitable. The sooner they learn about the importance of saving and investing, the better equipped they will be to become financially responsible adults. That benefits them, of course, and also us; the more financially responsible our children and grandchildren become, the less likely they'll have to rely on the largesse of the parents or grandparents. Mind you, we parents or grandparents must merely try to do the best we can. There are no guarantees that Junior will leap at the opportunity to learn about investing and become a poster child for good financial habits as a young adult. In fact, if you've got more than one child or grandchild, it's very unlikely that all of them will end up as you planned when it comes to the way they handle money (or the way they handle any other aspects of their life, for that matter). But, as far as money is concerned, you can stack the odds in your favor by creating a home environment that encourages learning about investing and other family financial matters. (See page 31.)

PONO'S LAW OF FINANCIAL EDUCATION

The more you teach your children or grandchildren about financial matters, the lower the probability that you'll have to support them in your old age.

HOW DID MUTUAL FUND MANAGERS LEARN ABOUT INVESTING?

A few years ago, I conducted a survey of over 1,000 managers of stock mutual funds to find out, among other things, what got them hooked on investing. The results were very intriguing. You'd think that the vast majority of these managers had majored in business administration in college, taking a healthy dose of courses on finance and investing. That wasn't the case. Many had academic training far afield from investing; they majored in engineering, psychology, and philosophy. (So there's still hope for you arts and sciences majors to become savvy investors.) But another part of the survey was even more revealing. When asked about their first exposure to the stock market, most indicated that they learned about investing from their parents and grandparents. Not formal instruction mind you—just hearing their parents and grandparents talk about family investments and the stock market. Were these managers from families that had tons of money and Brobdingnagian portfolios? A few were, but the vast majority came from families that were distinctly middle income. You can talk about investing with your kids just as easily if you own some funds through your 401(k) at work and 10 shares of AT&T as you can if you have a seven-figure portfolio. Perhaps it's even easier to teach your kids about money when your holdings are modest, because the families with big money probably have managers attending to the family wealth.

So by all means talk about investing with the younger generation. But don't expect them to ask for a subscription to *The Wall Street Journal* for Christmas. It will take some time for it to sink in, but chances are that they'll start to learn something about investing. After all, kids still listen to the older generation. If you don't think so, why is it that your five-year-old can repeat verbatim a naughty joke that she overheard you telling your spouse?

MY GRANDMOTHER'S INFLUENCE

I recall my parents' discussions about family investments, modest though they were. But the person most responsible for initiating my interest in investing when I was a youngster was my grandmother—the only grandparent I ever knew. She gave me 11 shares of General Motors and 11 shares of Chase Manhattan Bank stock on my eleventh birthday.

I have held onto those 11 shares each of GM and Chase and have participated in their dividend reinvestment plans for as long as they've been offered. Over the years, occasionally I made some optional additional investments totaling a few hundred dollars. Today, thanks to my grandmother, the value of these shares, which cost her just a few hundred dollars when she gave them to me in 1956, is more than $30,000. They pay annual dividends that aren't much less than she paid for the stock when I was 11, which I dutifully reinvest, of course. I'll probably use the money to help pay my kids' college tuition. I'm sure Granny would approve were she still with us.

My parents told me that when I originally got the stock, I didn't pay any attention to my "portfolio." But when the dividends started rolling in, they said that I slowly started to perk up. I'd check the prices in the paper and occasionally, when I was feeling flush with money, I'd buy a copy of *The Wall Street Journal*. By the time I was 15, I'm told, I was buying stocks through Mom and Dad's brokerage account. They actually saved some of the broker's statements, and most of my purchases were so small that the brokerage commission was more than the amount of my purchase. (These were the days before discount brokers and Internet trading.)

Incidentally, GM and Chase, while solid stocks, have not been stellar performers over the past 40-odd years, but I've held on anyway for sentimental reasons, I guess. In this, though, I urge you not to follow my example. Don't hold onto any investment for sentimental reasons. All too often, that sentimental investment turns into a mediocre one over time.

INVESTING 101

Even if you didn't get an exceptional financial upbringing, it's not too late to give yourself a chance at a successful financial future. Investing is important to your future, and the sooner you become familiar with it, the better.

Investing isn't that complicated. If it were, then the people who advise you on investing would be geniuses. When was the last time you met someone in the investment business who was a genius? If you can arm yourself with some basic investing knowledge, you can learn to make your own investing decisions and become your own investment adviser. It does take some effort to educate yourself about how to manage your money, but once you know the basics, it's really not that difficult. There are many excellent, understandable, and readily available resources on investing, but if you're new to investing or want a quick refresher, the following will help.

What Do You Want Your Money to Do for You?

The first step is to determine what goals you have for your money. Accumulating enough money to be able to retire comfortably is certainly a goal for all working-age people. Everyone should be concerned with retirement, even people who are young and see retirement as a long way off. There are other common goals that motivate people to invest their money. You may yearn for something more immediate, such as buying a car or taking a vacation. A house or college for the kids are other common milestones. Retired people are concerned about having enough income to live comfortably and to be able to keep up with inflation.

When Do You Want to Achieve Your Goals?

Once you've determined your financial goals, you next need to decide how soon you want to reach each one of them. If you need money for a goal within three years—to buy a car for example—consider that a short-term goal. A long-term goal is 10 or more years. Consider anything in between as a medium-term goal. As I'll explain later, the time when you need your money to meet your goals will be very important for making your investment choices.

Typically, we have goals in all three of these areas—short-term, medium-term, and long-term—and one key factor in deciding where to invest your money is how soon you're going to need it. For short-term goals, safety is the most important factor: With money you'll be spending soon, you don't want the value of your money to drop just before you need it. For long-term goals, growth is important: Your money needs to increase in value enough to stay ahead of inflation. Medium-term goals are less clear-cut. You may want some combination of growth and safety. Perhaps you'd want some growth to help build your savings and some income to help balance out the ups and downs of investing for growth. Deciding how much of each you need—how much safety and how much growth is a crucial part of deciding how to invest your money.

There is a third factor that is important to many people: income. Just as working-age people earn a paycheck, your investments can earn money for you that can be spent on day-to-day expenses or can be reinvested.

RISK IS NOT A FOUR-LETTER WORD

No one wants to risk losing money, especially losing money on investments. After all, it's hard enough saving money. Losing it is, in a word, depressing. But there are two kinds of risk: the kind you can see and the kind you can't. The kind you can't see is the risk that comes from inflation and what it means to the buying power of your income. Let me give you an example. At a 3½ percent inflation rate per year, your cost of living doubles every 20 years. It could go higher than that or, hopefully, it could stay lower, but I don't want you to risk your financial future by assuming that inflation will be nonexistent or very low. At 3½ percent inflation, for every $20 you spend today, you'll need $40 in 20 years to buy the same things, and double that again for the next 20 years. In 40 years, for the $20 you need today, you'll need $80.

So let's consider someone at age 25 whose living expenses are

$25,000 today. When he is 45, he'll be spending more than $50,000 for the same expenses if inflation averages 3½ percent per year. When he retires in another 20 years, he will need $100,000—or maybe $80,000 if he can live on 20 percent less in his retirement.

Here's another example that looks at inflation a little differently. It shows how inflation affects purchasing power. Someone who is planning for retirement figures that, in addition to Social Security, he'll need $25,000 per year in income for living expenses. Now $25,000 happens to be just what his annual retirement income is expected to be, so he thinks he's in good shape. But consider how inflation can affect the purchasing power of his $25,000 over his retirement years. If inflation is 3½ percent per year, after less than seven years our retiree has seen his purchasing power drop to $20,000. After 20 years, his purchasing power can be cut in half. So that $25,000 of income, which looked so good at the time he was planning his retirement, could be worth far less in terms of purchasing power later in life. These numbers are pretty scary, I admit, but they show how much risk is involved by just letting your money sit without growing enough to outpace inflation.

Some fear investing because they can see the stock market go up and down and interest rates go up and down. That's the kind of risk you can see. So they put their money somewhere where it will be safe but earning low interest. If you don't take into account what you can't see from inflation, you will really be missing the boat. Chart #5 compares the invisible risk of inflation with the visible risk—the one that scares all of us—of losing money on our investments.

Now you may conclude that there is a risk in everything. And there is, but you can minimize the risk that you can see—the visible risk from investments. You have more control over visible risk—that is the kind you have when you invest in stocks and bonds—because you can control how much and what kind of risk you take. There are several ways to reduce the amount of visible risk; one of the best involves diversifying your investments—spreading your money around among various kinds of investments.

CHART #5	
Inflation Risk vs. Investment Risk	
The Invisible Risk of Inflation	**Visible Risk from Investments**
• Means your money loses buying power over time	• Means the value of your initial investment could go up or down
• Is caused by increases over time in the cost of living	• Is caused by different factors that depend on the type of investment
• Is less of a potential problem in the short-term	• Is historically less of a problem over the long-term
• Can be managed by investing to try to get a rate of return that is higher than or keeps pace with inflation	• Can be managed by deciding how much and what kind of investment risk to take, and how much to diversify
• Is associated mostly with short-term investments	• Is associated mostly with stocks and bonds

THE THREE MAIN INVESTMENT CATEGORIES

There are three main types of investments, each geared mostly toward one of the three things you need from your money: growth, income, and safety. I say mostly, because an investment behaves very differently over the short term—say two to three years—than it does over the long term, say ten years or more. The same investments can behave very differently over different periods. There are three basic kinds of investments: short-term investments, bonds, and stocks.

SHORT-TERM INVESTMENTS

The short-term investments that most of us are familiar with are short-term CDs, bank savings accounts, money market funds, and U.S. Treasury bills. In essence, short-term investments maintain a stable value, pay interest, and can be easily changed into cash. Of the three types of investments, short-term investments pay the lowest rate of return. So why invest in them at all? Well, people buy these primarily for safety. You do get some income from them, but what's most important is their stability. When you go into a short-term investment, you can be pretty sure about how much money you'll get out of it. You are not taking much visible risk of losing money on your investment. The prices of these types of investments don't go up and down the way that other investments do.

So when would a short-term investment be a good investment? Well, if you're going to buy something in the next year or two, it's good to know the money will be there when you need it. On the other hand, if you're not going to need the money for a few years, you may not want to keep that money in a short-term investment, because you're facing much more invisible risk from inflation. Remember how inflation cuts your buying power over time? That's the danger with short-term investments. In effect, you are losing money—losing purchasing power—without even realizing it.

BONDS

Bonds are like IOUs. When you lend someone money, you get an IOU from the borrower. (Of course, if you lend money to your child and get an IOU, good luck trying to get the money back!) With a bond, you lend money to a corporation (corporate bonds) or a federal government agency (U.S. government bonds) or a state or local government (municipal bonds) in return for receiving regular payments of interest on the loan you made as well as the repayment of principal when the loan matures. The interest provides income. That's the most important reason people buy bonds. The income can help them pay their bills or it can be reinvested. The income can also help even out the ups and downs that both bond and stock prices go through. Bonds usually pay more interest than short-term investments, but like stocks, their prices can change. Bond prices and interest rates are like the opposite ends of a seesaw. When interest rates decline, bond prices rise. But when interest rates rise, bond prices will likely decline. That means that if you have money in bonds, the overall value of that investment could go down even though you are receiving interest income. Bond interest rates stay fixed until the bond matures, and they are, therefore often called "fixed-income investments." But their prices go up and down depending on what interest rates in general do. The longer the bond's maturity—that is, the amount of time until the loan will be repaid in full—the more the price can fluctuate.

STOCKS

When you own a share of stock, you own a share of a company. How much of the company you own depends on the number of shares you have. Stocks are sometimes called "equities" because they are like the equity in your house. You own a part of something—in this case, the company. If you have a mortgage on your house, you own a part of it and the bank has the rest of your equity. With stock, the other stockholders share the equity in the company. As a group, stocks go up and down in value more than any other type of investment over the short term. But over time, stocks have been one of the few types of investments that have beaten inflation. There's no guarantee that what has happened in the past will continue in the future, of course, but the average yearly return on stocks has been a little over 10 percent. Historically, stocks have grown much faster than bonds and short-term investments. People are often afraid of stocks because they hear about bear markets or stock market crashes. That should be a concern to investors who will need the money within just a few years, but over the long run, there is more risk of losing money to inflation if you don't invest in stocks. Yes, the visible risk of stocks periodically losing value is higher in the short term than other investments, but with proper investment diversification (which is discussed in Chapter 10) you can protect yourself from that risk *and* from inflation.

MUTUAL FUNDS

Many people think that mutual funds are a fourth kind of investment. They are not. Mutual funds are one way—often a very smart way—to put money into the three types of investments discussed above. Mutual funds help individuals protect themselves against the risks of investing in the stock of just one company or in the bond of just one lender. Mutual funds allow you to pool your money with other investors. With this shared capital, the fund manager picks one of the three types of investments to concentrate on and buys many different stocks, or many different bonds, or many different short-term investments. Some funds invest in both stocks and bonds.

Each fund has its own way of trying to make money—its "investment objective." Based on those guidelines, a professional manager decides which stocks and/or bonds to buy. Stock mutual funds and bond mutual funds are self-explanatory. Some funds, such as balanced mutual funds, invest in both stocks and bonds. Money market funds buy short-term investments.

For more information on the various investment categories and the role they might play in your portfolio, click on:

http://jonathanpond.com/investments.categories.htm

TOTAL RETURN

One other investment term that's important to understand is *total return*. Total return includes not only income earned from an investment through interest and dividends, but also any increase or decrease in the price of the investment. For example, if you get 6 percent interest on a bond, but the price of the bond drops 10 percent, your total return is -4 percent. On the other hand, if you get 6 percent interest on a bond and its price increases by 8 percent, your total return is +14 percent. Total return, rather than the interest or the dividend that an investment pays, is the best way to compare different types of investments and to evaluate how your investments have performed.

MANAGING INVESTMENT RISK—THREE FOR THE MONEY

Now that you understand the various types of investments, it's time to look at managing the risk that each poses. Here are three important ingredients for managing risk.

1. Put time on your side. Investing for long periods means you have a long time to ride out the ups and downs experienced by the stock market. As I said earlier, stocks can go up or down in the short term, but the historical trend over time has been up.

2. Avoid putting all your eggs in one basket. When you diversify by investing in many different stocks or bonds instead of just one, you reduce the impact of any one investment eroding your money. You can do this with mutual funds or by buying the stocks of several companies in different industries or several bonds from different issuers.

3. Put your dollars in all three types of investments: stocks, bonds, and short-term investments. The fancy term for this is *asset allocation,* or *investment allocation.* (See Chapter 10.)

Combining the types of investments you make can help minimize risks. If one type is doing badly, another may be doing quite well. That way, you don't have to do everything right, you just have to do more right than wrong. If everything is in one basket, you have only one chance to get it right. While you'll make a killing if you're right, there's risk and then there's stupidity. Investment allocation does not guarantee against a loss, but it can help you minimize both the visible risk of periodic investment loss and the invisible risk of inflation. Remember, stocks are generally for growth, bonds are generally for income, and short-term investments are generally for meeting financial needs in the near future.

If you're concerned about investment risk or you want to learn more about how to turn invest-ment risk to your advantage, click on:
http://jonathanpond.com/investments.risk.htm

The way you divide up your investments is up to your own circumstances and judgment, but it is terribly important to your long-term investment success. So devote some time to thinking about the best way to divvy up your investments. It will be time well spent.

Developing Your Own Investment Personality

A lot of people fear taking risk with their money when, in fact, the biggest risk in investing is in taking no risk at all. Even those investors who are comfortable with risk—or at least realize that they have to take investment risk—aren't quite sure how much risk they should be taking. It's all well and good for people in the financial media, including myself, to talk about "prudent risk," but it's also fair to ask what the heck we mean by that. I'm afraid it's very difficult to quantify risk in a way that investors understand.

I've never been a big fan of those questionnaires and software programs that supposedly assess your tolerance for risk. I suppose they're okay, but my concern is that they could lead those who are downright afraid of risk and those who really love risk into making unwise investment decisions. How can the questionnaires do this? If you answered all of the questions that are posed to you in the questionnaire or software at either extreme, the resulting suggestions are likely to do you no good or even do you harm. If you answer the questions in such a manner that indicates that you don't like risk, are afraid of risk, and want nothing to do with risk, the resulting recommendations will likely put you into no-risk (translate low-yield) investments such as Treasury bills or money market funds. Or, if you indicate that you absolutely love risk, live for risk, and couldn't imagine life without risk, the recommendations may well put

> ## POND'S LAW OF INVESTMENT RISK
>
> The biggest risk in investing is taking no risk at all.

you entirely into stocks. Then one bad afternoon could wipe out everything.

I don't think that either of these risk assessment outcomes is desirable for the vast majority of investors. Rather, money that's earmarked for long-term needs, such as retirement—and that's probably most of your money—should be invested primarily in stocks and/or stock mutual funds. While you may want to reduce your stock exposure somewhat as you near or enter retirement, you should still have a majority of your money in stocks; you're still a long-term investor even if you're well into your retirement years. I'm often asked, "If stocks are so superior to other investment categories, why shouldn't I put all of my money there?" If you can tolerate the risk, go right ahead. But as much as I like stocks, I couldn't sleep at night if I had all of my money in stocks. Remember 1929? How you invest is up to you. I urge you to spend some time developing your own investment personality rather than blindly following some risk assessment computer program or the opinions of others, my own included. Don't blindly accept or reject risk. As I said in Chapter 3, nothing in your financial life is "either/or." The best investors balance their investments.

SMART (AND PAINLESS) WAYS TO ADD TO YOUR INVESTMENTS

Human nature often gets in the way of the dual tasks of saving and investing. Saving is difficult enough, and once you've saved, it takes yet more effort to put those savings to work for you. But there are a couple of ways to easily accomplish both tasks without having to lift a finger. Both of them involve electronic transfers of money to an investment account. Ah, better living through electronics: It's impossible to get your hands on money that's transferred electronically.

1. **Automatic withdrawal.** Most mutual fund companies and brokerage firms allow you to invest automatically. You specify a fixed amount to be withdrawn at regular intervals from your bank or credit union account and put into your investment account. Many employers will permit money to be withdrawn from your paycheck and automatically transferred to a retirement or investment account. It's a great way to begin and stick with a regular investing program. For example, a lot of people who have the best of intentions about contributing to an IRA every year have trouble coming up with the money to make a contribution. The cash is just, well, gone. They should have money withdrawn each month ($166 and change a month if they want to do the full $2,000) and put into their IRA accounts.

2. **Dividend Reinvestment Plans.** If you have already purchased stock in a corporation, dividend reinvestment plans (DRIPs) are one of the smartest ways to purchase new shares in the company. Why? Because corporations will purchase the shares for you either through the automatic reinvestment of your dividends or by additional investments. The icing on the cake is that they'll process those transactions for a nominal (or even no) fee. Some companies even offer these shares to you at a slight discount. That's how my few, pitiful shares of stock turned into $30,000.

In order to participate in these dividend reinvestment and optional purchase plans, you must first buy at least one share of stock through a broker—usually. A growing number of companies are allowing investors to buy their first shares directly from the company and at no commission through DIPs—direct investment plans (see page 123).

Mutual fund companies also offer to reinvest dividends (and capital gains), and it makes a great deal of sense to do so unless you need the income. A growing number of brokerage firms will reinvest your dividends for you perhaps at a small fee. There is a drawback to any reinvestment program. You still have to pay taxes on any dividends or capital gains that are reinvested. But that's a small price to pay in exchange for conveniently building up your investments over the years.

DOLLAR COST AVERAGING

Investing regularly and painlessly through automatic withdrawal and/or dividend reinvestment plans is easy to do. It's also a very smart thing to do. While most investors don't realize it, by investing automatically you're actually dollar cost averaging. Dollar cost averaging is one of the best ways to add to your investments. It involves investing a fixed amount in a particular stock issue or mutual fund account on a regular basis. The trick is to stay with your schedule regardless of whether the share price goes up or down, and as long as you stick with your automatic investing program, that's exactly what you're doing. Because you're investing a fixed amount at fixed intervals, your dollars buy fewer shares when the stock or mutual fund price is high and more when it is low. As a result, the average purchase price per share is lower than the average market price over the same period of time.

For the latest information on automatic investing, including lists of companies that offer such programs and an illustration of both dollar cost averaging and value averaging, click on:

http://jonathanpond.com/investments.automaticinvesting.htm

THERE'S NOTHING WRONG WITH OLD-FASHIONED INVESTING USING OLD-FASHIONED INVESTMENTS

> Nothing is more admirable than the fortitude with which millionaires tolerate the disadvantages of their wealth.
>
> *Rex Stout*

A caller on a talk show asked me for some help with a tax problem a while back. She couldn't reconstruct her capital gains and losses because she'd been trading stocks rather actively. I asked how actively. She said she traded 50 to 100 times *a day*. No wonder she couldn't figure out her capital gains. Day traders are a curious species. I guess we all go through a stage when we fancy ourselves brilliant traders, but it doesn't take long for the inevitable comeuppance. If you're a day trader—or even an active trader—this chapter won't be too stimulating. Instead, this chapter will help you become better at:

➤ diversifying your investments
➤ rebalancing your portfolio
➤ investing overseas
➤ buying stock directly from corporations
➤ investing in real estate
➤ investing in—or avoiding—annuities

SOLVING THE MYSTERY OF SUCCESSFUL INVESTING

Investing successfully is crucial to your financial future, but there is no mystery to it—just a lot of common sense applied to techniques which have been used by successful investors for decades. The following sections will lead you through the process of assembling a diversified investment portfolio in just four straightforward steps.

A lot of people are frightened by investing. They have been led to believe that investing is complicated and the average Joe and Jane are simply incapable of making sensible investment decisions. Everyone can be a successful investor, and the way to success is through old-fashioned, dull investments.

IS INVESTMENT ALLOCATION PASSÉ?

There has been much discussion in the investment community about whether investment allocation is relevant anymore. Some critics of investment allocation cite the long bull market of the 1990s that rewarded large-cap U.S. growth stocks and left everything else, small caps, internationals, and bonds in the dust. These critics maintain that the "new economy" (see page 157) is so favorable to big U.S. growth companies that putting your money anywhere else is, well, a waste of money—especially in the 21st century. A lot of investors have been lulled into the cozy notion that the real action is in U.S. large caps. After all, that's where the action was in the late 1990s. If you owned anything else it did nothing more than drag down your investment returns. Truth be told, it did do something more: it lowered investment risk. The critics have lost sight of the reason to diversify: reducing risk. And if you diversify, you're bound to underperform the leading performance benchmark—the one that gets all of the attention. But you'll sleep like a rock.

Since investment allocation is far from

POND'S LAW OF HAPPINESS

Happiness is a dull portfolio.

dead, I'm going to explain how it works and how it will make you a more prudent and better investor. It involves four steps. Since most investors start out with mutual fund investments, and even experienced investors and investors with large portfolios make generous use of mutual funds, I'll illustrate allocation using those "everyman" treatments. These guidelines apply to all of your investments—mutual funds as well as individual stocks and bonds.

My illustrations include only stock and bond investments. Most investors put all or most of the money they're investing for the long-term into stocks and bonds—and mutual funds that invest in stocks or bonds. As mentioned in Chapter 9, short-term investments are most appropriate to meet short-term investment needs. They are discussed on page 136. Another investment category is real estate. If you're thinking about investing in income-producing real estate, I offer some tips on page 123.

STEP ONE: FIGURE OUT HOW MUCH TO INVEST IN STOCK FUNDS AND HOW MUCH TO INVEST IN BOND FUNDS

The first step is a simple calculation that helps you determine your allocation between stocks and bonds. In other words, of the total money you have available to invest, this determines how much should be invested in stock funds (and stocks) and how much in bond funds (and bonds).

Three different investment allocations are presented below. The one you select is up to you. It will depend upon how comfortable you are taking risk, what your goals are and your stage in life. If you are very comfortable with investment risk, then you will probably opt for the aggressive investment allocation. On the other hand, if risk makes you nervous, the conservative allocation may be for you. And for those who are somewhere in between, like me, there is a moderate investment allocation as well.

AGGRESSIVE PORTFOLIO ALLOCATION

If you are willing to accept risk in your investments in exchange for the possibility of earning high long-term investment returns, here is the formula for calculating an aggressive investment allocation:

Subtract your age from 120. The resulting amount is the approximate percentage of the money you have available for long-term investment that you should invest in stocks. The rest should be invested in bonds.

A 40-year-old investor who is quite comfortable with risk therefore wants an aggressive portfolio allocation. She would, according to the above formula, invest about 80 percent of her money in stock funds (120 - 40 = 80) and the rest, about 20 percent, in bond funds.

Moderate Portfolio Allocation

A moderate portfolio allocation still includes a fairly heavy weighting of stocks in the portfolio. To determine a moderate portfolio allocation, use the following formula:

Subtract your age from 110. The resulting amount is the approximate percentage of the money you have available for long-term investment that you should invest in stocks. The rest should be invested in bonds.

A 50-year-old investor wisely realizes that he needs to continue investing for growth as well as income during retirement, and a moderate portfolio allocation would fit the bill. According to the above formula, this investor would put about 60 percent of his money in stock funds (110 - 50 = 60) and the rest, about 40 percent, in bond funds.

Conservative Portfolio Allocation

If you are less comfortable with the ups and downs of the stock market, a conservative portfolio will still place some stock funds in your portfolio. Stocks are essential if your portfolio is going to grow over the years, but the proportion of stocks will be somewhat lower than the aggressive and moderate portfolios. To determine a conservative portfolio allocation, use the following formula:

Subtract your age from 100. The resulting amount is the approximate percentage of the money you have available for long-term investment that you should invest in stocks. The rest should be invested in bonds.

A 53-year-old investor who is a bit skittish about the stock market but still realizes that stocks are crucial to her long-term investment success should follow a conservative portfolio allocation. According to that formula, she would invest about 47 percent of her money in stock funds (100 - 53 = 47) and the rest, about 53 percent in bond funds.

Some Additional Guidelines

All three investment allocation formulas are based on your age, so as your age increases you will gradually invest more money in bonds and less in stocks. The older you become, the less time you have to make up for investment losses, and yes, there will be times when you suffer losses. So, as you age, your investment allocation will gradually become more conservative since bonds are a more conservative investment than stocks. The formula will change each year. That doesn't mean you need to change your investment allocation every year. These formulas should be rough approximations of how you should invest, not rigid standards.

The problem with investment allocation formulas that are tied to age is that they suggest a lower percentage of stocks for retirees than is prudent. So you may find that the above formulas result in a stock allocation percentage that is lower than you think is appropriate. If you're comfortable with a higher percentage of your money in stocks, by all means allocate your portfolio accordingly. I think most recent retirees should still have at least 60 percent of their money invested in stocks and veteran retirees at least half. After all, you're still a long-term investor whose living costs will rise and, therefore, whose investments need to rise accordingly.

STEP TWO: FIGURE OUT HOW MUCH TO INVEST IN EACH STOCK AND BOND MUTUAL FUND CATEGORY

Unfortunately, successful investing is a bit more complicated than simply putting all of the money you've earmarked for stocks in a single stock fund and all the money you've earmarked for bonds in a single bond fund. There are many different kinds of stocks and bonds, and so there are many different kinds of stock and bond mutual funds. This variety works to your advantage. There are four major categories of stock mutual funds:

- Large company U.S. growth (stocks that don't pay dividends)
- Large company U.S. growth and income (dividend-paying stocks)
- Small company (small cap)
- International

There are three major categories of bond mutual funds:

- Municipal
- U.S. government
- Corporate

The way you allocate your money in the bond categories depends on whether your investments are in retirement accounts and/or taxable accounts. Since the interest income from municipal bond funds is exempt from federal and, perhaps, state income taxes, you should invest in them only in a *taxable* investment account. Since the interest earned on corporate bond funds is subject to both federal and state income taxes, they are best suited for *retirement* accounts since the interest that would otherwise be heavily taxed is not subject to income taxes until you begin withdrawing.

For a detailed description of the many categories of stock and bond mutual funds, click on:
http://jonathanpond.com/investments.mutualfundcategories.htm

Assigning Percentages to Each Category

By now, you've assigned overall percentages to both stocks and bonds according to your age and the amount of risk you feel comfortable with. The way you allocate your money within those percentages is dependent upon the same things. If you are working age but not yet within a decade or so of retirement, you have a long time for your investments to grow. So the emphasis in the stock and bond categories should be on those with the best long-term growth potential. Of course, with growth comes risk. But for investors who won't need the money for a long time, history has shown that prudent risk is well rewarded. Pre-retirees—those within 10 years or so of retirement—often need to begin getting a bit less aggressive with their investments. But the emphasis should still be on investments that offer inflation-beating growth. Finally, retirees may want to be more conservative, while keeping enough money invested for growth so that they keep up with inflation.

Invest in all or most of these categories in reasonable proportions. By so doing, you will always have at least some money invested in thriving categories while not having too much of your money tied up in the dogs.

While everyone's situation is unique, Chart #6 shows an example of how someone who has both retirement accounts and taxable accounts might allocate their money within the various categories of stocks and bonds.

Investment allocation case studies that show people from all walks of life how to diversify may be found by clicking on:

http://jonathanpond.com/investments.allocations.htm

Recommendations for More Modest Portfolios

You probably need at least $15,000 to $20,000 to create a portfolio that includes all of the above-recommended investments. The reason being that most (but not all) mutual fund companies require minimum investment balances of $2,500 or more per fund, with lower minimums for IRA or other retirement accounts. If you're not at that lofty level, don't despair. If you have less than $5,000 to invest, select a balanced mutual fund (see page 131). These funds invest in both stocks and bonds, giving you a "balanced" portfolio in a single mutual fund. Once you have more than $5,000 to invest, you can begin to buy individual mutual funds in sequence, perhaps starting with a growth and income stock fund, a government bond fund, an international stock fund, a municipal bond fund, and so forth.

CHART #6			
Sample Fund Investment Category Allocation			
Stock Mutual Funds		**Bond Mutual Funds**	
Percentage of money you will invest in stock funds		Percentage of money you will invest in bond funds	
Growth	30%	Municipal	40%
Growth and income	40	U.S. Government	30
Small company	15	Corporate	<u>30</u>
International	<u>15</u>		
	100%		100%

Finally, if you have a 401(k) or similar plan where you work, remember to combine the money you're investing in that account, as well as all other investment accounts you might have, when deciding how to divvy up your money in a balanced and diversified fashion.

STEP THREE: SELECT AND MONITOR YOUR MUTUAL FUND INVESTMENTS

In the third step, I'll provide some guidance on how to select good mutual funds in each category and then monitor your fund investments periodically.

SELECTING GOOD FUNDS

The process of selecting good funds may seem overwhelming. After all, there are more than 10,000 available and the financial press is constantly highlighting the hot-performing ones. Every fund manages to find *some* performance measure that it can beat. It may seem that, depending on how you measure them, all funds are good funds. But they're not. Yet there are hundreds of excellent funds, and the challenge is finding the ones that are right for you.

Selecting good funds is not difficult. If you have access to the right resources, and your public library almost certainly does, you can find the right funds for you in no time. If you rely on someone else to recommend a fund, be sure to ask why he or she is high on the fund, especially if you're paying for the advice. In my experience, I have rarely encountered a situation where a paid adviser is recommending sub-par funds. In fact, when asked to review a portfolio of mutual funds prepared by a broker or other adviser, I almost always have nothing but praise for the selections.

PONO'S FIRST LAW OF MUTUAL FUNDS

A heretofore-excellent mutual fund's performance will deteriorate right after you buy it.

An Abundance of Resources

If you want to select your own funds, go to the library and check out one of the mutual fund monitoring services such as *Morningstar* or *Value Line Mutual Fund Survey*. Also, the major financial newspapers (particularly *The Wall Street Journal* and *Barron's*) and the financial magazines provide regular coverage of mutual funds. I particularly like the monthly mutual fund coverage in *The Wall Street Journal*, published on the first Monday of each month, and the quarterly mutual fund wrap-ups published in both *The Wall Street Journal* and *Barron's* shortly after the end of each quarter.

While many publications provide extensive fund coverage, be very careful about blindly following their recommendations. History has shown time and again that some of the funds that they tout end up being short-term wonders and long-term whimpers. On the other hand, lists of recommended funds can provide a good source of names for your further investigation. The important thing is not to purchase a fund just because you read about it in a magazine or newspaper or heard someone tout it. Do your own research.

How to Identify Winning Funds

There are several ways to identify possible fund candidates worthy of including in your portfolio. If you're starting from scratch in locating good funds, check the resources mentioned above. Use the following criteria as a first cut:

- *Morningstar:* Overall ranking of four or five stars
- *Value Line Mutual Fund Survey:* Overall ranking of one or two
- *Wall Street Journal* Monthly mutual fund performance: Ranking over the past one, three, and five years of "A," "B," or "C" (particularly if the fund has earned no more than a single "C" ranking in those three time periods)

The more ranking services you can use to check on a particular fund, the better. Ideally, you should be able to identify a fund that not only consistently ranks above average in comparison with its peers but that is also highly regarded by the various ratings services. Each of these services uses different criteria to evaluate past fund performance. So if you find a fund in a particular category that is well regarded by all of them, you probably have a winner. Finally, be sure to read a fund's prospectus and most recent performance report before investing to make sure you're comfortable with the fund's investment philosophy and its individual holdings.

PON'S SECOND LAW OF MUTUAL FUNDS

The performance of a fund will collapse shortly after it is featured by a financial publication as one of the best.

MONITORING FUND PERFORMANCE

The great advantage of mutual funds is that you are paying someone else a small amount of money to lie awake at night worrying about how your money should be invested. But you still need to check up periodically on how the funds you own are doing. It's quite simple, and it is important. You don't want to discover five years from now that the wonderful fund you bought has turned into a stinker.

How often?

Review your funds' performance every six months. If you really want to get into your investments you might do it quarterly, but those who review their investments too often are likely to overreact to what they see as a disappointing problem. Every fund, even the best ones, will periodically underperform its peers. If you are checking a fund every month and you see that it is consistently underperforming, you're liable to pull the plug on the fund just before it—as so often happens with good funds—comes roaring back.

How to Review Your Funds

Reviewing fund performance takes only a few minutes. You need to make sure the performance of each fund you own is up to snuff. That doesn't necessarily mean that a fund you own must have outperformed its peers over the past six months, but it is important to know if it has badly underperformed them. It is also important to make sure your stock and bond allocations remain on target (see Step Four on page 120). Here are the steps for making periodic evaluation of your fund holdings.

1. **List all of your fund investments.** Organize a list according to investment category—growth, small company, U.S. government bond, etc.
2. **Determine what the total return performance of each fund has been within the most recent period.** Note this performance next to the fund names on your summary. The financial newspapers list the total return performance of each fund for the year-to-date (YTD).

3. **Compare each fund's performance to the performance of its peer group.** The peer group performance record can be found in the summaries that the mutual fund monitoring services provide or in *The Wall Street Journal.* Make sure that you are accurately comparing each fund with its peer group average.

4. **Gather more historical data for laggards.** If you are concerned that your fund has underperformed its peer group average, review its performance over the past couple of years. If you determine your fund has been a laggard for a lot more than just the last six months or so, this may be the time to consider a change. On the other hand, if it has just begun to lag, you should probably wait a while to see if, as is often the case, the fund rebounds. See page 132 for tips on deciding when to sell a fund.

It's also important to remember that the ways the mutual fund monitoring services classify funds are far from precise. For example, most stock mutual fund managers use one of two investment "styles" for managing their funds (some mangers use a blend of both styles):

- **Growth style.** Managers who prefer investing in stocks with rapidly growing sales and profits, *or*
- **Value style.** Mangers who prefer investing in stocks that they think are undervalued and underappreciated by Wall Street

Usually, one style is doing better than the other, and therein lies the dilemma. The ranking services could assign a higher rank to a fund whose management style is in favor and a lower rank to a fund whose management style is lagging even though the funds are in the same general category—small company funds, for example. Consider the late 1990s when the growth style of investing was producing much better returns than value. As a result, value funds suffered in the mutual fund rankings. But just because your fund's management style happens to be out of favor doesn't mean you should dump the fund. That style will inevitably come back into favor. Incidentally, studies have shown that over long investment periods, the total gains posted by value-style and growth-style funds are just about equal, with a slight advantage to value.

5. **Determine your investment allocation status.** Summarize your investment allocation status as part of your periodic review. Compare the percentage

of total fund assets in each investment category with your investment allocation objectives as discussed in Step Two. If you find a significant variance between where your investments stand and your target, you should consider rebalancing to return to your target percentages. This is the subject of the fourth and final step.

STEP FOUR: PERIODICALLY REBALANCE YOUR INVESTMENT ALLOCATION

If you follow the first three steps described above you should achieve very good investment results. Periodically rebalancing your investment allocation should help you achieve even better results. The reason for this is quite simple. Rebalancing your investments forces you to do the right thing, even if it requires you to go against the current outlook of Wall Street experts. Going against the Wall Street crowd is often not such a bad thing to do. Here's how rebalancing works. About every six months, summarize your investments to see how they're allocated. Be sure to combine all of your investment accounts. Rebalancing is a waste of time if you fail to consider all of the money you have available for investment. Figure out for your combined portfolios what the current percentages are in each of your investment categories—typically growth stock funds, growth and income stock funds, small company stock funds, international stock funds, municipal bond funds, U.S. government bond funds, and corporate bond funds. Chances are that you'll find that the percentages you now have in stocks and bonds vary from the allocation you want. (See Chart #6 on page 115 for an example.) That's because stock and bond values fluctuate. What rebalancing does is bring your investment allocation back to the percentages you determined in Steps One and Two. Here's a brief example:

> Barry Berry wants to maintain a 70 percent stock/30 percent overall allocation. But stock prices have declined over the past six months to the point where stocks now account for 63 percent of his portfolio's total value. What should he do? Rebalance by selling enough of his bond investments and use that money to add more to his stock investments so that he brings his portfolio back to his 70 percent stock/30 percent bond target allocation.

By periodically rebalancing your portfolio, you force yourself to make very sensible changes in your investment portfolios. In the above example, the stock market had declined rather sharply over the previous six months, and you're buying stocks *after* they've declined in value. Would this not be a bad time to be buying a *small amount* of stock investments? If the market has de-

POND'S THIRD LAW OF MUTUAL FUNDS

A mediocre mutual fund will begin to outperform its peers right after you sell it.

clined sharply, the investment experts are flooding the airwaves with a very pessimistic outlook. You're probably buying some of your stocks at a time when the great majority of investors are selling. But that's okay. Rebalancing also forces you to sell some of your stock investments if the stock market has risen and add to bonds when interest rates have risen. By following this formula, you're buying cheap and selling dear.

How Often Should You Rebalance?

You might be thinking that if rebalancing is such a great thing, you should do it all the time. It takes some time, and you don't want to burden yourself by doing it too often. While rebalancing once a year may be appropriate for many investors, my recommendation is to rebalance about every six months *unless* there has been a major change in either stock prices or interest rates (which affect bond prices). Then, you might want to rebalance in less than six months.

Some Important Things to Consider

There are some important matters to consider before you rebalance. Sometimes, the costs or inconvenience of rebalancing may outweigh the benefits.

Before rebalancing, carefully analyze what, if any, tax consequences would result, and avoid making sales where there may be costly tax consequences. Instead, find alternatives that will result in you owing little or no taxes—rebalancing in a retirement account, perhaps, since no taxes are owed until you start withdrawing money from the retirement account.

Also, be mindful of investment costs. The benefits of rebalancing can soon be lost if fees and commissions eat away at your portfolio. Rebalance through no-load funds or load fund families that allow no-cost switches within the family.

Finally, you may find that the necessary rebalancing involves such a small amount of money that it isn't worth your time and effort. Perhaps you should wait another six months before doing it. But you can't reach that conclusion without finding out exactly where your portfolio stands.

Rebalancing causes a lot of confusion for investors. For some examples and work sheets that will take the mystery out of rebalancing, click on:

http://jonathanpond.com/investments.rebalancing.htm

WHY INVESTING OVERSEAS MAKES SENSE (AND DOLLARS)

A lot of people tell me that they have international investments because the U.S. stocks they own (either individually or in their mutual funds) derive a lot of revenues and profits from foreign operations. Certainly, many U.S. companies do very well overseas, and overseas expansion has most definitely bolstered their bottom lines. But the reason you invest internationally is to take advantage of the opportunities offered by the many excellent companies that are based overseas. This is most easily done through an international or global mutual fund but can also be done by buying shares of foreign corporations that trade on the U.S. stock exchanges. These shares are known as American Depository Receipts, or ADRs.

While the lackluster performance of foreign stocks in the 1990s caused many people to get rid of them, their time in the sunshine will return. (Actually, foreign stocks didn't do all that badly. U.S. stocks just performed spectacularly.) While foreign stocks did drag down the investment returns of a well-diversified portfolio a bit, the reason you put some money overseas is to decrease the overall risk in your investment portfolio. That's right. As risky as they may seem to a U.S. investor, adding foreign stocks to a portfolio that consists primarily of U.S. stocks actually *decreases* the risk in that portfolio.

For some additional ideas on ways to prudently add a foreign flavor to your investments, click on:

http://jonathanpond.com/investments.international.htm

Buying Stocks Directly from Corporations

In the early 1970s, a handful of companies began offering dividend reinvestment plans (DRIPs), which allowed shareholders to automatically reinvest their dividends and buy additional shares (see page 107). DRIPs caught on and now about 1,000 corporations offer them. In order to participate in a DRIP, however, you had to first buy some shares of stock in the company through a stockbroker—usually.

In recent years a new investor-friendly program, direct investment plans (DIPs), has been introduced. Several hundred companies now permit investors to make direct *initial* purchases of stock from the company (called DIPs). You can buy shares from these companies without a broker and still participate in their DRIPs. Minimum initial purchases typically range from $200 to $1,000, and your local library has directories with phone numbers so that you can contact the corporations directly.

For the latest information on DRIPs, DIPs, other automatic investment programs, and a list of the companies that offer them click on:

http://jonathanpond.com/investments.automaticinvesting.htm

A Quick Way to Evaluate a Contemplated Real Estate Investment

It's too bad more people don't invest in income-producing real estate because it's one of the best ways for people of average financial means to create wealth. True, being a landlord is no picnic, but a lot of people don't seem to mind it. If the real estate bug ever catches you, here are

POND'S LAW OF REAL ESTATE PROFIT MAXIMIZATION

The best place to advertise a property that you want to sell is in the local medical journal because doctors are notorious for overpaying for real estate.

some suggestions that will help you avoid the biggest sin inexperienced (and even a few experienced) real estate investors commit: overpaying. If you pay too much, the property is almost a sure loser from the outset.

The simplest way to evaluate a property is to compare the price you'd have to pay for it with its current gross yearly rental income—called the "rent multiplier." Any property selling for much more than seven or eight times total annual rental is likely to yield a negative cash flow; in other words, your rental income won't be sufficient to cover your mortgage and operating expenses, let alone make a profit. To determine the rent multiplier, which compares the total selling price with the current gross annual rental, use the following formula:

$$\text{Rent multiplier} = \frac{\text{Selling price}}{\text{Gross annual rental}}$$

The asking price of a duplex is $165,000 and it generates $15,000 in annual rent. The rent multiplier is calculated as follows:

$$\text{Rent multiplier} = \frac{\$165,000}{\$15,000} = 11$$

In other words, the property is selling for 11 times annual rental. As I just mentioned, any property that is selling for much more than seven times the gross annual rental is probably not going to be a particularly good investment. Also remember that if you put a sizable cash down payment into the property to assure a positive cash flow, you're only fooling yourself; there's an opportunity cost associated with tying up a lot of cash that could otherwise be earning income. Incidentally, professional real estate investors generally do not pay more than five to six times gross annual rental.

The Lowdown on Annuities

Everyone's heard about annuities, but many people's eyes glaze over when trying to figure them out. So here's a quick and dirty explanation. These are the four characteristics of annuities:

➤ An **immediate annuity** is one that begins making regular payments to you as soon as you put your money into it. Immediate annuities are usually used by retirees to receive a regular, assured income for the rest of their lives.

➤ A **deferred annuity** is one in which you invest your money now, let it grow inside the annuity tax deferred, and later withdraw it in a lump sum, by receiving regular payments until the money runs out or by rolling the money into an immediate annuity for ongoing income.

➤ A **fixed annuity** grows or makes payments at a fixed rate of return.

➤ A **variable annuity** invests the annuity money in a variety of mutual funds of your choosing.

Therefore, there are actually four kinds of annuities based upon these characteristics:

➤ **Fixed deferred annuity**—a tax-deferred investment account that grows in value based on a fixed investment return

➤ **Variable deferred annuity**—a tax-deferred investment account that grows in value based on a variable investment return depending on the performance of the underlying mutual funds selected for investment

➤ **Fixed immediate-pay annuity**—an investment account that makes fixed regular payments to you either for a certain period of time or for the rest of your life

➤ **Variable immediate-pay annuity**—an investment account that makes regular payments to you either for a certain period of time or for the rest of your life. The amount of the payments varies according to the performance of the underlying mutual funds that you select for investment.

I'll discuss deferred annuities next. You can find some suggestions on immediate annuities on page 193.

Should You Invest in Deferred Annuities?

A lot of people are buying (actually they're probably sold) deferred annuities who shouldn't be doing so. The current income tax structure taxes long-term capital gains—capital gains for investments that aren't sold for at least a year at a lower rate than income from other sources. The attraction of deferred annuities is that you can invest as much money as you'd like in a tax-deferred annuity (but the money you put in is not deductible), and it will grow tax-deferred, just like an IRA, until you eventually withdraw the money, presumably when you're retired.

But the current tax rules have taken a lot of the bloom off the annuity rose. Let me explain. As with any long-term investment, and that's what deferred annuities are supposed to be, you should invest the money primarily in stock funds or stocks to achieve inflation-beating growth. Let's assume for a moment that you have a choice between investing excess money in a deferred annuity or in a taxable investment account. If you invested money in the annuity, the tax rules dictate that you will eventually pay taxes on the annuity's gains at the same rate as your other income from dividends and interest, in other words, at a higher rate than you would for capital gains. If instead of the annuity, you simply kept the money in a taxable investment account and invested it in tax-efficient investments such as individual stocks and index funds, the taxes you pay would be primarily at a lower rate than you would have to pay from the deferred annuity. (See page 171 for more information on tax-efficient investing.) True, you may have to pay some taxes along the way in the taxable account, which would have been avoided in the deferred annuity, but studies show that in order to receive a benefit from the deferred annuity, the money has to be in there a long time.

This doesn't mean that tax-deferred annuities aren't worthwhile; they may be in some instances. But I've been finding that a lot of people are getting into deferred annuities who shouldn't be. Here are some rules that will help you decide whether a deferred annuity makes sense for you and, if so, how to pick a good one.

1. **Max out your other retirement plan investments before buying a deferred annuity.** It doesn't make any sense to buy into a deferred annuity if you haven't contributed the maximum to all other types of retirement plans that are available to you. They're all better retirement investments than the deferred annuity. If someone who is trying to sell you a deferred annuity tells you otherwise, they, er, don't have your best interests in mind. Also, never, never, never put a deferred annuity into an IRA or other retirement account. Putting an investment that is tax advantaged already (the deferred annuity) into an account that is also tax advantaged makes about as much sense as paying your income taxes twice.

2. **Don't buy a deferred annuity unless you intend to hold on to it for at least 20 years.** It takes many, many years for the tax advantages of a deferred annuity to offset its fees (which can be considerable) as well as the higher eventual tax rate described above. Thus, anyone over 50 needs to take an especially hard look at buying a tax-deferred annuity. Sadly, many retirees are being sold deferred annuities that have no place in a retiree's investment portfolio. I have yet to speak with any retiree who, when they fully understood what they had been sold, didn't regret it.

3. **Ignore the insurance feature.** One selling point that is often offered with tax-deferred annuities is insurance. Some insurance. All the insurance usually offers is to pay your estate the equivalent of what you originally invested in your deferred annuity if you die and the annuity's value is less than your original investment. While some insurers are sweetening the insurance provision a bit, this insurance is of dubious value, particularly when (if) you find out how much you're being charged for it each year.

4. **Select a low-fee deferred annuity.** If you decide that a deferred annuity is a worthwhile addition to your retirement investment arsenal, make sure you choose one that levies low fees and offers mutual funds with strong past performance records. Fees vary widely among insurance companies that offer deferred annuities. If you're willing to do a little shopping on your own, check with the big no-load mutual fund companies. Several offer deferred annuities, which have lower fees, less restrictive penalties if you want to switch to another company or withdraw money within a few years, and excellent mutual funds within the annuity.

For a rundown on the latest information on both immediate and deferred annuities and companies offering annuities, click on:

http://jonathanpond.com/investments.annuities.htm

SLEEP-TIGHT INVESTING

Several years ago, one of the Boston newspapers interviewed me about my investment philosophy. I was delighted to see my picture on the first page of the business section accompanying the interview. The caption under the photo read: "Jonathan Pond advocates dullness and passivity." All well and good until an acquaintance called my wife that morning to tell her about the photo and the caption. What the acquaintance didn't say was that I was talking about investing. For some reason my wife thought the article was in the "Family Life" section which caused her to respond: "What's Jonathan doing talking about our love life in the newspaper?" But, when it comes to investing, I still think dull is beautiful. In this chapter, I want to show you some ways to sleep better at night and not worry about your investments.

My five-year-old loves to tell her two older sisters and her parents to have "sweet dreams" before she reluctantly retires for the evening. While the information that follows probably won't give you sweet dreams, I hope it will help you avoid losing sleep over your investments.

WHAT TO DO IF YOU HAVE A LOT OF CASH TO INVEST

There may come a time (or that time could be right now) when you have a lot of money sitting in a checking or savings account or other low-yield securities that you want to invest. There are a couple of events that could give rise to this. Either you haven't done anything about investing all or a large chunk of the money you've saved, or you have recently received a cash windfall (an inheritance or a distribution from your retirement plan or a large bonus). Whatever the situation, the $64,000 question is how fast should you go about investing the money?

TWO SCHOOLS OF THOUGHT

There are two schools of thought about how to invest a sizable amount of cash. The first school says, "Invest it all at once," and it has history on its side. More often than not, the stock market is rising — in fact, it rises about 80 percent of the time. Therefore, by investing all of the cash at once, the odds are in your favor. Studies that have compared immediate investing with gradual investing do show that there is a slight advantage to investing all the money at once.

Now for the second school of thought. Let's call it "Jonathan's Sleep-at-Night Approach." I prefer investing a cash windfall gradually. I'm not alone in this theory, by the way. A lot of investment pros think that history be damned, you don't want to risk buying a fortune in stocks just before the market declines or cornering the market in bonds just before interest rates shoot up.

The way to reduce the risk of ill-timed investing is to devise a plan to invest your money gradually. Don't get me wrong. If you can accept the risk of investing all of the money at once, then do it. As I said, history is on your side. But a lot of us are a bit

> ### POND'S LAW OF INSOMNIA
>
> For every ten minutes you spend during the day worrying about your investments, you will lose one hour's sleep that night.

too skittish to do that. Investing your money gradually is, in essence, much like the dollar-cost averaging technique that is widely and successfully used for investing in individual stocks or mutual funds. (See page 108.)

You can find examples of strategies and timetables for investing a substantial sum by clicking on:

http://jonathanpond.com/investments.timetables.htm

The Case for Balanced Funds (and Balanced Investing)

A lot of people ask me to recommend a single mutual fund. Often, they're first-time investors or they want to set up an investment account for a younger generation family member. Fortunately, there are a lot of mutual funds that combine two or more investment categories in a single fund. The ones I recommend fall under one of these two categories:

- **Balanced funds.** While there is some variation in the allocation, the typical balanced fund invests 60 percent of its money in stocks and the remaining 40 percent in bonds. This, by the way, isn't such a bad overall allocation anyway, so you can combine both stocks and bonds in good measure with a single fund. I often refer to balanced funds as "the one fund to own if you own only one fund."
- **Asset allocation funds.** Funds in this category have a bit more flexibility in how they divvy up their investors' money among various investment categories. Some of these funds have target dates, such as 2010, which means the manager selects the investments with that time horizon in mind. The longer it is until the fund's target date, the more money that is allocated to stocks.

Balanced fund managers have a shorter leash in that they usually have to hew to a more stringent stock/bond allocation than asset allocation fund managers, but you can find good individual funds in either of these categories.

KNOWING WHEN TO SELL A MUTUAL FUND

Talk about losing sleep. Countless investors have tossed and turned because they're not sure what to do with a sub-par mutual fund. The basic rules for selling a fund apply in both strong and weak investment markets. Consider the following unfortunate, but common, scenario. An investor chooses a stock mutual fund based solely on its strong recent performance. Over the next several quarters, however, the fund's performance begins to lag behind its peers. Disappointed, the investor sells in favor of another fund with stronger recent performance. Shortly thereafter, the fund that was sold begins to rebound, once again posting the solid results for which the investor originally purchased it, while the recently purchased fund begins to lag. To such an investor it must seem as if he can do no right. An investment veteran once counseled a similarly frustrated part-time stock market player by reminding him that "the stock doesn't know you own it." In the case described above, however, the problem was not with the fund, but with the investor. And the problem is knowing when to sell.

There are several factors that need to be considered before selling a mutual fund. If a fund's performance deteriorates, as in the case described above, you've got to make an assessment of the cause of the poor performance. Is it performing badly compared with other categories of funds or is it performing badly compared with similar funds?

BAD PERFORMANCE COMPARED WITH FUNDS IN OTHER CATEGORIES

It doesn't matter how well or how badly the market is performing. If your fund investments are diversified, you're bound to have some whose return is downright anemic compared with the top-performing funds that get all the attention in the business press each quarter. But just because your fund made only 3 percent while some other funds made 13 percent last quarter doesn't mean you should offload the one you've got. Just as trading a shortstop for failing to hit enough home runs makes little sense to a major league baseball manager, selling a small company stock fund for failing to keep pace with a roaring bull market that rewards large company stock funds makes little sense to an experienced investor. If the out-of-favor fund is, in fact, doing what it's supposed to be doing, and you're still comfortable maintaining an investment in that category, then abandoning the fund on the basis of underperformance with other fund categories is the wrong decision.

BAD PERFORMANCE COMPARED WITH SIMILAR FUNDS

If your fund is underperforming compared with the average for similar funds (for example, other small company funds), you have a potential problem, but don't be too quick to dump the fund. First, make sure you're comparing apples to apples when comparing the fund with its peers. If your fund emphasizes value investing, don't compare it with funds that emphasize growth investing (see page 119). Second, if it is under performing its peers, find out why. Often, the manager simply emphasized some group of stocks or some type or maturity of bonds that didn't do too well. But if the manager is consistent, chances are that his or her preferences will eventually pay off. That's why I recommend holding on to a fund unless and until it underperforms its category average for two consecutive years. If you picked a good fund in the first place, but it has temporarily fallen on hard times, chances are very good that the fund will begin to turn in performance numbers that are well above average. By the way, as I mentioned earlier, the rebound occurs right after quick-triggered investors have sold the fund.

For additional guidance on evaluating mutual fund performance, click on:

http://jonathanpond.com/investments.mutualfundevaluation.htm

MANAGEMENT CHANGE

A change in management may or may not be a reason to sell a fund. In such cases it's important to assess the likelihood that the fund will be able to continue in the same manner as it has in the past. Compare it to cuisine. At one restaurant a star chef cooks up specialties each night according to his whims, while at another restaurant the recipes are rigorously followed night after night. Clearly, at the former a change in chefs is a major event (whether good or bad), while at the latter it doesn't much matter who's cooking from night to night. Getting back to funds, don't automatically sell a good fund if it changes managers. More often than not, the new manager is up to the challenge of continuing the fund's strong performance.

CHANGE IN YOUR INVESTMENT GOALS

Last, but perhaps most important, you might sell a fund when your own goals have changed. This is easy to overlook especially if a fund is performing well in a rising market or is holding up well in a declining market. An investor who has racked up substantial long-term gains in a growth fund may be reticent to sell despite an increasing need for retirement income. Similarly, an investor whose nest egg is earmarked for a young child's college education needs to rethink her strategy if her goal changes to the purchase of a home. For these reasons, it is a good idea to reassess your investment goals at least once a year.

The decision whether or not to sell is far simpler for the investor who understands why a fund was purchased in the first place. From that point on, the investor need only monitor the fund to make sure that the reasons for which it was purchased are still in force. The tendency of some investors to overtrade brings to mind a study conducted in the late 1980s that correlated the practices of stock fund managers to the performance of their funds. The one trait that was unmistakably correlated to success was discipline. It is a trait you would be wise to look for in your funds, and in yourself.

YOUR INVESTMENT ADVISER'S WORST NIGHTMARE

If I ever need somebody to explain something in a way that no one will ever be able to understand, I'll hire a big investment firm. Their investment performance statements are the apogee of obfuscation. No one, not even a Ph.D. in finance, could figure out how their investments have done based on the information that these firms provide in their statements.

Sadly (for big investment firms), it is quite easy to provide a statement that tells the investor precisely what happened to his or her investments over the past month, quarter, or year. Chart #7 contains a form that you can take straight to whoever oversees your investments. (Please don't tell your adviser where you got this, or I'm going to get some unkind mail.) If you manage your own money, you should fill it out yourself.

In just six lines, you can receive an informative summary of just how your investment account performed. Then you don't have to count sheep wondering how your investments *really* did. I don't think anyone could argue that it's unfair to request this summary.

PONO'S LAW OF STOCK SELECTION

The price of a stock will decline just after you buy it. The price of a stock will rise just after you sell it. (The same applies to mutual funds.)

CHART #7

Investment Performance Summary

Name:_____

Period measured: From: ___/___/___ To: ___/___/___   Example

                    Mo/day/year   Mo/day/year

		Example
1. Beginning balance in investment account	$_____	$50,000
2. Plus: Money added to account	_____	6,000
3. Subtract: Money withdrawn from account	(_____)	(2,000)
4. Subtract: Commissions and fees	(_____)	(500)
5. Add or (subtract) investment gains or (losses) for the period	_____	$ 3,500
6. Equals ending balance in investment account	$_____	$57,000

How to Invest Money That You're Going to Need within a Few Years

While you benefit from taking a long-term view when selecting and managing your investments, there are times when you need to be assured you can tap into some money in just a few months or in a year or two without risking a large loss in principal. Such situations may arise when college tuitions need to be paid, you're planning to buy a first or second home, you're planning home improvements, or another big ticket item is on the horizon. The mutual fund industry offers a couple of alternatives that can provide attractive short-term returns with little or no risk to principal. Both money market mutual funds and short-term bond funds offer okay, albeit unspectacular, returns with virtually no risk in the case of money funds, and with low risk of principal loss in the case of short-term bond funds. CDs are another possibility.

By carefully comparing the yields offered by various short-term investment securities, you can make the most of your money. After all, why settle for a 3 percent return in a savings account when you may be able to get almost twice that in other safe, short-term investments? In fact, with most short-term investments you can change from one to another quickly and without concern about capital gains taxes or fees.

Finding the Best Returns on Short-Term Investments

As opposed to stocks and bonds, short-term investments are pretty straightforward. With a little bit of effort, however, you can make the most of these otherwise mundane investments. The keys to maximizing the interest you'll fetch are

➤ Determining the current interest rates paid by various kinds of short-term investments

➤ Comparing after-tax interest rates to find the investment with the best return—after taxes are taken out

The first step is pretty easy. The financial pages of most newspapers regularly show the interest being paid on most types of short-term investments. If you really want to do a bang-up job, buy a copy of *Barron's*, the weekly financial newspaper for investment fanatics, at the newsstand. It has extensive and up-to-date data on the interest paid on all types of short-term investments, including most money market funds.

Once you've determined the interest that's being paid on the various short-term investments, the next step is to find out which pays the most—after considering taxes. Chart #8 summarizes the way short-term investments are taxed.

So if a money market deposit account at the bank pays 3.5 percent interest, but your mutual fund company offers a tax-exempt money market fund that pays 2.8 percent, it may seem that the bank money market deposit account is better. However, the interest income on a tax-exempt money market fund is not subject to federal income tax, while the interest on the money market deposit account is. Even though the stated interest rate on a particular short-term investment may be lower, it's how much you get to keep after taxes that counts.

CHART #8
Summary of How Short-Term Investments Are Taxed

Type of Short-Term Investment	Interest Income Is Subject To:	
Available through banks:	Federal Income Taxes	State Income Taxes
Savings accounts	Yes	Yes
Money market deposit accounts	Yes	Yes
Available through mutual funds or brokers:		
General money market funds	Yes	Yes
U.S. Treasury money market funds	Yes	No
Tax-exempt money market funds	No	Yes
Single-state tax-exempt money market funds	No	No
Available through banks or brokers:		
U.S. Treasury bills	Yes	No
Short-term CDs	Yes	Yes

Here are a few other suggestions to help you make the most of your short-term investments.

CD Shopping

If you're in the market for a CD, a little shopping around—even outside your hometown—could reap some rewards. First compare rates among banks in town; banks are in hot competition with each other these days. If you have a broker, check with him or her about CD offerings that the brokerage firm may have. Finally, *Barron's* lists the highest yielding CDs in the country. Remember, as long as the issuing bank is FDIC insured, you really shouldn't care where your CD comes from. You just want the best yield.

Compare Money Market Fund Yields

If you have an account with a mutual fund or a broker offering several different kinds of money market funds, be sure to compare yields to make sure the one you select offers the best after-tax return. This may require you to periodically compare the returns among various money market funds, but, hey, if you can improve your return by periodically switching among money market funds, it's more money in your pocket.

Save on Treasury Bill Purchases

If you regularly buy T-bills, consider buying them directly from the U.S. Treasury at no cost. Simply call the nearest Federal Reserve bank or branch and ask for some information on their "Treasury Direct" program. If you don't want to go through the effort of buying T-bills directly from the Fed, compare fees between your bank and your brokerage firm.

For additional information on the variety of short-term investment alternatives, including formulas for computing after-tax returns and a list of those that are most attractive now, click on:

http://jonathanpond.com/investments.short-term.htm

INVESTING FOR COLLEGE

I lose some sleep whenever I look at the projections of how much it's going to cost to educate my kids. When I add it up for three kids, college costs look more like the federal debt than a bill I will have to pay.

Don't even think about trying to save every last cent that it's going to cost to educate Junior. It will require putting aside more money than you could possibly afford. Instead, plan on setting aside each month an amount that you can reasonably afford—perhaps enough to cover 30 to 40 percent of the cost. Avoid setting your college savings sight too high; if you find that you can't save what you set out to, you may become discouraged and not save at all.

Don't begin saving for college unless and until you've maxed out all retirement plan contributions you can make. While it's great to save for college, it's more important (and more financially advantageous) to put money away in retirement plans.

How you invest money that's earmarked for college depends a lot on how long it is before you'll need to use the money. And that, of course, depends on your child's age. The nearer the child is to entering college, the less risk you can afford with the money that will be needed to meet college costs. There aren't many times in our lives when we are investing for the short term, but one of those times is when a child nears college age.

➤ **Preteens.** If the child is under thirteen, invest the money just as you would your retirement money. The majority of the money—certainly at least 60 percent—should be invested in stock mutual funds and perhaps individual stocks.

POND'S LAW OF COLLEGE SAVING

You only need to save about one-third of your children's college costs by the time they enter college. Just having them out of the house will save enough money to pay the other two-thirds.

➤ **Teenagers.** As if having a teenager isn't worrisome enough already, you're also going to fret about how much risk is prudent in the college savings fund. The trick here is to gradually shift your money out of stocks into more conservative investments. Why? Because you're becoming short-term investors; college is now just a few years off. You don't want to risk having too much invested in stocks that could, of course, take a tumble just before the tuition bills come due.

Chart #9 contains a suggested timetable that gradually changes the college fund allocation as the child approaches college age.

THE FAMILY WEALTH FACTOR

Moving to a more conservative investment allocation as the child nears college age is particularly important if you have limited resources outside of the college nest egg to draw upon. If, on the other hand, you're fortunate enough to have enough money to be able to pay the tuition bills from other sources, then you may not need to become as conservative with the college funds as I outlined above. In other words, you have enough backup money to be able to continue taking some risk with the college fund.

CUSTODIAL ACCOUNT?

Should you keep the college savings fund in your name or your child's name? There certainly are tax advantages for putting at least *some* of the

CHART #9
Timetable for Gradually Changing Investment Allocation as College Age Approaches

Age	12	13	14	15	16	17	18
Stock Funds	60%	50%	40%	30%	20%	10%	10%
Bond Funds	30%	30%	30%	20%	10%	10%	
Short-Term Investments	10%	20%	30%	50%	70%	80%	90%
	100%	100%	100%	100%	100%	100%	100%

money in the youngster's name. A limited amount of investment income earned in a custodial account for a child under age 14 is taxed at the child's lower tax rate; for the 14-and-over set, there are no such "kiddie tax" limitations. (See page 182 for an example of how tax advantageous it can be to put investments in a child's name.)

But putting too much money in a child's name can backfire. First, there is no absolute guarantee that your darling will spend the money on a Princeton education. Once children reach the age of majority, age 18 in most states, they can't legally be stopped from using the money any way they want. Imagine this scenario: In lieu of going to college, your daughter joins a cult and falls in love with the chief guru. His highness urges her to "release" herself from all worldly goods (so that he can buy another Rolls Royce with your money, of course). This has happened!

Second, building up a cache of money in your child's name could be a liability if you think you may qualify for financial aid. Why? Because under the complex formula for calculating how much aid a student is el-igible for, the child is expected to contribute a higher percentage of her investments than you are of yours. In other words, putting all the money in Junior's name can wipe the dough out, but leaving it in your name can preserve some capital for your feeble years.

So what's the upshot here? My advice is to put some money in a young child's name—to take advantage of the lower taxes. Once the child reaches the teen years, and you can be at least somewhat more cer-tain about his responsibility and college aspirations, shift more money to the child—if you're pretty sure you won't qualify for financial aid.

STATE TUITION SAVINGS PLANS

Many states now offer tuition savings plans. Are these a worthwhile place to invest college money? As with most matters financial, it depends. The after-tax money you contribute to these plans grows tax free. Some of the programs are quite attractive, others not so. In general, the investment re-turns are best if the child goes to one of the participating colleges—usu-ally a state school. But if the child opts for another college—and most parents would prefer not to restrict their kid's college choice—then the returns will be much lower. If you are attracted to your state's tuition savings plan, go ahead and participate, but with only some of your college savings—25 percent, perhaps. Consider this money to be a rock-solid foundation for your college savings, but don't go overboard here. You can probably get higher investment returns elsewhere.

THE FAMILY HOUSE AS A SOURCE OF TUITION PAYMENTS

I'm not talking here about taking out a home equity loan to help pay college costs, although that may become necessary. Instead, some families try to pay off the home mortgage by the time their kids go off to get their higher learning. No mortgage means more money each month that can be used to pay college costs. Not a bad idea, if you can afford to pay off the mortgage that soon.

QUALIFIED STATE TUITION PROGRAMS

I've saved the best for last. QSTPs, sometimes called Section 529 programs (after the Internal Revenue Code section that authorized them) are the hot new thing. Most states have developed their own programs, selecting an investment adviser that is typically one of the big mutual fund companies. The dollars contributed are after-tax, but the money grows tax-deferred. While distributions are subject to tax, it is only in the year the funds are used to pay college expenses, and then only at the student's lower tax rate. Also, for purposes of qualifying for financial aid, the money in the QSTP is deemed to be owned by the parents and not the student.

These plans are very flexible. You don't have to reside in the state to participate in its program. The money can be used to pay tuition at any college (compared with the state tuition savings plans that typically limit the colleges). There are no income levels for participation, and you can contribute up to $100,000 to a QSTP in a single year for a child. QSTPs will become the most popular way to invest for college in the New Century.

Investments to Avoid

Although you may be told differently, there are a couple of investments that don't make much sense for college savings. Don't get me wrong; these are certainly better than nothing, but you can do better. Cash value life insurance—insuring you, your spouse, or worse, your child—won't deliver the kinds of returns you need to build up a sizable college nest egg. U.S. savings bonds were once an okay investment, but when the rules changed in 1995, they spoiled them.

Saving and investing for college is a challenge for every parent. For current information on college investment strategies, including the latest news on the exciting Qualified State Tuition Programs, click on:

http://jonathanpond.com/investments.college.htm

Chapter 12

■ BULLS MAKE MONEY, BEARS MAKE MONEY, BUT PIGS AND LAMBS GET SLAUGHTERED

> Anyone who thinks there's safety in numbers hasn't looked at the stock market pages.
>
> *Irene Peter*

Which species are you: bull, bear, pig, or lamb? This chapter contains some examples of what could happen to pigs and lambs and also provides some suggestions that will help you avoid their fate. Bull markets have a way of making investors unrealistic. I've had several people tell me in no uncertain terms that the stock market will rise by 25 percent per year indefinitely. If so, your money will grow tenfold in just 10 years. In 25 years a mere $10,000 investment will be worth over $2.5 million. Imagine how rich we'll all be if these people are correct. They're not. If you're up there in the clouds with other optimistic investors, this chapter will hopefully bring you a bit closer to terra firma. If you're just a plain old investor who's concerned about doing well when the market's doing well and not doing horribly when it's not, I'll provide some suggestions that will help you do just that.

THE DANGER OF BEING OVERLY OPTIMISTIC
ABOUT THE STOCK MARKET

If there is one positive outcome of the periodic market corrections of the 1990s it was that a lot of investors were reminded that stocks don't simply rise forever. When they do fall, they can fall sharply and swiftly. Still, some investors shrug off these corrections. They have convinced themselves that stocks would rise at a rate of 15, 20, even 25 percent—forever. But there's a real danger, in my humble opinion, being lulled into a sense that a constantly rising stock market will be your ticket to financial security.

I prepared an analysis that points out the danger of being too optimistic when estimating stock market returns. It can be hazardous to your financial health if you're unrealistic about how much your investments will earn. My example involves someone—a couple in this case, but it doesn't matter—who wants to retire in 25 years. They've looked back at the performance of stocks over the 1990s (risen about 18 percent per year), and they're confident that they'll be able to earn an average of 15 percent on their money. Based on that assumption—a 15 percent annual return—they're putting away enough money each year so that they'll have enough in 25 years to be able to retire comfortably.

Let's assume they've been too optimistic. Instead of their investments averaging a 15 percent return, they average 10 percent. (That, by the way, is about what stocks made on an annual basis before the great bull market of the 1980s and 1990s.) Here's what happens. Instead of being able to retire in 25 years, they will have to work an extra 11 years—in other words, it will take them 36 years to rack up the amount of money they need. So, overstating how much your investments will earn can have serious consequences.

POND'S LAW OF INVESTMENT ANXIETY

The higher the stock market rises, the more anxious investors become. When it reaches all-time highs, investors start hoping for a decline to relieve their anxiety.

Now the hypothetical people cited in

my illustration aren't going to want to defer their retirement by 11 years. One alternative is to increase their level of annual savings to make up for the fact that they might earn 10 percent on their money rather than 15 percent. That will require that they more than double their annual savings! This gets back to a point that I find very troubling. Many working age people are using a high investment return assumption as a reason not to save enough money for retirement.

The Eleventh Commandment

Though shalt not covet thy investment profits because the stock market will not rise forever.

Too many retirees are doing the same—overstating future investment returns—to justify spending more than they should in retirement. I recently spoke with a woman who had just retired and who was assuming a 17 percent return on her retirement money. She was drawing almost twice as much money out of her nest egg as she should. If investment returns get

Do You Fret Over Your Investments All the Time? Not to Worry.

I used to be concerned about people who obsess over their investments—those who check on how their portfolios are doing every day or every week. Some use the Internet to download prices into their portfolio throughout the day so they can find out how much money they made or lost in the past 30 minutes. I used to caution them that there's nothing to be gained from doing all that checking except a lot of needless stress. But in my old age I've decided not to worry about them anymore. Life has a way of balancing things. People who fret over their investments will not do as well with their money because their constant worry will cause them to make unwise changes to their investments. But life has a self-correcting mechanism. The worrywarts probably don't need to accumulate as much money as their more laid-back contemporaries because their self-inflicted stress will shorten their lives. The shorter your life span, the less money you'll need.

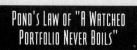

POND'S LAW OF "A WATCHED PORTFOLIO NEVER BOILS"

The more frequently you check how your portfolio is performing, the worse your portfolio will perform.

back to normal—the 10 percent range— she'll run out of money before she's 80.

By the way, I think expecting a 10 percent return is still too optimistic. To be safe you ought to assume even less—say around 7 to 8 percent. A 10 percent return requires having all your money in stocks, and I think most people shouldn't do that. Don't get me wrong when I suggest that you assume a more conservative rate of return on your investments. I hope stocks continue to rise as they have over the past decade, but I just don't want you to bet your financial future on a booming stock market. That way, if the market booms, we'll all be pleasantly surprised. But if it doesn't, we won't be confronted with having to defer or cut back on our retirement.

THIS MUTUAL FUND "ONE-TWO PUNCH" CAN KNOCK THE STUFFING OUT OF YOUR NEST EGG

Here are two of the biggest mistakes mutual fund investors make:

➤ Bailing out of a fund that has turned in a disappointing performance compared with some measure of stock performance that is completely unrelated to the fund

➤ Buying whatever fund has recently turned in a stellar performance

Each of these mistakes is, well, a mistake. But if you're really talented, you can combine the two and make a really big mistake. Here's how:

Peggy Porcine had just seen the quarterly mutual fund wrap-up on one of the financial news channels. The commentator noted that while most funds were up modestly for the quarter, the Super Internet Stock Fund rose a spectacular 82 percent. The program interviewed the fund's manager who, of course, exuded confidence that his fund had just begun to tap into the Internet gold mine. Peggy was sold, but since she was short of money, she had to sell one of the funds she currently owned. She reviewed the performance of each fund and found one apparent laggard, a small cap fund that had the audacity to lose 5 percent over the past quarter. (It turns out that small company stock funds suffered relative to other stock categories over the quarter with an average loss of 10 percent.) "Why hold onto that dog," Peggy opined, "when I can make 80 percent plus with the Super Internet Fund." So she sold the small company fund and bought Super Internet.

> ### POND'S LAW OF BULL MARKETS
>
> A bull market causes people to live higher off the hog. The stronger the bull market, the higher off the hog you live—until your consumption habits resemble the eating habits of a pig. Oink, oink.

If you've been down the same road that Peggy just traversed, you probably know the all-too-common outcome. Super Internet Fund tanks over the ensuing quarter while the small company fund rebounds sharply. Peggy's done the old double whammy. She bought a recent hot-performing fund that was, as most of them are, a disaster waiting to happen. At the same time, she sold a well-performing small company fund that, while it had lost 5 percent, actually outperformed most of the other funds in its category.

IT'S OKAY TO MAKE RISKY INVESTMENTS, BUT . . .

It's easy to feel like a chump when you hear about all the money that's being made on hot stock sectors—in the late 20th century it was Internet stocks. It's no help either when your friend brags about quadrupling her money in a month with a hot new technology stock. (Isn't it funny how people love to talk about their investment winners, but somehow never mention their losers?)

You may be surprised to hear this, but if you want to join the "Hot Stock Chasers Club," I say go right ahead. Take a small portion of your money, perhaps 5 percent, and shoot for the stars. You may do quite well, but if you don't, it's not the end of the world. In fact, it may be a low-cost lesson that, when it comes to stocks that seem to go nowhere but up, the law of gravity hasn't been repealed. It's okay to buy risky stocks, but don't risk too much of your money on them.

INVESTMENT EXPENSES DO MATTER

Do you pay attention to investment expenses? Do you just assume that expenses don't really matter or there's nothing you can do to reduce things such as brokerage commissions and mutual fund loads and expenses? When the stock and bond markets are sailing along earning double-digit returns, investment expenses don't take much of a bite out of your profits. If investment returns get back to normal—which they will—then investment expenses do make a difference. Chart #10 shows just how much a difference investment expenses can make over the years. Pay closer attention to your investment expenses because it could make a sizable difference in how well your investments perform in the future.

To find information on the expenses of mutual funds that you own or are considering buying, click on:

http://jonathanpond.com/investments.fundexpenses.htm

DELAY OF GAME PENALTY: THE PERIL OF INVESTING TOO CONSERVATIVELY

Do you think of investing as a game that thrusts naive people into the jaws of the Wall Street monsters, only to chew them up and spit them out upon the arrival of the next bear market? True, the stock market is like a game, but it's a game that every long-term investor should get comfortable playing.

Those who don't pay a big penalty by keeping too much money in supposedly safe, low-yield accounts. These "investments" always lose ground to inflation after you pay taxes on the interest. Rather, give

POND'S LAW OF DAY TRADING

Anyone who becomes a day trader will reinvest any and all winning investments until such time as he or she has lost all past gains—and then some.

your money a chance to grow. Consider poor Larry in the following example:

Larry Lamb prefers safe investments. The only retirement plan he qualifies for is an IRA, and he puts his $2,000 per year allotment into CDs. He doesn't want to risk any of his money. He recalls his grandmother talking about the great stock market crash of 1929. His parents worked for companies that had pension plans, and they didn't have many investments or worry about retirement. But Larry realizes that it's up to him to provide for his own retirement. He's accumulated $10,000 in his checking account that he wants to put into a savings account for the golden years. His friend is trying to convince Larry to invest the money in mutual funds, to which Larry responds, "In the savings account my money will earn three percent—*guaranteed*."

Chart #11 shows the penalty that Larry will pay, because the savings account is not only guaranteed to preserve his principal, it's also guaranteed to seriously impair his prospects for a financially comfortable retirement. If he puts the money into a savings account, sure it'll earn "guaranteed" 3 percent interest. But he'll have to pay combined federal and state income tax of 30 percent on that interest. His friend suggests that Larry put $2,000 into a money market fund and invest the other $8,000 In some conservative and tax-efficient stock mutual funds.

In addition to assuming that the savings account averages a 3 percent

---

CHART #10

Investment Expenses Do Count

This table illustrates how much a 1 percent difference in mutual fund expenses means to your long-term investment nest egg. It compares a $10,000 investment in two different mutual funds, both of which produce 10 percent annual returns, but that's before mutual fund expenses.

Annual Fund	Return Over Number of Years Investment Is Held				
Expenses	5 years	10 years	15 years	20 years	25 years
0.75%	$16,000	$24,000	$38,000	$49,000	$91,000
1.75%	$15,000	$22,000	$33,000	$59,000	$73,000

SOMETIMES THE BEST THING TO DO WITH YOUR INVESTMENTS IS NOTHING

A good friend of mine who is a very successful stockbroker as well as a radio talk-show host related the following true story to me: "A few years ago a recently retired steelworker came into my office to ask for some investment advice. He said that he was very embarrassed about his situation and had avoided speaking with an investment adviser about it for many years.

"About 25 years earlier he had inherited $40,000 worth of stock from his father. He told me that at that time he didn't know anything about investments although he recognized the names of all the companies whose shares he had inherited. So he put the stock certificates in his safe-deposit box, where they sat for 25 years. He then went on to say that he had been receiving dividend income all along, and he noted that it had increased considerably over the years.

"I told him to retrieve the certificates from the safe-deposit box so we could figure out what they were worth. Well, as you might suspect, his stock was worth more than $500,000. He hadn't paid one cent of income tax on the more than $450,000 of appreciation in value because he had held on to the shares. His annual dividend income was almost $20,000, which is half of what the total stock investment itself was worth 25 years earlier!"

annual pre-tax interest rate, the money market fund is assumed to average 4 percent pre-tax annual return and the mutual fund money 8 percent. The results in Chart #11 are rather startling. When Larry retires in 25 years, he should have almost three times as much money if he follows his friend's very reasonable advice. The moral of the story: If you feel comfortable keeping a lot of money safe, you'll end up paying a big price for that supposed comfort. Instead, give money that you're not going to need for a long time a chance to grow.

CHART #11

Larry Lamb's Decision

Here's how much Larry's $10,000 will be worth after taxes under each investment scenario:

At the end of	Investing $10,000 in a savings account	Investing $2,000 in a money market fund and $8,000 in stock funds
5 years	$11,000	$14,000
10 years	$12,000	$18,000
15 years	$14,000	$25,000
20 years	$15,000	$35,000
25 years	$17,000	$48,000

PITY THE MARKET TIMER

I've long been amused by those persons who maintain that they can time the market. No one can, although there are a lot of otherwise rational people who disagree. The best analogy to market timing is natural family planning. As a concept (please excuse the pun), it certainly sounds doable. And as a short-term strategy, it may even work. But, over the long-term, its failure will be announced with a lusty cry.

THE ALLURE OF MARKET TIMING

The allure of market timing is certainly understandable. Long bull markets make investors skittish. Quick market downturns scare everyone. The notion that you or someone who is trying to sell you his or her investment savvy can actually get out of the market just before it takes a dip and then get back into the market just before it rebounds is terribly attractive. It reminds me of a time when I was in college and was obsessed with the stock market. My roommate and I spent long hours (my grades reflected it) devising a model, based on past stock performance, that predicted with 100 percent accuracy that a particular stock was going to rise or fall in value. All a stock had to do was satisfy our 80 different statistical criteria and, bingo, it was sure to rise. The trouble was that we couldn't find any stock that satisfied even half of the criteria, much less the 80 required for a slam-dunk.

SO IT GOES WITH MARKET TIMING

As you read this, there are undoubtedly scads of people who are devising models to predict stock market turns. They are, like I was back in college, chasing a pipe dream. The stock market—and the bond market—behaves in perverse ways. The great bull market of the 1980s and 1990s defied all past stock market logic. When the Dow reached 5000, pundits were warning that stocks were overpriced. When it hit 7000, Wall Street bears were forecasting a huge crash. At 10000, a level that a decade ago would have been thought impossible to attain in a lifetime, just about everyone was scared to death. What happened next? The Dow reached 11000 just 24 trading days later. That's the perversity of the market. When it's doing great, people get scared; when it's tumbling, people get scared; when it's going nowhere, people get scared.

With the Dow over 9000 in mid-1998, it did drop almost 2000 points, attributed to severe deterioration in many overseas economies and slowing profit growth here in the U.S. The market timers came out of the woodwork saying "I told you that stocks were overpriced." And, of course, they gloated that they had gotten themselves or their clients out of stocks in the nick of time. But a funny thing happened on the way to the bear market of 1998. Against conventional wisdom (Asian problems still persisted, corporate earnings growth was slowing), the market posted a spectacular rebound in late 1998, pushing it back up to all-time highs. Stocks regained all of their losses—and then some—over a period of just a few weeks.

A ROUND-TRIP TICKET THAT'S HARD TO WIN

The big problem with trying to time the stock market is not so much getting out of the market before it drops as it is deciding when to get back *in*. Some investors manage to get out in time, but all too often they get out in anticipation of a drop that doesn't occur. The real challenge is getting back in just before the inevitable rebound. Usually, stock prices surge quickly after a drop, and the jump occurs just when gloom and doom permeate Wall Street. Those few timers who managed to get out of stocks before they plummeted usually miss the rebound. It reminds me of a caller on a radio talk show who told me he had gotten out of stocks entirely and he was wondering if it was a good time to get back in. I suggested that any time is a good time to invest in stocks. But, since all of his money was on

> ## Pond's Laws of Market Timing
>
> 1. Anyone who tells you that he or she can time the market is delusional.
> 2. Anyone who sells their investments just before or during a market decline will not buy them again until the market has risen to a level that is higher than when they sold.

the sidelines, I encouraged him to reinvest the money gradually—over the next year or two. I asked this chap when he got out of stocks. He said that it was right after the Crash of 1987. At the time of his call, the Dow Jones Industrial Average was 8100. The Dow was under 2000 in late 1987. This would-be market timer was a little late getting back in. All the while he was wondering if this was a good time to reinvest, the Dow stocks had quadrupled!

The Lesson

Don't ever try to time the market. Develop a balanced and diversified investment strategy and stick with it, even when you've lost money and the Wall Street pundits are spewing nothing but awful forecasts for stocks. Keep investing, using the power of dollar-cost averaging. Remember, if history is any indicator, stocks will come roaring back and you want to be there to enjoy the party. Chart #12 illustrates how strongly and consistently the stock market rebounds.

CHART #12

Post-1950 Market Rebounds

The far left column shows all of the years since 1950 in which the Standard & Poor's stock index has declined. The far right shows the gain in the Standard & Poor's stocks during the subsequent year. Incidentally the stock market crash of 1987 didn't even make the list, because stocks were actually up for the year.

Down Market Year(s)	Amount of Decline	Gain in Following Year
1953	-1.0	+52.6
1957	-10.8	+43.4
1962	-8.7	+22.8
1966	-10.1	+24.0
1969	-8.5	+4.0
1973–1974	-37.3	+37.2
1977	-7.2	+6.6
1981	-4.9	+21.4
1990	-3.2	+30.5

Chapter 13

NEW CENTURY, NEW INVESTMENT OPPORTUNITIES

> There are two classes of people who tell what is going to happen in the future: Those who don't know, and those who don't know they don't know.
>
> *John Kenneth Galbraith*

The biggest challenge to investors in the 21st century is the quickening pace of change in American and foreign industries. This is no longer "your parents' stock market." In the old days, you could invest successfully simply by putting your money in the old standbys, "the generals," as in General Electric, General Motors, and General Foods. As technology becomes more and more dominant in our lives and in the lives of companies that provide us with goods and services, that is changing. The technological revolution will accelerate just as the industrial revolution did a century ago. Arguably, there will be even more investment opportunities in the New Century. But because the pace of change and innovation is so rapid, investors will have to spend more time keeping abreast of the investment markets and make investment decisions more quickly. On the other hand, you shouldn't simply abandon all of the rules that guided sound investing before. Some have suggested that there is a "new economy," and that both business cycles and inflation are yesterday's news. While I'll certainly listen to their arguments (and, generous soul that I am, I summarize them

below), I don't think we should bet our financial futures on such speculation.

One thing you can go to the bank on is how quickly things change
in our economy, the world economy, and in the investment markets. So,
the agile investor will need to understand three important investment
techniques that I believe will become crucial to successful investing over
the next decade:

➤ Taking advantage of attractive industries by investing in sector funds
➤ Using index funds to build an investment foundation and earn attractive returns
➤ Emphasizing tax-efficient investing to enhance investment performance

THOUGHTS ON THE SO-CALLED "NEW ECONOMY"

In the past several years, numerous articles have been written about a
"new economy" to which historical beliefs about economic behavior
and business cycles no longer apply. Proponents of the new economy
theory say the structure of the American economy has changed to a more
robust and stable form that's not subject to the boom-and-bust cycles of
the past. They even suggest that the high stock market levels reached in
the late 20th century did not reflect an overvalued market.

INVESTMENT DECISIONS AND THE ECONOMY

Typically, strategic investment decisions—when to pull back from the
market, when to buy shares of a foreign stock fund, when to take capital
gains—are influenced by factors such as an investor's immediate need
for cash or expectations about a change in market behavior. The stock
market's daily, weekly, and monthly tweaks and twitches are closely followed, and active traders use increasingly refined market timing methods that are as inaccurate as the blunt instruments of old. Economic

factors feature prominently in explanations of market behavior, but com-
mentators sometimes use "the market" to mean "the economy."

The stock market is *not* the economy. Thoughtful investors understand the state of the economy rather than track the daily, weekly, or
quarterly changes in the state of the stock market. The ultimate success
of strategic investment decisions—from overall investment allocation to
individual stock, bond, or mutual fund selection—will be rooted in an
understanding of the forces driving the economy, not the market. It's the
state of the economy that determines the state of the investment climate,
not the reverse. Understanding long-term economic trends also allows
investors to make informed assumptions about key decision factors such
as interest and inflation rates. Following the market's every gurgle and
burp will keep market timers glued to their computers and cell phones,
but until they realize that the market and the economy are not one, busy
is all it will keep them.

THE OLD ECONOMY: BOOM AND BUST

In the early part of the 20th century, the American economy grew
through brisk population growth, huge capital investment building the
country's infrastructure, and a stock market dominated by a small number of very large companies. Volatility was built into the structure of that
high-growth economy as a result of periodic investment surges and the
boom-and-bust business cycles of heavy industry.

THE NEW ECONOMY: SLOW AND STEADY

Many economists believe the U.S. economy has experienced several
fundamental changes during the last hundred years, changes that can be
expected to endure for some time to come. The most important of these
changes may be significantly reduced rates of economic growth and
volatility. Over long periods of time, real economic growth has an almost
one-to-one relationship with population growth, and the significant slowing of America's population growth rate contributes to the past decade's
slow, steady economic growth rate. A second key to the slowed growth

rate is the major, and continuing, shift in capital investment from the building of the country's infrastructure to its maintenance and retooling—an inevitable shift as the country matures. Finally, the economy's evolution from a manufacturing base to a growing reliance on services also smooths its course. Besides slowing the economy's growth rate, these changes have resulted in far briefer and gentler business cycles, reducing the economy's volatility.

The new economy is making some investors (and some economists) a bit nervous: in some ways, it seems too good to be true. Certain unpleasant historic benchmarks are no longer reliable indicators of cause and effect. (The lowest unemployment rate in more than two decades, for instance, unaccountably failed to trigger an increase in the also low inflation rate.) Many seasoned investors seem to be worried simply by the unprecedented length of the late 20th century's bull market cycle.

What's going to happen next, and when, can't be precisely anticipated, despite the swelling chorus of detailed—and conflicting—predictions. But there seems to be some agreement among economists that nothing is likely to change substantially until the early years of the New Century, and perhaps not even then. Some believe that consumption will ease off. We'll see a slowdown in retail sales accompanied by smaller profit margins and reduced capital expenditures, which will lead to a moderate downturn. They also believe that interest and inflation rate fluctuations will be comparatively minor.

POND'S LAW OF STOCK MARKET PREDICTION

The most successful Wall Street prognosticators are able to predict accurately whether the market will fall or rise 50 percent of the time.

THE LESSON FOR INVESTORS

While it's usually not possible to distinguish between a short-term blip and the start of a long-term trend, it will certainly be possible, even with far from perfect information, for investors to make reasonably informed and reasonable decisions in any economy we're likely to see in the foreseeable future. You may find it useful to keep the following considerations in mind when making long-term investment decisions:

➤ Short-term economic trends should not be confused with the basic economic structure or accorded as much importance. For example, a single month decline in consumer confidence doesn't necessarily portend a long-term trend.

➤ Market behavior, especially in the short run, can be at least as dependent on investor expectations as on "reality." That's why a sharply rising market often tends to overreact to temporary bad news. Investors fear the worst, but when the reality turns out to be not so bad, the upward trend in the market continues.

➤ The market is not the economy, and the behavior of the market does not predict the economy. In fact, the reverse is true.

➤ Investor expectations are based on relative perceptions. A 60-year-old investor won't even blink at an 8 percent long-term Treasury yield, but her 28-year-old investment adviser might be spooked by high interest rates into making some very bad decisions.

➤ Respected economists believe the stability of the new economy's structure will prevent the investment climate from deteriorating significantly over the long term.

How Deflation Could Affect You

There's been a lot of talk lately about the possibility of deflation—a decline in prices—arriving on our shores. Although it's far from a certainty right now, several economists are flat-out predicting deflation. Nevertheless, forewarned is forearmed; it's helpful to get some understanding of how deflation may affect you so that you'll be better prepared if and when we do see prices declining. Some prices are already dropping. Car prices, for example, have experienced some year-to-year price declines. Other evidence of possible impending deflation: Consumer prices have been rising at the slowest rate in over a decade. Wholesale prices in the U.S.—prices of items sold to manufacturers and retailers—have been declining in order to compete with foreign manufacturers, whose faltering economies have forced them to reduce their prices on items exported to the U.S.

It would seem that deflation would be a welcome occurrence. After all, no one likes *inflation!* It be wonderful if the prices of the goods and services that we buy drop, wouldn't it? In fact, deflation would not bring all good news by any measure.

INVESTMENTS

Stock prices could decline in a deflationary environment. Stock prices rise, in large measure, because a company's revenues or profits are rising. But with deflation, corporations will be unable to raise prices and may in fact have to lower them. While material costs may also decline, labor costs will not, and profits will be squeezed. While there are few eternal truths in the stock market, one is that declining corporate profits hurt stock prices.

CONSUMER PRODUCTS

With deflation, prices of a lot of products, particularly those that are not labor intensive, will decline. On the other hand, the prices for labor intensive products and services will probably continue to rise. Confusion will result, and consumers may hold back on making purchases in hopes that products will decline further. If so, this could be very detrimental to our economy and to the stock market.

EMPLOYMENT

If companies are scrambling to cut costs in the face of having to lower prices and seeing demand slacken, they may be required to reduce employment. Even in the best of circumstances, employers will have little opportunity to increase pay or provide bonuses in deflation-driven markets.

So deflation is certainly not as attractive as it might seem at first blush. Keep abreast of economic reports so that you will at least be prepared for the possibility of deflation.

Attractive Industries for the New Century

Identifying the next Microsoft or AOL or Amazon.com is a tough and elusive challenge for most individual investors. But one way to become more selective in your investing is to spot promising industry sectors, and then either pick promising stocks within these sectors or let mutual fund managers do the work of identifying promising stocks within them. The long-term prosperity that we've been enjoying won't last forever. Some segments of the economy will probably experience lackluster growth in the New Century while others will rise to lead the market. In fact, we are in the midst of a fundamental transition in our stock market. The old blue chip manufacturing companies that dominated industry after World War II are rapidly being replaced by a new generation of 21st century blue chip companies. You might say that the old blue chip stocks are becoming cow chips.

In my view, a handful of sectors will most likely continue to prosper in the early part of the 21st century, although they, like all industries, will periodically experience some tough times along the way. Among them are technology, real estate, financial services, health-care, and biotechnology.

Technology

The U.S. is changing from an economy based on manufacturing to one based on information and communications. The dramatic growth of the high-tech sector, which includes software, computers, semiconductors, networking, and communications, reflects this. In the New Century the high-tech sector will continue to lead the market. While there will always be product cycles, and some segments within the sector will inevitably experience ups and downs, the industry as a whole will remain the growth engine of the information era. Analysts believe technology will soon rise to an astounding 15 percent of the gross national product from the current level of less than 10 percent.

At present, the industry is benefiting from relentless technological advances. The convergence of computers, consumer electronics, and communications is fueling demands for compelling new hardware and software with high power and connectivity. The economy may slow in the coming years, accompanied inevitably by some reduction in capital outlays, but most companies will continue to invest in new technology. That's the solution to higher efficiency and long-term growth.

Many U.S. high-tech companies are now dominant suppliers in the international arena. Even if domestic revenue slows, demand for electronic products from overseas markets is expected to be strong so long as the overseas economies regain their strength. With this foreign interest buttressing the domestic industry, the technology sector will continue its strong growth.

REAL ESTATE

A combination of low interest rates and a healthy economy has sparked a rebound for both commercial and residential real estate in most areas of the country. Both residential and commercial real estate markets report a positive outlook for the early part of the 21st century. Commercial real estate looks particularly attractive. The lackluster new construction activities during the early 1990s has resulted in a shortage of commercial rental space in many regions, pumping up property prices and rents and spurring more construction. Of course, the commercial real estate market goes through boom and bust cycles, so investors will have to be always wary of the next bust.

FINANCIAL SERVICES

Continued robust growth is also expected in the banking and financial services industry. Bank stocks are benefiting from a confluence of factors: Lower interest rates and high loan demand have raised profits; record-breaking mergers and acquisitions have brought increased efficiency in operations; new technology, such as computer banking, has enabled banks to provide lower-cost services; and lucrative new sources of fee income are boosting profits. So long as interest rates remain low, banks stand to benefit. Low interest rates lower borrowing costs (isn't it poetic justice that banks have to borrow, too?) and help boost profitability. The brokerage business has also boomed in recent years as the merger, underwriting, and securities trading businesses have soared.

One worry is that a deterioration in credit quality—an increase in bad or doubtful loans on the books of banks—could end the good times. Both the industry and investors have been watching for the classic signs of a bubble, but analysts think it unlikely to happen in the foreseeable future. Not only are banks better managed now than they were in the past, but they have put a great deal of effort into reallocating capital toward more stable higher-margin activities. Banks now generate a large portion of revenues by providing fee-based services. To prevent any loan quality problems, many banks have also tightened lending standards. Industry watchers agree that it is hard to see banks facing problems on a scale similar to those in the early 1990s. Banks are now well managed and enjoy a very profitable asset base.

Health Care

Amid rising health-care costs and a near-record level of mergers and acquisitions, the health-care industry has come under pressure to maintain profitability. As hospitals, medical groups, managed-care, and health insurers continue pairing up to win a competitive edge, the pace of health-care consolidation is likely to continue. These moves will pay off in more efficient operations and more cost savings. It's good for us as investors even though we hate it as patients. Health-care providers are also striving to improve their administrative systems.

Attractive investment opportunities also abound within the research- and development-oriented companies who are introducing pharmaceutical and medical device innovations to improve the quality of life and reduce health-care costs.

Biotechnology

Formerly a subset of the health-care industry, biotechnology has emerged as a sector in its own right. New biotech products are being introduced at a staggering rate, and many more innovative drugs and treatment devices are expected in coming years. The growth potential here is enormous: One new drug for a major disease could rapidly become a multibillion-dollar product.

Unlike in the area of information technology, where a new product could quickly become obsolete, biotech innovations generally have long life cycles, measured in years rather than months.

You can find the latest scuttlebutt on the economy and an update on what Wall Street thinks are the most attractive industries by clicking on:

http://jonathanpond.com/economy.outlook.htm

A SIMPLE STRATEGY FOR INVESTING PROFITABLY IN SECTOR FUNDS

While you can certainly buy individual stocks in these or other sectors that you find attractive, buying a sector mutual fund is a lower risk way to invest since the fund's manager will invest in many companies within that sector.

A sector fund (also known as a specialized fund) is not a mutual fund in the pure sense. While the fund is diversified insofar as it invests in stocks of many companies, a sector fund restricts those investments to a single industry.

I usually discourage investors from putting a lot of their money into sector funds. Sometimes I feel I'm fighting a losing battle because sector funds almost always dominate the lists of best-performing mutual funds over a past quarter or past year. That shouldn't come as a surprise. If a particular sector is flying high, chances are that its sector funds will be beating the daylights out of the more diversified ones. All too often, however, that same high-performing sector fund ends up on next year's list of worst-performing funds. While a garden variety mutual fund that is di-versified across several different industries won't suffer too much if a par-ticular industry falls on hard times, a sector fund that's in that hapless industry could suffer big time.

Nevertheless, sector funds do provide an easy way to invest in an industry that you think is attractive. But please don't bet the ranch on them. Also, don't buy a sector fund just because it was a recent high performer. I'll bet you'll be financially worse off if you do so. Instead, pick a sector fund because you are excited by the prospects for stocks of a particular industry. And this leads me to my strategy.

STRATEGY

My strategy for investing in sector funds involves first identifying industries that are considered to have very attractive prospects over the next year or so. There are a couple of ways to do this. If you have an account with a full-service brokerage firm, your broker may be able to provide you with some reports that identify attractive industries. Or, you could go to the library and check the *Value Line Investment Survey,* which ranks over 90 different industries for expected performance over the next year. But whatever your source, if the industry is expected to do well, you could then go about the task of identifying a good sector fund. This process is no different from the process of locating any good mutual fund. (See page 116.) In spite of their popularity, sector funds are not yet available for many industry categories. Here, however, are some industries that have a sufficient number of sector funds available:

➤ Energy/natural resources
➤ Financial services
➤ Health care
➤ Precious metals
➤ Real estate
➤ Technology
➤ Utilities

THREE FOR THE MONEY

I have to admit an attraction to three particular sectors. In fact, I think most investors, once they've got enough money to invest in a few diversified mutual funds, should strongly consider investing in these three important and attractive industrial sectors.

1. **Health-care funds.** You might think that with all of the problems the health-care industry is going through that this is an industry to be avoided. But there are a lot of health-care companies that are in the business not only of improving our health but also of reducing the costs of keeping us healthy and treating illness. It takes a pro to separate the good health-care stocks from the also-rans. You'll get such a pro when you buy a solid health-care fund.

2. **Real-estate funds.** There are three major long-term investment categories: stocks, bonds, and real estate. While most investors can't afford to buy real estate or don't want to be landlords, real-estate mutual funds are an easy and inexpensive way to add this important investment category to your portfolio.

3. **Technology funds.** I really like the prospects for the technology industry over the next decade. In fact, as I mentioned earlier, I think we're in the midst of a major transition away from the old industrial companies to a whole new generation of wonderful companies aching to take their place. What industry will these companies be in? Without a doubt, technology. But it's very difficult to put together a well-diversified portfolio of individual stocks in the volatile and rapidly changing technology industry. So the best way to play this exciting sector is with a technology mutual fund, and there are many good ones out there.

For a rundown on resources to help you select funds in sectors that interest you, click on:
http://jonathanpond.com/investments.sectorfunds.htm

INDEX FUNDS SHOULD PLAY A ROLE IN YOUR PORTFOLIO

Index funds arrived on the scene quite a while ago, but over the waning years of the 20th century, they have proven themselves to be a very worthy addition to any long-term investment portfolio. Many investors, especially inexperienced investors and those with insufficient time to devote to following their investments, have found the indexing idea appealing.

An index fund is a mutual fund designed to mimic a particular stock or bond index, such as the Standard & Poor's 500 Stock Index. Proponents of indexing argue that it is futile for mutual funds to try to beat the market. Studies show that few experienced investment managers consistently beat the market indexes. So why pay a manager when simply buying a fund that equals the market average will work just as well—if not better?

ADVANTAGES OF INDEXING

Index funds offer a number of advantages, including low expenses. Because index funds are passively managed, there is no need to pay expensive analysts or managers for doing research. The annual expenses for an index fund are much lower than those of actively managed funds. Index funds have posted excellent performance, but remember, the market in general has been up since index funds have become particularly popular. It is in up markets where they will do very well. Index funds are broadly diversified across many industries. For investors with a limited amount of money to invest, index funds can be an excellent way to achieve diversification. Finally, index funds can be very tax-friendly in that they tend to distribute very low capital gains compared with actively managed funds. Therefore, index funds are particularly efficacious for your taxable investment accounts (page 172).

LIMITATIONS OF INDEXING

With all the compelling advantages of indexing, however, it is not the magic solution to all of your investment needs. For example, you must be happy to achieve average market returns (whatever they may be), because that is the best an index fund can do. Index fund managers are usually prohibited from using any defensive measures, such as moving out of stocks if the manager thinks stock prices are going to decline. So index funds will not be able to protect your investment in the event of a market downturn. Thus, in comparison with some actively managed stock funds that periodically take defensive measures when the market turns down, index funds tend to be more volatile.

Types of Index Funds

Index funds are now available in a host of flavors, designed to appeal to just about any particular interest of investors. Here are some of the more popular ones:

➤ S&P 500 index funds
➤ Wilshire 5000 stock index funds
➤ Small-company index funds
➤ International stock index funds
➤ Bond index funds

Index funds are not the only way to invest in a broad stock index. You can also buy stocks on the stock exchange that represent a specific stock index. For example, SPDRs (Standard & Poor's Depositary Receipts) trade on the stock exchange and represent the S&P 500 Index. Industry-specific "Spiders," as SPDRs are called, are also available on the stock exchange. Each of them is a group of stocks within the S&P 500 Stock Index that represents a single industry.

Do the many permutations and combinations of index funds offer the same advantages of the granddaddy—the S&P 500 index funds? Conclusive answers have not yet been found. Some reports have indicated that actively managed small-company funds and actively managed international stock funds have a better chance of outperforming their respective indexes. Analysts believe that there is more opportunity for managers to identify attractive investments in the small company and international stock markets than there is in the U.S. large-company stock markets. So, while indexing has evolved into a very respectable method of investing, the results are mixed. For some markets, indexing has worked very well, not so in others. In all, index funds could certainly play a role in your investment accounts. You may first want to anchor a portion of your portfolio in an S&P 500 index fund or a Wilshire 5000 index fund which combines large-cap, mid-cap, and small-cap stocks in the same fund. But remember that appropriate investment allocation calls for more than indexing, and indexing is more than buying just one index fund.

For some suggestions and an illustration on how you can assemble a diversified portfolio that includes index funds as well as an update on available index funds, click on:

http://jonathanpond.com/investments.indexfunds.htm

TAX-EFFICIENT INVESTING—THE NEW MANTRA THAT NO ONE'S PAYING ATTENTION TO

You may have heard or read about "tax-efficient investing." While the notion of investing in a fashion that minimizes the income taxes you have to pay on those investments has always made good sense, it is particularly advantageous since capital gains rates were lowered in the late 1990s. Before the drop in capital gains tax rates, most taxpayers paid the same rate of tax on long-term capital gains (28 percent) as they did on other types of income, including interest and dividends (also 28 percent for most taxpayers but potentially as high as 40 percent). In those days, it didn't much matter whether your investment income came from dividends, interest, or capital gains since it was taxed at the same rate. But now, long-term capital gains rates are, for most taxpayers, 20 percent. All you have to do to qualify is hold on to the investment for more than one year. If you hold on to it for a year or less, it's a short-term capital gain which, for most of us, is taxed just like other kinds of income at a rate ranging from 28 percent to almost 40 percent. So with long-term capital gains rates now lower than the taxes on other income, the more investments you can hold on to for more than a year, the better.

Tax-efficient investing can easily add a percentage point or two to your annual investment returns. While it may not seem like much, that can make a lot of difference in what you accumulate over the years. By emphasizing tax-friendly investments in your taxable* accounts and tax-unfriendly investments in your retirement accounts, you can improve your annual investment returns by a couple of percentage points.

TAX-FRIENDLY INVESTMENTS

Perfect for taxable investment accounts, tax-friendly investments are those investments that tend to pass on very little taxable income. Here are examples of tax-friendly investments:

➤ Index funds
➤ Tax-efficient or low-turnover mutual funds
➤ Municipal bonds and municipal bond funds
➤ Individual stocks

Index funds (page 168) are very attractive investments. Several mutual fund companies have introduced tax-efficient mutual funds whose managers, in addition to striving for good overall investment returns, also endeavor to distribute a minimum of taxable income each year. Low-turnover mutual funds are also usually tax-friendly. They are funds whose managers don't do a lot of buying and selling in the fund's portfolio.

The next tax-friendly investment should be obvious to most investors—municipal bonds and municipal bond funds whose interest is generally federally tax exempt and may also be exempt from state income taxes. Buying and holding individual stocks is also tax friendly because you don't have to pay any gains on the stock's appreciation in value until you sell it. So with individual stocks, as opposed to most mutual funds, you decide if and when to incur a capital gain. (See page 181.)

TAX-UNFRIENDLY INVESTMENTS

Tax-unfriendly investments generally belong in retirement accounts, because, as I hope you know, no taxes are payable in a retirement account

---

*Tax-efficiency is not a concern with your tax-advantaged retirement accounts (as opposed to your taxable accounts) since the investment income from these accounts, whether they come from capital gains, dividends, or interest, is not subject to income taxes until you start making withdrawals.

until the money is withdrawn. The two tax-unfriendly investments that are particularly appropriate for retirement accounts are:

➤ High-turnover stock funds
➤ Corporate bonds and corporate bond funds

High-turnover stock funds are the funds that tend to pass on a lot of highly taxed short-term capital gains. Corporate bonds and corporate bond funds are tax unfriendly because the interest they pay is subject to federal and state income taxes. You get slaughtered when you have high-turnover stock funds and/or corporate bonds in a taxable account. If you can, put them in your retirement accounts. It could save you a lot of money over the years—a good thing unless you derive pleasure from giving extra money to the government. See page 179 for more guidance on tax-efficient mutual funds.

Here is an example that shows why you need to pay attention to tax-efficient investing in your taxable investment accounts.

Roger Rodgers has $25,000 to invest for the long term outside his retirement accounts. He's in the 36 percent tax bracket, and he's considering three different investments, all of which, he assumes, will earn 9 percent per year.

The first alternative is a mutual fund whose manager actively trades stocks. Roger would expect that all of the income would be taxed as short-term capital gains and dividends, in other words taxed at 36 percent.

The next is another stock mutual fund run in a tax-efficient manner. He expects the 9 percent annual return of this fund to consist of 3 percent dividends and short-term capital gains, which would be taxed at 36 percent, and 6 percent long-term gains, which are taxed at 20 percent.

Finally, Roger is considering investing in a few individual stocks that pay a 1 percent dividend and, he forecasts, will return another 8 percent annual growth for a total annual return of 9 percent.

Here are the after-tax returns of each of Roger's three alternatives.

	After-tax value of $25,000 investment earning 9% per year		
Investment alternative	10 years	20 years	30 years
1. Tax-unfriendly fund	$44,000	$77,000	$134,000
2. Tax-friendly fund	48,000	92,000	176,000
3. Individual growth stocks	55,000	117,000	253,000

As you can see from the table, Roger is much better off with the more tax-friendly choices. Both the tax-friendly fund and the individual growth stocks provide much higher returns than the tax-unfriendly fund. One point of clarification: The individual growth stocks are assumed to have been held throughout the 10-, 20-, and 30-year periods. If they are sold, a substantial long-term capital gain would have to be paid, so the advantage of individual growth stocks over the other two alternatives may not be as great as it seems. Nevertheless, under each of the three holding periods, individual growth stocks still win out over the other two alternatives—but they also carry greater risk.

The best tax-efficient investment strategies under current tax rules can be found by clicking on:

http://jonathanpond.com/investments.taxefficient.htm

DEATH AND TAXES MAY BE LIFE'S ONLY CERTAINTIES, BUT AT LEAST DEATH DOESN'T GET WORSE EVERY TIME THE CONGRESS CONVENES

T axes are a depressing subject. The Internal Revenue Code is a nightmare. Some of the smartest people in the world can't figure out many of its provisions. Here, for example, is an attempt by congressional tax writers to *clarify* some tax gobbledygook. By the way, this is one sentence.

In determining the amount of an education credit, qualified tuition and related expenses paid during the taxable year must be reduced by any amount paid to, or on behalf of, a student during the taxable year with respect to attendance at an eligible education institution during an academic period beginning in that taxable year that is a qualified scholarship that is excludable from income under section 117; a veterans' or member of the armed forces' educational assistance allowance under chapter 30, 31, 32, 34 or 35 of title 38, United States Code, or under chapter 1606 of title 10, United States Code; employer-provided educational assistance that is excludable from income under section 127; or any other educational assistance that is excludable from gross income (other than a gift, bequest, devise, or inheritance within the meaning of section 102(a)).

Give me strength! No wonder more than half of us feel compelled to pay someone else to fill out our tax returns. That's a disgrace. The vast majority of Americans are honest taxpayers. They are willing, albeit un-happy, to fork over what the regulations say they have to fork over—if they could figure it out! Every attempt by Congress to simplify the tax rules ends up making the rules more complicated. Unfortunately, I don't see any simplicity on the horizon. However, tax changes enacted in the late 1990s do provide some wonderful benefits to investors, home-owners, and families struggling to pay for college even if they make the tax code yet more complicated.

By the way, as attractive as it sounds, don't hold your breath for a flat tax. It sounds great, but it's rife with problems. It will never happen. A true flat tax would do away with all tax deductions and simply tax all of our income at a lower specified percentage. But in order to do that, you'd have to do away with, among other things, the mortgage interest deduc-tion and the charitable contribution deduction. This would make both home ownership and contributing to charity less attractive, hardly a good thing. They are so important to our society that these deductions will be forever present in our tax rules. With a flat tax, interest on U.S. Treasury bonds and corporate bonds would be taxed at a much lower rate than they now are. If that happens, municipal bonds, whose interest is gener-ally exempt from federal taxes, will become less attractive. So in order to compete for investor money, states and municipalities will have to in-crease the interest they pay on their bonds, effectively increasing the cost of running state and local governments and raising state income taxes. I'd love to see tax reform or any other tax changes, so long as they lower *my* tax bill. As Senator Russell Long of Louisiana was said to have said: "Don't tax you, don't tax me, tax the fellow behind that tree." But I don't think a flat tax will be enacted without a lot of exceptions and complexities.

As bad as taxes are, you still need to be-come familiar with ways to reduce them. There's no easier (or more satisfying) way to cut your expenses than finding sensible

POND'S LAW OF CONGRESSIONAL WISDOM

The longer members of the House or Senate are in office, the more they think that they're bet-ter able to spend our money than we are.

ways to reduce taxes. And as complex as most of the changes in the tax rules have been since the mid-1980s, one thing has remained true: Actions you now take to reduce your taxes will enhance your financial well being.

➤ The mortgage interest deduction encourages home ownership, which enables you to take control of your housing costs rather than being subject to a landlord's rent hikes. (See Chapter 8.)

➤ Tax credits and other breaks for college students and their parents help middle-income families educate their children without severely impairing their retirement nest eggs. (See Chapter 4.)

➤ The tax deferral and, in many cases, the tax deductions associated with contributions to retirement plans encourage setting aside money for retirement. (See Chapter 16.)

➤ A long-term capital gains rate that is lower than the rate imposed on short-term gains and other types of income encourages a sensible, buy-and-hold investment strategy for investments held in taxable accounts. (See page 171.)

➤ The possibility of reducing income taxes during retirement through the Roth IRA. (See page 201.)

➤ Generous exclusions from profits on the sale of a personal residence allow those who are downsizing, including retirees, to keep more money from the sale of a home. (See page 90.)

➤ The ability to pass on more of an estate to your heirs without having to resort to elaborate estate-planning techniques. (See page 252.)

If you're still one of the dwindling number of Americans who prepare their own income tax returns, some helpful hints, including ways to use the computer to help, can be found by clicking on:

http://jonathanpond.com/taxes.preparation.htm

"I'M NOT GOING TO MAKE THAT INVESTMENT BECAUSE CONGRESS IS GOING TO CHANGE THE TAX RULES"

I've lost count of the number of times I've heard that excuse. What's worse is that a lot of people have been advised by none other than their tax and financial advisers to avoid making a sensible financial decision because the tax rules are going to be changed. I guess these professionals must have an inside track on the exact tax rule changes that Congress is going to enact over the next 20 years. Come on! Even Congress doesn't know what changes will be made in the tax rules—not 20 years from now, not even next year. Any time you start fiddling with your financial decisions based upon what you or your adviser thinks is going to happen in the future, you're going to make the wrong decisions.

Most recently, I've heard countless people say they're not going to do a Roth IRA because the rules are going to be changed. I've been around long enough to recall that the same thing was said when the original IRA was established. A couple of other favorites are "I've got a big profit in a stock, but its share price is declining. But I've got to hold on for another year because Congress is going to lower the capital gains tax rate." "I'm going to start collecting my Social Security benefits as soon as possible because Congress is going to cut the benefits. If I start collecting now, I'll be able to lock in a higher benefit."

Here's my advice: Never avoid making an otherwise sensible financial decision based upon what Congress may do. No one can predict what Congress will do for us or, more likely when it comes to taxes and Social Security, *to* us.

READ THIS AND WEEP

Taxes take a big bite out of our paychecks, but for whatever reason, most Americans gripe about taxes only when they file their tax returns. By Memorial Day, taxes are only a memory. There are ways to reduce your tax bill, but unless you keep taxes in mind throughout the year, you probably won't take maximum advantage of tax-saving techniques.

Here's my public service message on taxes. I hope you keep the following table in mind throughout the year. It shows how much you have to earn to have enough money left over after taxes to buy the things you need.

If this expenditure:	Costs this much:	Here's how much you have to earn to pay for it:
Personal car loan	$300	$450
Rent	$750	$1,150
College tuition	$10,000	$15,500

Here's a tip for renters: If you're paying $900 in rent, you could own a house or condo with a $135,000 mortgage and pay no more than $900 a month after tax savings from mortgage interest and property taxes are taken into consideration.

Remember, finding a sensible way to reduce your tax bill is like finding money on the sidewalk. Money doesn't come any easier than by uncovering tax deductions or tax-advantaged investments.

INCLUDE SOME TAX-EFFICIENT MUTUAL FUNDS IN YOUR TAXABLE INVESTMENT ACCOUNTS

Each year at tax time, mutual fund investors face some unpleasant surprises. Mutual fund companies are required to pass along their realized capital gains, interest, and dividends to their shareholders. Taxes can greatly reduce a fund's performance. Tax liabilities are rarely a concern of most fund managers whose role is to obtain the highest total (before tax) return, except when tax efficiency is among the fund's objectives. Therefore, it's up to you to

POND'S LAW OF TAX POLICY

When imposing more taxes on the rich, Congress will always define "rich" as someone earning more than the salary of a member of Congress.

choose funds that are right for your tax situation. Yet most investors pay little heed of this—to their financial detriment. (See page 171.)

Of course, when you put a fund into a tax-deferred retirement account, taxes are of no immediate concern. It's when you put funds into a taxable investment account that it gets ugly.

TAX EFFICIENCY OF MUTUAL FUNDS

The relative tax efficiency of a mutual fund depends largely upon the fund's investment objective and the way in which it is managed. At one extreme, all or virtually all of the income distributed by single-state municipal money-market funds is tax-exempt. At the other end, stock funds striving for growth often distribute large capital gains to shareholders. And for funds that trade frequently, many of these capital gains could be short term, which bumps up the capital gains tax rate. Between the two extremes are endless varieties in terms of tax efficiencies.

Funds that invest in municipal securities are the most tax efficient because of the federal and perhaps state exemption of muni interest income. Nevertheless, any realized capital gains earned by a muni fund—or any fund for that matter—are subject to tax.

With respect to stock funds, index funds are more tax efficient than actively managed funds. (See page 168.)

There are some funds within most stock fund categories that are intentionally managed to minimize taxes. These funds go one step further than index funds in their efforts to minimize tax liabilities. They may employ a number of strategies, including:

➤ Deliberately selling losing investments to offset capital gains from other stocks
➤ When only part of a position is sold, selling shares with the highest tax cost basis (the higher the tax basis, the lower the capital gains tax)
➤ Minimizing turnover (turnover is the measure of how frequently the fund manager buys and sells securities in the fund. High turnover funds tend to have higher capital gains distributions)
➤ Avoiding stocks that pay high dividends

Of course, you shouldn't let taxes override other considerations that are often more important, including past investment performance and how a particular fund complements your other investment holdings. Taxes should, however, receive at least some consideration when you select a mutual fund for a taxable account. After all, income taxes can easily consume one-third or more of your investment income. Anything that can be done to minimize that bite while still meeting your overall investment objectives merits your serious attention.

BUY INDIVIDUAL STOCKS SO THAT YOU CAN DECIDE WHEN TO PAY CAPITAL GAINS TAXES

The way the rich get richer is by buying and holding individual stocks (or real estate), letting them appreciate in value throughout their lifetimes, and then passing them on to their ill-deserving heirs, who inherit the stocks not at the price their ancestors paid for them, but rather at the price of the stock when the dearly departed departed. Now, you might think, these people must have been pretty rich if they didn't have to sell any stock along the way. Well, they may have lived off the dividends, which probably increased at a rate greater than inflation over the years. The beauty of individual stocks is that you aren't having to pay capital gains every year as you would with most stock mutual funds. In short, owning individual stocks is a very tax-wise way to invest in your taxable investment accounts. Of course, if you eventually do sell a stock that you've owned a long time, you could be in for some hefty capital-gains taxes. But remember, the most that Uncle Sam will extract from you is 20 percent of the profit you made on the stock. Unpleasant? Yes, but you'll still end up with most of your money.

> ### POND'S LAW OF BRACKET CREEP (OR DON'T CRY OVER MORE MILK)
>
> There are worse things in life than moving into a higher tax bracket . . . like moving into a lower tax bracket.

TAKE ADVANTAGE OF YOUR CHILD'S LOWER TAX RATE IF YOU ARE INVESTING FOR COLLEGE

Make sure that you take advantage of the lower tax rate enjoyed by youngsters. For children under 14, there are limits to the amount of investment income they can earn. If it exceeds that amount, they are taxed at the parents' tax rate. There is usually no reason not to put enough college-earmarked money in the child's name (using a custodial account) to earn investment income up to the limit. Beginning at age 14, all income earned by a youngster will be taxed at the child's tax rate. As Chart #13 shows, taking advantage of a child's lower income tax rate can save hundreds of dollars in taxes each year. For more information on planning to meet the high costs of a college education, see Chapter 4.

You can obtain more suggestions for tax-advantaged ways to invest for college by clicking on:
http://jonathanpond.com/investments.college.htm

50 USEFUL IRS PUBLICATIONS (THEY'RE FREE, TOO!)

The IRS wants to be your friend. Honest. These publications, available free from the IRS, can be very helpful in understanding income tax mat-

CHART #13		
The Advantage of Investing in Your Child's Name		
	Investment in Parents' Name[1]	**Investment in Child's Name**
Taxable investment income	$1,000	$1,000
Subtract income taxes	(330)	(100)
After-tax income	$670	$900
Tax savings by investing in child's name ($900 - $670) = $230		

[1]Parents are assumed to be in the 33 percent federal and state income tax bracket.

ters that pertain to you. You can order any of them by calling (800) 829-3676 or by going on the IRS web site address noted below.

Publication #	Title
1	Your Rights as a Taxpayer
17	Your Federal Income Tax
54	Tax Guide for U.S. Citizens and Resident Aliens Abroad
225	Farmer's Tax Guide
334	Tax Guide for Small Businesses
448	Federal Estate and Gift Taxes
463	Travel, Entertainment, and Gift Expenses
501	Exemptions, Standard Deduction, and Filing Information
502	Medical and Dental Expenses
503	Child and Dependent Care Credit
504	Tax Information for Divorced or Separated Individuals
505	Tax Withholding and Estimated Tax
508	Educational Expenses
514	Foreign Tax Credit for Individuals
520	Scholarships and Fellowships
521	Moving Expenses
523	Tax Information on Selling Your Home
524	Credit for the Elderly or the Disabled
525	Taxable and Nontaxable Income
526	Charitable Contributions
527	Residential Rental Property
529	Miscellaneous Deductions
530	Tax Information for Homeowners (Including Owners of Condominiums and Cooperative Apartments)
531	Reporting Income from Tips
533	Self-Employment Tax
534	Depreciation
535	Business Expenses
537	Installment Sales
544	Sales and Other Dispositions of Assets

You can download these publications as well as copies of tax forms directly from the IRS web site by clicking on:

http://www.irs.gov/prod/forms_pubs/index.html

Chapter 15

It's Never Too Late—or Too Early— to Plan for a Comfortable Retirement

> **Not everyone wants to be a millionaire; many are content just to live like one.**
>
> *Anonymous*

Everyone has several personal financial goals—things they want to accomplish with their money—such as buying a home or paying for the kids' college education. The one goal that every working-age person has in common is being able to afford to retire. Most of the financial things we do during our working years (contributing to retirement plans, paying down the mortgage, protecting our savings and income with insurance, for example) are directly or indirectly geared toward being able to afford to retire. But in the New Century, to paraphrase an automobile ad, that is not your father's retirement. Several factors came into play in the latter part of the 20th century making it steadily more challenging for working-age people to realize their retirement dreams. While the spectacular rise in the stock market in the 1980s and 1990s helped some people accumulate the retirement money they're going to need, other factors are working against them. There's no arguing that it's going to be tougher to retire comfortably in the 21st century than it was for our parents. Once you recognize the reasons why, you can better appreciate what you're going to need to do between now and the time you get your gold watch. (Does anyone get a gold watch anymore?)

The Challenges of Achieving a Financially Secure Retirement

Several changes are coming in the retirement landscape, and they will affect your planning. These four trends make it all the more important for you to take the action necessary to achieve a financially secure retirement as soon as possible.

1. **Long life expectancies.** Longevity has increased dramatically since the beginning of last century. The idea of letting workers retire at age 65 originated about a century ago. Some enlightened employers in Europe decided to allow those few people who made it to 65 to retire. I guess they wanted to let them enjoy a few months of leisure before they died. What a difference a century makes. Now, a person who retires at 65 should plan on living another 25 years; many will live well beyond that. You may work for 35 or 40 years, during which time you will have to accumulate enough retirement funds to last 25 years or more. If you retire early, you could spend as many years retired as you did working.

2. **Inflation.** Inflation poses two challenges. First, inflation makes it tougher to accumulate sufficient resources in advance of retirement. Second, inflation makes it tougher to keep up with steadily increasing living costs throughout a long retirement. One of the biggest mistakes people make in planning for their retirements is to ignore or underestimate the effects of inflation. Even though inflation is much lower now than it was during the double-digit years of the late 1970s and early 1980s, it still takes its toll on your purchasing power. Incidentally, the average annual inflation rate during the 1980s, including the high rates of the early 1980s, was 4.7 percent. During the 1990s, a decade of supposedly very low inflation, inflation averaged almost 3 percent per year. While a 3 to 4 percent inflation rate may seem low, it means that the cost of living will double every 18 to 25 years. Retirees, therefore, are likely to see their cost of living double—or more—during their retirement years.

3. **Social insecurity.** Fiscal pressures on the government and employers are

increasing the likelihood that to assure an adequate retirement income, we will have to rely less on Social Security and company pension plans and more on personal investments and savings. With respect to company pension plans, an unmistakable shift is taking place. The burden of funding retirement income is moving away from the employer to the employee. As happy as the employees are when their companies offer a 401(k) plan, the employers are even happier. After all, it's the employees who end up footing most or all of the bill for the contributions to their accounts, and it's a heck of a lot cheaper than a pension plan. Those employees who don't contribute to these plans had better win the lottery.

4. **Great expectations.** Most of us have very ambitious retirement expectations—we expect to maintain the same style of life when we retire as we had during our working years. Moreover, almost half of working-age people want to retire early. Previous generations expected to cut back somewhat when they retired and didn't expect to retire before 65. There's nothing wrong with setting high retirement expectations—as long as you're willing to take the actions necessary to achieve them.

It's easy to feel overwhelmed when planning for retirement, particularly if you're one of the many late starters. For some inspiration and tips, click on:

http://jonathanpond.com/retirement.latestarters.htm

 The Social Security Administration has a very helpful web site which can be reached by clicking on:

http://www.ssa.gov/

You can use this site to obtain Form SSA-7050, Request for Social Security Earnings Information, if you haven't received an earnings and benefits statement automatically from the Social Security Administration.

Will Social Security Be Around When You Retire?

It's very fashionable for people to say that they're not factoring Social Security into their retirement planning because it won't be around when they retire. True, the system faces trouble largely because there aren't enough generation Xers and Yers around to support the huge number of baby boomers retiring. Is the system in trouble? Yes. Is some tough medicine required to fix the system, like raising the age when full benefits can be received or imposing more means-based tests on retirees? Definitely. Is Social Security going kaput? Of course not. Name a single member of Congress who will vote to end Social Security.

But even though Social Security will always be around, the most important thing to remember is that Social Security is only intended to provide a minimal retirement income, perhaps enough to support you for one week of each month. If you want to live the other three weeks, and I have yet to meet anyone who doesn't, it's up to you to come up with the difference. But don't join the crowd who say that Social Security is going away. They know not of what they speak.

Prepare Your Retirement Income and Expense Projections

Whether you're working age or retired, it's important to find out where you stand on retirement. The only way to do this is to put pencil to paper (or fingers to computer keyboard) and prepare a forecast of your retirement expenses and income. If you're still working, your projection will also show you how much you need to save. Your projections are only as good as your assumptions, and here are three important assumptions I strongly recommend you use:

1. **Inflation.** Use at least 3 percent. While there's a good chance that inflation will continue to be quite low, you shouldn't risk your financial future on it. If you use 3 percent and inflation averages less than

that, then you'll probably be in better shape when you retire than the projections will show. Better to beat your projections than come up short.

2. **Life expectancy.** Assume you'll live to age 95, and I hope you do. That seems like a long time to most people, and it is. Nevertheless, the odds are pretty good that you'll make it to 90 or more. In fact, a couple both reaching age 65 has a last-to-die life expectancy of 25 years. Let me translate that into English: if you and your spouse both reach age 65, you've got a very good chance of at least one of you surviving another 25 years, in other words, reaching age 90. So, while you may not be attracted to the idea of becoming a nonagenarian, you'd better plan financially for such an eventuality.

3. **Investment gains.** Use 7 to 8 percent to project your average annual investment gains. Hopefully they'll be better than that, but don't wager your retirement ranch on it. There's an example on page 146 that shows the danger of overestimating your investment returns when preparing retirement income and expense projections.

You may be tempted to fiddle with my suggested assumptions, but don't fiddle too much. While I hope you're optimistic about your financial future, don't let that optimism cloud your sound judgment in planning. I want all of your future financial surprises to be pleasant ones!

There are a lot of available work sheets, inexpensive software programs, and web sites that you can use to help you forecast your retirement income and expenses. For a list of my favorites, as well as more suggestions for preparing your all-important retirement projections, click on:

http://jonathanpond.com/retirement.projections.htm

Do You Want to Retire Early?

Many people aspire to, or are forced to consider, early retirement. If you are offered an early retirement incentive plan, review it carefully with the

No Good Deed Goes Unpunished

A couple of years ago, in the course of a brief interview by a major publication, I opined that:"The average 45-year-old couple will need to amass $1 million by the age of 65 which, when combined with Social Security, will enable them to retire in reasonable comfort." I thought this was a pretty benign and helpful observation until I started to receive the hate mail. While most of my mail is complimentary (or at least civil), you can't please all of the people all of the time. Some have called me an "idiot." Recently, I achieved an even higher level of criticism when a letter began with:"Jonathan Pond is a complete idiot." But I've never received so much criticism for a single statement than I did from the "millionaire-by-65" statement. Many accused me of pandering to the rich and scaring middle-class people. Others said they could retire rich on half that money. In retrospect, I wish I had indicated how much retirement income $1 million plus Social Security would provide for a couple 20 years hence. A $1 million nest egg plus Social Security would seem to be enough to provide a lot of income—if the income were being taken out today. But in my example, the $1 million won't be available for another 20 years. In the meantime, as it always does, inflation will drive up living costs. While $1 million plus Social Security might provide an income of around $75,000 today, that same amount of money in 20 years will only provide about $45,000 of purchasing power in today's dollars in the first year of retirement. Is $45,000 a comfortable retirement income? Certainly. Is it a "rich" couple's retirement income? Hardly.

Pond's Law of Early Retirement Incentive Plans

All early retirement incentive plans offer a lot less than meets the eye.

help of a CPA or experienced financial planner. Despite the candy coating by your employer who, after all, is trying to persuade you to leave, such plans usually require you to sacrifice a lot of future income compared with staying until normal retirement age.

Keys to Successful Early-Retirement Planning

If you want to retire early, take heed. If there's one common characteristic of people who can afford to retire early, it is sacrifice. This is how they do it:

1. **They plan early.** You can't decide when you're 50 that you want to retire at age 55—unless you're filthy rich. It doesn't take years of planning—it takes decades. Many successful early retirees begin planning for their dream in their 20s and 30s. They work for companies with generous pension plans and avoid hopping jobs so that they can accrue substantial benefits. Some couples make the decision not to have children so they won't incur the expenses of raising them. Many live in low-cost cities and towns.

2. **They sacrifice during their working years.** Where most people have trouble saving 10 percent of their salary, successful early retirees realize that they need to save 20 or 30 percent of their income during their working years. They are experts at living well below their means. They often live in inexpensive housing, and they become experts at keeping their living expenses low. Those that own homes get out from under their mortgage as soon as they can and certainly no later than when they plan to retire.

3. **They sacrifice after their working years.** Even though they have spent many years living modestly, successful early retirees cut back even further when they retire. They realize how much money they will have to continue saving in order to make ends meet 30 or 40 years hence. They relocate to low-cost areas of the country. Some even move out of the United States to settle in countries whose living costs are much lower.

> ## Pond's Law of Early Retirement
>
> Anyone who needs to collect Social Security benefits before age 65 to meet living expenses will run short of money later in life.

INFLATION'S TOLL ON EARLY RETIREES

Inflation is even more of an issue if you retire early. You'll be spending more years in retirement, and, therefore, you will be more heavily affected by inflation. Chart #14 illustrates how much more severely inflation affects early retirees. It shows how much living expenses will increase between retirement and the time you reach age 80.

The lesson here is quite simple. While everyone should take inflation into account when planning for retirement, the earlier you retire, the more inflation will affect you. Early retirees may well see their costs of living *triple*. Failure to take that into account could seriously jeopardize your financial health at a time in life when re-entering the work force would be difficult, if not impossible.

For more information on early retirement and how to evaluate an early retirement incentive plan, click on:

http://jonathanpond.com/retirement.earlyretirement.htm

CHART #14	
Effects of Inflation on Early Retirees	
Retirement Age	**If Your Living Expenses When You Retire Are $40,000, Your Living Expenses at Age 80 Will Be***
65	$67,000
60	$80,000
55	$95,000
50	$112,000

*Assuming a 3.5% annual inflation rate

One of the Most Important Financial Decisions of Your Life: Choosing Between a Lump Sum and an Annuity

There are only a handful of watershed moments in people's lives. Their graduation from college, their wedding day, the birth of a child are all days that one will never forget. But for many of us, one of the most important financial decisions of our lives is still before us—how to handle a distribution from our retirement plan when we retire.

Is it better to take a lump-sum payment at retirement or to take an annuity? The answer is anything but simple, the ramifications can be huge, and it is made even more perplexing by the general lack of objective advice on the subject. Investment advisers will likely encourage a rollover, while those in the annuity business will quote chapter and verse on the virtues of annuitizing.

True, some pension plans make it easy: They don't give you a choice, requiring you to take an annuity when you retire, period. On the other hand, many company plans (as well as any retirement plans that you have contributed to like 401(k) plans and IRAs) allow you the option of taking a lump-sum payout. This option affords you the advantage of more control over your financial destiny and must be considered carefully.

Key Considerations

Here in a nutshell are the key considerations when making this key decision:

1. **Investment risk.** Once you take possession of your lump sum, what happens to it is your business. If you lose it in unwise investments— or even "wise" ones that go sour anyway—there's no recourse but to suffer in silence. Unless you are confident of your own investment abilities—or those of a competent adviser—you may be better off taking the annuity.

2. **Liability risk.** Lump-sum distributions are not protected from liability. They have to be used up to pay major medical (or other) expenses, including nursing home costs, if you exhaust other resources. In many cases, though, annuities are not subject to this liability.

3. **Inflation risk.** While some annuity plans are adjusted (at least partly) to offset the effects of inflation, most are not. The reality of a fixed-payout annuity—barring a 1930s style deflation—is a steady loss of purchasing power. If you take the lump sum, you have a good, but by no means assured, chance of investing it to keep up with inflation.

4. **Anticipated income.** Generally, annuity payouts give you less income than you could make if you were investing the money on your own. Reason: The payout schedules tend to be figured very conservatively to minimize the annuity company's future financial risks. Find out the exact monthly or quarterly stipend you'd receive from an annuity and compare this figure to your anticipated rate of return if you were investing a lump sum on your own.

5. **Mortality risk.** Traditionally, annuity payments cease when you do. Consequently, if you die prematurely, your estate is considerably poorer than it would have been if you'd taken a lump sum. Note, though, that many annuity plans—both the corporate type and the kind you buy on your own—make some sort of provision for this event. Typically, it's a continuation of some lesser stream of payments for the benefit of a surviving spouse, or the option of receiving a lump-sum payout of a portion of the money that was originally put into the annuity.

LUMP SUM OR ANNUITY?

Each payout method has advantages and disadvantages, and no financial decision is "either/or." (See Chapter 3.) Many retirees will benefit from taking an annuity for part of the money and investing the rest. If you do decide on an annuity, be sure to shop around. Don't assume that your company annuity or the first annuity you come across is the best. Chances are it isn't. And if you decide to accept a lump-sum payment, make sure you examine the best way to put more of your retirement dollars in your pocket and less in Uncle Sam's.

If you decide to annuitize all or part of your retirement money, you may want to take a lump-sum distribution of the entire amount and use some of it to purchase an annuity. It doesn't have to be all at once. For example, some retirees wait until they are in their 70s to annuitize. By postponing the decision, you can increase the amount of income that the annuity will pay out since the payments are tied to life expectancy.

For more information on the all-important decision about how to withdraw retirement plan money when you retire, click on:

http://jonathanpond.com/retirement.payouts.htm

Chapter 16

LET UNCLE SAM HELP BANKROLL YOUR RETIREMENT NEST EGG

> I'm proud to be paying taxes in the United States. The only thing is—I could be just as proud for half the money.
>
> Arthur Godfrey

Believe it or not, Uncle Sam can be your partner in helping you save for a financially comfortable retirement. By investing in tax advantaged retirement plans, you will enjoy at least one of these tax-saving benefits:

➤ **Tax deferral.** All retirement savings plans share one thing in common: Investments inside these plans are not subject to taxes on the income you earn on your investments—interest, dividends, and capital gains—until you begin making withdrawals.

➤ **Tax deduction.** Many retirement savings plans also allow you to take a tax deduction for money you put into the plan or allow you to reduce your salary by the amount of your contribution, which is the same as a tax deduction.

➤ **Tax-free withdrawal.** In the case of the delectable Roth IRA, the money you withdraw when you're retired is generally tax-free.

So, thanks to the federal government's beneficence (not to mention it's fervent desire to make you, rather than Uncle Sam, responsible for bankrolling your retirement) there are all sorts of ways you can put money aside for retirement. This money stays outside the clutches of the tax collectors until you begin withdrawing the money or, in the case of the Roth IRA, forever. People who don't take advantage of these plans are, quite simply one sandwich short of a picnic because they're sacrificing their financial futures. I've never met anyone who thought they put too much money aside for retirement, but I've met a lot who wish they had the chance to do it over again.

A Lot of Tax-Advantaged Investment Choices

Here's a list of the available tax-advantaged investment opportunities. Most involve retirement plans, but there are also some individual investments that offer a means of achieving tax-deferred growth outside of one.

Deductible Tax-Deferred Investment Plans

➤ 401(k) (salary reduction) plan
➤ 403(b) plan for employees of non-profit organizations
➤ SIMPLE (Savings Incentive Match Plan for Employees) plan for employees of small businesses
➤ SEP (Simplified Employee Pension) plan for the self-employed and their employees
➤ Keogh plan for the self-employed and their employees
➤ Tax-deductible IRA

Nondeductible Tax-Deferred Investments and Investment Plans

➤ Nondeductible traditional IRA
➤ Roth IRA
➤ Holding individual stock or real estate
➤ Deferred annuity

Tax-Free Investments

➤ Municipal bonds and municipal bond mutual funds

For a glossary that explains the retirement plans and other tax-advantaged investments listed above, click on:

http://jonathanpond.com/retirement.glossary.htm

Chart #15 summarizes the tax-advantaged features of these retirement plans and tax-advantaged investments.

SOME TAX-ADVANTAGED INVESTMENTS ARE BETTER THAN OTHERS

Choosing the best tax-advantaged investments can be confusing. But, depending on your own circumstances, some tax-advantaged investments are superior to others. In general, any that permit you to contribute tax-deductible dollars are where your money should go first. If, on top of the tax deductibility going in, your employer offers a match, all the better.

But after you've maxed out on all tax-deductible retirement plan

CHART #15			
Tax-Advantaged Investment Categories			
Category	**Contributions**	**Investment Earnings**	**Examples**
Deductible Tax-Deferred	Deductible	Tax-deferred until withdrawal	• 401(k) • 403(b) • SIMPLE • SEP • Keogh • Deductible • IRA
Nondeductible Tax-deferred	Not deductible Roth IRA withdrawals usually tax-free	Tax-deferred until withdrawn or sold;	• Nondeductible IRA • Roth IRA • Individual stock and real estate investments • Deferred annuity
Tax-free	Not deductible capital gains are taxable	Interest is tax-exempt;	• Municipal bond • Municipal bond mutual fund

investments, you'll still probably want and need to contribute to other tax-advantaged investments. This is when the situation gets more complicated. Chart #16 should help you identify those tax-advantaged investment accounts and investments that are best for you based on your employment status. In addition, whether you're working age or retired, if you have a traditional IRA and qualify, you should also consider a Roth IRA conversion (page 206).

CHART #16
The Best Tax-Advantaged Investments For You

Check your Status:

☐ I am an employee	☐ I am self-employed	☐ I am an exployee but I also have some self-employment income	☐ I am retired or have no self-employment income

Here are Your Best Tax-Advantaged Investments:

Best	401(k), 403(b), or SIMPLE if available from your employer	SEP or Keogh plan	401(k), 403(b), or SIMPLE if available from your employer	Delay withdrawing retirement plan investments (traditional IRAs, etc.)
Second Best	IRA[1]	IRA[1]	SEP or Keogh plan	Buying and holding individual stocks and real estate
Third Best	Buying and holding individual stocks and real estate	Buying and holding individual stocks and real estate	IRA[1]	Municipal bonds and muni bond funds
Also Worth Considering	Deferred annuities[2] Municipal bonds and municipal bond funds	Deferred annuities[2] Municipal bonds and municipal bond funds	Buying and holding indiviudal stocks and real estate Deferred annuities[2] Municipal bonds and bond funds	

[1] If you qualify, the Roth IRA is usually preferable to a nondeductible traditional IRA and may be preferable to a deductible IRA.
[2] Deferred annuities are not recommended for most people over age 50. (See page 126.)

Are You Eligible for a Particular Retirement Plan?

> ### Pond's Law of Hardheadedness
>
> Employees who don't participate in their company's retirement savings plan when an employer match is offered have cement between their ears.

As good as they are, you may not qualify for all of the available retirement plans. The "Infernal" Revenue Code has, in its own inimitable way, imposed all sorts of restrictions and phase-outs on retirement plan participation, most of which defy logic. According to our elected officials, the reason they deny some people the ability to participate is so that the "rich" won't benefit too much from saving and investing for the future. How do they define the rich? If you look back over the past 20 years of legislation, you'd find that a "rich" person was pretty consistently defined as anyone who was earning more than the salary of a member of Congress. This is not a joke. Of the retirement plan and tax-deferred investments categorized in Chart 15, the only ones that aren't burdened by some restrictions are holding individual stocks and/or real estate, deferred annuities, and municipal bonds or muni bond funds. Everyone can own those investments; otherwise, you need to find out if you qualify.

The qualification rules for retirement plan participation are regularly being revised by Congress. To obtain the latest rules, click on:

http://jonathanpond.com/retirement.planrules.htm

Roth IRAs

Of the nondeductible plans, the one that everyone who qualifies should be taking advantage of is the Roth IRA. It is truly a retirement plan for the New Century! The Roth IRA is the best tax break that's been introduced in a long time. Every working-age person who qualifies should be mak-

Do You Have Too Much of Your Own Company's Stock in Your 401(k) Plan?

If you work for a big corporation, you may hold some of its stock in your 401(k) plan account. It's not unusual for 401(k) participants to be overinvested in their own company's stock thus putting their retirement money at significant risk from lack of diversification. Some people have made a lot of money by investing heavily in their own company's stock, of course, but countless other 401(k) plan participants have had years of savings wiped out in a matter of months. Your retirement money is too important to risk on the price fluctuations of a single stock. And do you really want to depend on one company for your career *and* your retirement income? As optimistic as you might be about your company's future, I don't think you should invest *any* of your 401(k) money in your employer's stock, and certainly no more than 10 percent. If the company offers a stock purchase plan, buy the stock through that plan—not through the 401(k). In fact, if the stock purchase plan offers the stock at a discount, you're crazy not to participate.

ing annual *contributions* to a Roth IRA. The Roth IRA *conversion*—that's where you transfer money from your traditional IRAs into a Roth IRA— is also well worth examining for anyone who qualifies, working age or retired. (See page 206.)

The Roth IRA offers more flexibility than the traditional IRA (also sometimes called the regular IRA). In fact, the Roth IRA is so flexible that it probably shouldn't even be called an individual "retirement" account. It allows you to make *nondeductible* annual contributions and, if you adhere to the not-too-tough rules, you can withdraw money *tax-free* and *penalty-free* for important financial needs other than retirement.

ADVANTAGES OF THE ROTH IRA

I spoke with Senator Roth shortly after his legislation was passed. He said that the reason he authored the legislation was to give retirees a break. With traditional retirement savings plans, retirees end up having to fork over a lot of taxes during their retirement years when they can least afford it. The Roth will reduce the tax burden on seniors.

➤ You can generally withdraw original contributions at any time, for any reason, without penalty.

➤ Money can be withdrawn from the Roth IRA tax-free during retirement. This is the big advantage of the Roth. Imagine being able to withdraw money from your Roth IRA totally tax-free when you're retired and can really use all the money, rather than having to share it with Uncle Sam as would be required with a traditional IRA.

➤ Roth IRAs allow penalty-free withdrawals for higher education expenses.

➤ You can make contributions after age 70½ if you continue working.

➤ Distributions are not required after age 70½. Traditional IRAs require minimum annual withdrawals after age 70½. (See page 262 for more information on the estate-planning advantages of the Roth IRA.)

➤ You can name a new beneficiary for a Roth IRA at any time, including after age 70½.

By the way, these advantages generally also accrue to Roth IRA conversions, which are discussed on page 206.

IS THE ROTH IRA BETTER THAN A DEDUCTIBLE IRA?

A Roth IRA is worth considering even if you qualify for a tax-deductible IRA. It's a flexible way to save for other important goals in addition to retirement. (That's why they also make a great gift for a child or grandchild who has job income. See page 35.) You may be better off financially in the long run paying taxes now to fund a Roth IRA than you would be taking the tax deduction.

Are You Eligible?

Alas, not everyone qualifies for the Roth IRA. In order to qualify, your income must be under the specified eligibility requirements. If your income is just a wee bit above the thresholds, you may qualify for a partial Roth IRA deduction under the phase-out rules. If this sounds complicated, that's because it is. But the following table lays out the income requirements.

Do You Qualify for a Roth IRA Contribution?		
Allowable	**Adjusted Gross Income Limit**	
Contribution	**Single**	**Married and Filing Jointly**
$2000	Less than $95,000	Less than $150,000
Less than $2000 (determined by formula)	$95,000-$110,000	$150,000-$160,000
None	$110,001 or more	$160,001 or more

The Roth IRA rules are regularly changed by Congress. For the latest rules and information about the Roth IRA, click on:

http://jonathanpond.com/retirement.planrules.htm

To Roth or Not to Roth? That Is the Question

Is the Roth IRA too good to be true? We have become so skeptical of our public officials that many think there must be some hidden catch to the Roth IRA. According to the tax experts, the Roth IRA offers those who are eligible a tremendous opportunity—one that you'd be foolish to pass up.

You should do some calculations based on your own situation. You need to factor in two important matters: first, how long it will be until you're going to need to withdraw your Roth IRA money (the longer it is, the better the Roth will be); and second, what your expected income tax bracket will be when you begin to make withdrawals (if you think it will be the same or higher, the Roth should work to your advantage). Many financial services firms, particularly mutual fund companies and brokerage firms, provide the software necessary to make the calculations on their Internet sites.

Not only could the Roth IRA accumulate more after-tax earnings than a deductible IRA, but it might also be preferred over a 401(k) plan contribution. Consider making the minimum contribution to your 401(k) plan required to receive the full employer match, then contribute to the Roth IRA for tax-free earnings. Of course, if you're going to achieve your retirement dreams, you should be contributing the maximum to your 401(k) and contributing to a Roth IRA.

Schoolteachers, hospital employees, and other people who work for public, nonprofit institutions often have limited choices in their 403(b) savings plans. Most of the options may be for relatively expensive insurance-based products, such as fixed or variable annuities. The Roth IRA offers a new option for a portion of the money that might otherwise go into such a plan. Instead of taking the tax deduction, you can pay the taxes now, open a Roth IRA, and invest in mutual funds that assess lower fees. (It's best to do both to the max if you can swing it.)

Many retired people have income that is just below the level that would trigger a tax on their Social Security benefits. A Roth IRA may make it easier for them to stay below that level, because the withdrawals probably won't be included in taxable income.

Need an additional push to join the Roth IRA club? Consider the following examples:

> Brian Brilliant is trying to decide whether to change his annual IRA contributions from a nondeductible traditional IRA (he doesn't qualify for a deductible IRA) to a Roth IRA. He's 20 years away from retirement and expects to contribute $2,000 each year. Once he retires, Brian expects to withdraw the IRA money over 25 years. Is he better off making nondeductible IRA contributions or Roth IRA contributions? This is a pretty complicated matter, but that's why we have computers. And the computer tells us that if Brian is able to earn an average of 8 percent per year on

POND'S LAW OF IRA CONTRIBUTION DENIAL

None of the reasons people give as to why they're not contributing to an IRA have any validity.

his investments, he will be able to withdraw $158,000 in after-tax dollars from his nondeductible IRA over the course of his retirement years. Not bad. But the Roth IRA is even better, providing Brian with $214,000 in after-tax dollars.

Clarissa and Clarence Clever are contemporaries of Brian's, and they also expect to be contributing $2,000 each to an IRA over the next 20 years and then withdrawing the money over 25 years of retirement. Clarissa and Clarence qualify for a *deductible* IRA, but they've been hearing that the Roth IRA, even though it's not deductible, may actually be better than a deductible traditional IRA. What does the computer say? If they make deductible IRA contributions but don't invest the tax savings they would enjoy from the tax deduction, they could withdraw $290,000 in after-tax dollars during their retirement years. If they have the self-discipline to invest the deductible IRA's tax savings in a non-IRA account, they would accumulate even more—enough to be able to withdraw $372,000 in after-tax dollars during their retirement years. But the Roth IRA is even more advantageous. It results in after-tax income of $428,000. (That's twice as much as Brian Brilliant will withdraw from his Roth IRA, since Clarissa and Clarence are contributing a combined total $4,000 each year into their IRA accounts as opposed to Brian's $2,000). So, the Roth provides a greater return than a deductible traditional IRA.

For the latest information on Roth IRA contributions, including useful web sites that can help you determine if Roth IRA contributions make sense for you, click on:

http://jonathanpond.com/retirement.rothiracontributions.htm

CONVERTING TRADITIONAL IRAS TO ROTH IRAS

In addition to making annual contributions to a Roth IRA account, the tax rules also permit many people who already have traditional IRAs to *convert* them into Roth IRAs. While you'll have to pay taxes when you convert a traditional IRA into a Roth IRA, you'll be able to withdraw the Roth money later totally free of federal income taxes. Even if you don't have a traditional IRA now, you may in the future when you roll over your company tax-deferred retirement plans when you change jobs or retire. (As I will explain shortly, you're never too old to consider a Roth conversion, and many retirees stand to reap substantial benefits from doing so.)

One of the questions I'm most frequently asked is: "Should I consider converting my traditional IRAs to a Roth IRA?" While everyone's situation is different, the following information will help you make the right decision. To qualify for a Roth IRA conversion, your adjusted gross income (AGI) in the year you make the conversion must be $100,000 or less (not including the income you'll have to add to your AGI as a result of doing the conversion) whether you're single or married.

Staying within the Income Limit to Qualify for Roth IRA Conversions

The limitations on converting a traditional IRA to a Roth IRA disqualify a lot of people. However, some may be able to "manipulate" their income for the year in which the conversion is made. You need qualify for that year alone. For example, a retired person with a lot of investment income who wants to convert to a Roth IRA might sell investments in one year and, early the next year, buy one-year Treasury bills payable the following year. Interest paid on the T-bills will not be taxable until the bills mature. Or a taxpayer could hold tax-free municipal bonds for a year. Owners of family businesses might be able to pay themselves less for a year. For example, you might pay yourself a bonus in December of one year and again in January, 13 months later, and draw a smaller salary in the intervening year.

Three Questions to Answer before Converting to a Roth IRA

The younger you are when you convert to a Roth IRA (as well as make annual contributions to a Roth), the better. But it's probably never too late to consider a conversion, even if you're already retired. Here are three important matters to consider:

1. **How long will it be before you expect to make withdrawals from a Roth?** A Roth conversion will probably work if you don't need to tap into the money for at least 10 years, but the longer you can wait, the more tax-deferred, tax-free growth you'll be able to enjoy. This means that even retirees may benefit from a Roth. A good portion of the money you have in traditional IRAs when you retire won't be accessed for at least 10 years. (If all of it is likely to be needed within a decade, you're in trouble.) By converting this long-term IRA money to a Roth IRA now, you'll enjoy a higher after-tax income in your later retirement years.

2. **Do you expect to be in the same or higher tax bracket when you're retired?** If so, the Roth should be beneficial. If you expect to be in a lower tax bracket (most retirees won't) then a Roth conversion (or contribution) may not be worthwhile.

3. **Can you afford to pay the taxes due from the Roth conversion out of money that is outside your retirement accounts?** It doesn't make sense to take money out of retirement accounts (which will be subject to taxes and, perhaps, penalties) to pay the taxes due from a Roth conversion. You'll need to have enough nonretirement account money to be able to pay the taxes.

THE TIME TO CONSIDER A ROTH IRA CONVERSION IS NOW

You have a lot to gain by considering a Roth IRA conversion, but you need to do some homework first. If you have a tax adviser, make an appointment. Most financial services firms, including banks, brokerage firms, and mutual fund companies offer worksheets and software on their Internet sites. By using these resources you can figure out how much you stand to benefit from a Roth IRA conversion. Chances are, you'll find that a Roth IRA conversion will reward you with a higher retirement income. While the younger you are, the more time you'll have to allow the Roth IRA to work its magic, Roth IRA conversions can work at any age, even for those who are already retired. Consider the following three case studies of people of different ages:

Sean Shrewd is a long way from retirement. But he has already accumulated $25,000 in an IRA from some annual contributions and a rollover from a 401(k) plan at a former employer. Although 30 years away from retirement, Sean is considering a Roth IRA conversion since he's been hearing that it's well worth the taxes that he would have to pay up front. He ultimately expects to withdraw the money over 25 years of retirement. Sean assumes that he'll make an 8 percent annual return on his investments. (All 6of the other examples in this chapter also assume an 8 percent annual return.) Even though he'll have to pay over $8,000 in income taxes for the conversion, he'll still be far better off during retirement by making the conversion. In fact, the Roth IRA conversion will provide over $100,000 more after-tax retirement income ($545,000 if he converts to the Roth IRA compared with $435,000 if he doesn't). Incidentally, I didn't fudge the numbers. I took into consideration the taxes that would have been paid by converting to the Roth. (I also did the same for the other examples in this chapter.) But even after Sean paid that hefty tax, he still beats the traditional IRA because the Roth IRA can be withdrawn tax-free during retirement.

Samatha Sagacious wants to convert a $100,000 traditional IRA to a Roth IRA. She plans to hold on to the money for 20 years. After the 20-year accumulation period she expects to withdraw the money over 10 years. If Samantha decides not to convert to a Roth IRA, she will be able to withdraw $480,000 in after-tax dollars. But if she does convert, she'll enjoy $575,000 in after-tax dollars. That's 20 percent more after-tax income by converting to a Roth IRA!

Leonard Learned is about to retire, but he heard that Roth IRA conversions can be beneficial even for people who are nearing retirement or who are already retired. He's thinking about converting $100,000 of his IRA money into a Roth. He knows he won't need this money for at least ten years because he will tap into other IRA money as well as Social Security over the next decade. Leonard also figures that after allowing the converted IRA to grow for ten years, he will then withdraw it for 20 years. Does the Roth IRA make sense, even at this relatively late time of life? If he keeps his money in a traditional IRA, the computer says he'll be able to withdraw $355,000. If he converts to a Roth IRA, however, he will be able to enjoy after-tax retirement income of $407,000. Thus, the Roth IRA conversion results in almost 15 percent more after-tax retirement income.

For the latest information on Roth IRA conversions, including useful web sites that can help you determine if a Roth IRA conversion makes sense for you, click on:

http://jonathanpond.com/retirement.rothiraconversion.htm

THE BEST OF BOTH WORLDS: COMBINING A ROTH IRA CONVERSION AND ANNUAL ROTH IRA CONTRIBUTIONS

If you're still on the fence about the Roth IRA, consider the grand plan of Penelope Perspicacious. She's 35 years old, already has a $25,000 traditional IRA and has developed the very good habit of making $2,000 annual nondeductible IRA contributions. She wants to know how much she will benefit by converting her traditional IRA to a Roth and by changing her future annual IRA contributions to a Roth IRA. Penelope is in for some good news. The combination of the $25,000 Roth IRA conversion plus the annual Roth IRA contributions will provide her with over 30 percent more after-tax retirement income compared with not converting and continuing to contribute to a nondeductible traditional IRA. Her income-producing capital during retirement would be $800,000 if she didn't make any changes, compared with $1.1 million by Rothifying. For those who qualify, the Roth is a no-brainer decision.

Chapter 17

■ WILL YOUR GOLDEN YEARS BE GOLDEN? HOW TO THRIVE THROUGHOUT YOUR (AND YOUR PARENTS') RETIREMENT YEARS

> Live within your income, even if you have to borrow to do so.
>
> *Josh Billings*

Financial planning doesn't stop when you retire. Even people who have successfully made the transition from the working world to retired life cannot rest on their laurels. As for the retiree who did not plan adequately, careful attention to financial planning is especially necessary. The planning process continues as long as you live.

In this chapter, I'll discuss some matters that are important to retirees (and their children who will, sooner or later, likely be called upon to advise their retired parents on various financial matters). They include:

➤ Important financial planning concerns of retirees
➤ Investing when you're retired
➤ Making sure you never run out of money
➤ Avoiding problems when making minimum IRA withdrawals

CONTINUING FINANCIAL PLANNING IN RETIREMENT

Retired people, like their working counterparts, need to manage their debts wisely, invest appropriately, and in many instances continue the savings programs they began in their working years. Keeping records in good order is especially important for retirees. The sudden onset of a disability could result in a child or relative having to assume responsibility for the disabled person's financial affairs. Should a disability occur, thorough, well-organized records will make matters a great deal simpler. Retirees also need to maintain comprehensive insurance coverage, although life insurance can usually be scaled back. Retired people have to pay special attention to their estate plans in order to see that they are appropriate and up-to-date.

KEEP AN EYE ON YOUR FINANCIAL FUTURE

Unfortunately, all too many older people assume that because they succeeded in meeting their retirement savings goals, they no longer need to worry about planning. Yet people of all ages need to establish financial goals. They impose discipline and force you to consider where you want to be in the future. For retirees who have a comfortable amount of discretionary income, reasonable financial goals might include saving money for extensive travel, increased charitable giving, and transferring wealth to heirs before (and after) death.

One of the first things you should do when you retire—or even before—is take a hard look at what your retirement living expenses are likely to be. The last thing the retiree wants is to run out of money. Like everyone else, the new retiree needs to establish a workable budget. Hopefully, the income derived from pensions, Social Security benefits, and personal investments will be sufficient to make a lifestyle change unnecessary.

Many older people think that retirement is a time to adopt a super-conservative approach to investing. However, playing it overly safe can be just as disastrous as being wild and reckless. The retiree is faced with a dual challenge: He or she must continue to nurture an investment portfolio while ensuring that it provides a comfortable level of current income. Unlike younger investors, who generally rely on their salaries to meet living expenses, retirees often depend heavily on the performance of their investment portfolios for income. Because retirees are so aware of their dependence on income from investments, they tend to be excessively conservative in their investment habits, leaving them with an ever-declining standard of living.

For more details on financial planning matters that are unique to retirees, click on:

http://jonathanpond.com/retirement.retireeplanning.htm

INVESTING WHEN YOU'RE RETIRED

There's a myth going around that once you're retired, you've got to make some major changes in the way you invest. Wrong—assuming you have invested wisely during your working years.

TIME TO TAKE CHARGE OF YOUR INVESTMENTS

When you retire, you will be delighted to find that, perhaps for the first time in your life, you have the time to focus on your investing. And all I can say is, "go for it." With experience and time on your side, you'll become a much better investor—whether you make all your investment decisions yourself or rely on someone else to guide you. I am acquainted with one woman who had never done any investing until just after she retired. To make a long story short, in 20 years she has turned $100,000 into well over $2 million. And she is still a very successful, active investor in her mid-80s.

RETIREES NEED TO INVEST FOR BOTH GROWTH AND INCOME

Whenever I hear retirees on the radio talk shows review their portfolios—consisting of CDs, savings accounts, and bonds—I cringe. Why? Because, while most retirees certainly need income from their investments to help meet living expenses, they also need growth. Take a gander at Chart

> ### POND'S LAW OF RETIREMENT
>
> The greatest financial pleasure in retirement is telling your children how much you enjoy spending their inheritance.

FINANCIAL CHALLENGES OF YOUR RETIRED PARENTS (AND YOU IF YOU'RE A SENIOR CITIZEN)

All of our parents say: "We don't want to be a burden on you." Well, chances are they will be. While most of us won't have to provide financial support, as your parents age they are likely to become more and more dependent on their children, close relatives, or acquaintances to help them manage the inevitable financial challenges of senior citizens. Here are four particularly important matters to attend to as your parents (or you) age.

❶ Housing. I wish they would pass a law in this country that would require anyone who reaches age 65 to discuss with their family members various housing options. And by "housing options," I mean, of course, the possibility of having to go into a nursing home. Because if it's not discussed before the decision has to be made, you can pretty much be assured what the response of your mother or father will be: "Shoot me rather than put me in a nursing home." This is unfair. It sends the child on a permanent guilt trip when, if these matters had been discussed earlier, the possibility of having to go into a nursing home could have been discussed more rationally.

❷ Insurance. Make sure your parents keep and maintain the right kind and amount of insurance. A lot of seniors are either victimized by unscrupulous insurance agents or they go out on their own and buy narrowly defined coverage (cancer insurance, for example) that's a waste of money.

❸ Health care. A lot of seniors are reticent to ask for the health care that they deserve and are entitled to. Sometimes a younger generation family member will have to intervene to make sure that the senior is receiving appropriate health care.

❹ Day-to-day money concerns. Finally, look for situations where there might be money problems. A sudden change in spending habits, late filing of tax returns, late payment of bills may indicate that a senior is simply unable to maintain his or her day-to-day finances. It doesn't necessarily mean that a parent is having trouble making ends meet, but the assistance of a child or other family members is probably necessary. Another matter to be wary of is that seniors are all too often the victim of scam artists. They are easy marks and are often too embarrassed to complain to anyone. If you're a child, relative, or close friend of a senior, encourage him or her to check with you before making any major expenditure. Whether it's an investment, a driveway paving job, or whatever, encourage the senior to get your independent opinion. Just telling the "salesperson" that you have to check with a relative before making a decision is enough to make most scam *artistes* flee. We have a "$500 rule" in the Pond family. If the parents are going to spend more than $500 on anything, they first check with one of the kids. This has avoided several problems.

If your parents live quite a distance away, most cities have agencies that are available to meet the basic needs of the elderly, from home health care to companionship and escort services. For help in locating agencies and services, contact:

The National Association of Area Agencies on Aging
927 15th Street, NW
Washington, DC 20005
Telephone: (202) 296-8130; Web address: *www.N4A.org*

Special Note to Adult Children

If you're not expecting to receive much in the way of an inheritance, don't hold that against your parents. Imagine how much more money they'd have available to pass on to the next generation if they didn't have to raise you.

#17, which shows just how much living costs can increase, with a modest 3½ percent inflation rate, over a (hopefully) long retirement. How, pray tell, can anyone keep up with inflation if his or her portfolio doesn't grow?

Ralph Retiree, age 65, is getting ready to call it a day and he estimates that his living expenses in his first year of retirement will be $30,000. Ralph is a little surprised to see how much his cost of living will increase at a 3½ percent rate of inflation (and inflation could be higher than that). By age 75, his cost of living will go up by almost 50 percent. It will cost him $42,000 to live like he had lived for just $30,000 a decade earlier. And it gets worse. By age 85 his cost of living will have doubled, and if he makes it to age 100 (and more and more seniors are), his cost of living will have more than tripled, to $100,000!

You can find more information and case studies on investing during your retirement years by clicking on:

http://jonathanpond.com/retirement.retireeinvesting.htm

CHART #17

Why Investing for Growth Is Important for Retirees

Age	Annual Living Expenses Adjusted for 3 ½ Percent Average Annual Inflation					
65	$20,000	$30,000	$40,000	$50,000	$60,000	$70,000
70	24,000	36,000	48,000	59,000	72,000	71,000
75	28,000	42,000	56,000	71,000	85,000	99,000
80	34,000	50,000	67,000	84,000	100,000	117,000
85	40,000	60,000	80,000	99,000	119,000	139,000
90	47,000	71,000	94,000	118,000	142,000	165,000
95	56,000	84,000	112,000	140,000	168,000	196,000
100	67,000	100,000	133,000	167,000	200,000	233,000

For additional guidance on helping your aging parents or other aging family members, click on:

http://jonathanpond.com/general.agingparents.htm

MAKING SURE YOU NEVER RUN OUT OF MONEY

One of the big differences in our personal finances in the New Century compared with the 20th century is that retirees are now having to rely more and more heavily on their own savings and investments. It used to be that company pension plans and Social Security could cover most retirement needs. Since employers have cut back drastically on pension plans and it's unrealistic to expect Social Security to provide a high proportion of your retirement income, we have to rely on our own money to survive—and hopefully thrive—during our retirement years. It's up to you to make sure that you never deplete your retirement nest egg—or at least not before you die. While your children or other heirs won't agree, the best thing to try to do is to use up your assets right before you die.

Chart #18 will help you avoid making either of two big mistakes during your retirement years:

➤ Investing too conservatively
➤ Withdrawing too much of your nest egg

EMPHASIZING GROWTH AS WELL AS INCOME WITH YOUR RETIREMENT INVESTMENTS

Despite being sensibly risk-averse, retirees are still long-term investors whose cost of living will increase substantially. So, in addition to producing income, their investments still need to provide growth for the future. Consider Chart #18 which shows the number of years money will last at a given withdrawal rate. To illustrate how the chart works and how important it is to approach these matters realistically, consider the following example.

CHART #18

How Long Your Money Will Last

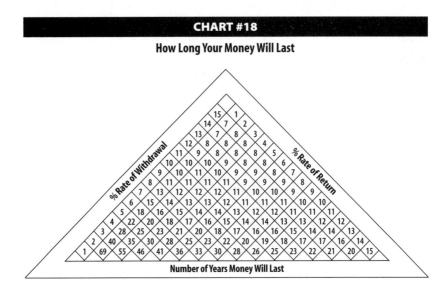

Number of Years Money Will Last

Carlisle Conservative likes to keep his money safe, so he puts his retirement stash in a combination of Treasury bills, bank savings accounts, and his checking account. The combination of safe investments provides him with a 3 percent average annual return. Greta Growth, on the other hand, likes dividend-paying stocks as well as some bonds. She's pretty confident that she can earn at least 7 percent on her money. Both Carlisle and Greta are withdrawing 7 percent of their retirement money this year. How long will their retirement nest eggs last?

The answers will show you how important investing for growth can be. The pyramid chart shows that Carlisle Conservative's money will run out in 18 years (on the pyramid, look for the intersection of the 7 percent rate of withdrawal column and the 3 percent rate of return column). On the other hand, Greta's money, since she expects to earn 7 percent as opposed to Carlisle's 3 percent, will never run out. (If the intersection of the columns is off the chart, it means that the money should never be exhausted.) Investing too conservatively could tarnish your golden years.

PRUDENT WITHDRAWAL RATE

The other danger, one which far too many retirees succumb to, is withdrawing too much from their retirement nest egg each year. Setting a reasonable percentage rate of withdrawal early in your retirement years will help you avoid what could be the most serious financial mistake of your life. Unfortunately, many retirees won't discover their mistake until it's too late and will end up having to severely cut back on their living standard late in life or, worse, running out of money altogether. Here's an example that, with the aid of Chart #18, will show what can happen if you establish a pattern of withdrawing too much of your retirement money each year.

Both Geraldine Greedy and Paul Prudent have recently retired and know how important it is to invest retirement money so that it can continue to grow during their retirement years. While their money has grown in the double-digit range during many of the years of the 1990s, both Geraldine and Paul feel that an 8 percent average annual return is a reasonable assumption for the future. But there the similarity ends. Geraldine plans to withdraw 14 percent of her total retirement investments during her first year of retirement and pretty much continue that pattern throughout. Paul, on the other hand, is planning to withdraw 7 percent in his first year and maintain that rate.

As the pyramid chart indicates, while Paul is in pretty good shape, Geraldine may be headed for trouble. Using an 8 percent rate of return and a 7 percent rate of withdrawal, Paul needn't worry about running out of money. (Remember, when the intersection of the columns is off the chart, the money should last indefinitely.) The chart indicates that Geraldine, on the other hand, will run out of money in 11 years if she continues the pattern of a 14 percent withdrawal rate while earning 8 percent on her investments.

As you plan your retirement, by all means run your own numbers against the information contained in the pyramid chart. Remember also, that this chart assumes a level rate of withdrawal. If, as is more realistic, you increase your withdrawal rate each year to account for inflation, the money won't last as long as the chart indicates.

THE MOST IMPORTANT FINANCIAL DECISION OF YOUR LIFE

I think the most important financial decision of your life (short of marrying someone who has $50 million) takes place when you retire. As you've just seen, the amount of money that you withdraw from your nest egg during your first year of retirement can influence your financial security for the rest of your life. If you establish a pattern of taking out too much money, you risk running short later in life. So how much can you safely withdraw from your retirement nest egg?

➤ If you retire at age 65 or soon thereafter, you can safely withdraw 6 percent of your money in your first year of retirement, but no more than 7 percent.

➤ If you retire early—in your late 50s or early 60s, you should hold your first year withdrawal rate to around 5 percent—or 6 percent at most.

Every year after your first year of retirement, you can increase the amount you withdraw by the amount of inflation during the preceding year. If you withdraw more than these amounts, you run a big risk of coming up short late in life. If you want to be ultra safe, hold your withdrawal rate to 4 percent.

BEWARE OF POTENTIAL SNAFUS WHEN YOU BEGIN MAKING MINIMUM IRA WITHDRAWALS

Beware! A minefield awaits you when you reach the age of 70½. While you may not celebrate your half birthday anymore, you'll still need to do some serious thinking. It's time to begin making minimum withdrawals from your traditional IRAs and to name a beneficiary. You'll have to stick with the minimum withdrawal decision for the rest of your life, and then some. If you make the wrong withdrawal decision or end up naming an inappropriate beneficiary, you may end up with some IRA money in your estate and your heirs may end up handing it over to Uncle Sam. Don't rest easy if your investment adviser, bank, brokerage firm, or mutual fund company advises you on how to structure your withdrawals or name beneficiaries either. They have been known to give the wrong advice. Once you elect a withdrawal method, you're stuck with it for life. In addition to just plain bad advice, stories abound of financial institutions that have lost beneficiary forms or been given IRA distribution checks in error. Any of these miscues could end up costing the heirs a tremendous amount of money.

So what's the big deal? No later than April 1 of the year after you reach age 70½, you must designate a beneficiary for your IRA as well as choose a method for making IRA withdrawals that is based on life expectancy. (If you miss the deadline, big penalties may be assessed unless you can convince the IRS that the reason you didn't was due to reasonable mistakes.) Those choices will not only determine the minimum amounts you'll have to withdraw for the rest of your life, but will also determine the way your beneficiary or beneficiaries can receive the money after you're gone.

Two minimum withdrawal methods are allowed: the recalculation method and the term-certain method. Each method has advantages and drawbacks. One of the most common pitfalls involves the selection of the recalculation method when a spouse or your estate is named beneficiary. It could require your survivors to speed up their withdrawals of the inherited IRA, leading to a big tax bill and foregoing the opportunity to allow the inherited IRA to continue growing tax deferred.

What's worse, many financial institutions simply apply the recalculation method if you don't step in and specify the term-certain method. By the way, the recalculation method or a combination of both methods may be the better choice in some instances. If it sounds complicated, it is. That's why, unless your IRAs are very small, you should pay an expert, a CPA or lawyer, perhaps, to advise you on the best decision. There's too much money riding on it to rely on the financial institution that holds your IRA to advise you. They'll be glad you got professional advice as well.

Watch out for Higher Taxes If You Make Two IRA Withdrawals in the Same Year

Remember, the latest you can make your first minimum withdrawal is April 1 (April Fool's Day, no less) of the year after the year in which you attain the age of 70½. But it may be better from a tax standpoint to take your first distribution (withdrawal) during the year you reach 70½ rather than at the last minute. Each subsequent withdrawal after age 70½ must be made in the current calendar year, so you could end up making two IRA withdrawals in that first year. For example, if you reach age 70½ in the year 2001 and make your first withdrawal in 2002 (on or before April 1), you'll have to make your second withdrawal in 2002 as well (but no later than December 31). If two IRA withdrawals in the same year will move you into a higher tax bracket, be sure to make your first withdrawal in the year you turn 70½ to avoid the higher tax otherwise brought on by having to make two withdrawals in the same year.

Roth IRA to the Rescue!

Scared to death of making a mistake with your traditional IRAs? The Roth IRA may be your salvation. With the Roth, you don't have to set up a minimum withdrawal program when you reach age 70½, so you avoid the potential pitfalls you've heard about. You can also change beneficiaries after age 70½. Your estate doesn't have to pay income taxes on a Roth after you leave this earth, which may well allow your heirs to receive a lot more money than they would have had the money been in a traditional IRA. For the scoop on Roths, see Chapter 16.

Chapter 18

Avoiding Mistakes in Your Financial Life

> It is a rather pleasant experience to be alone in a bank at night.
>
> *Willie Sutton*

We all make mistakes in our financial lives (as well as in every other aspect of our lives). Thankfully, most mistakes put only a small dent in your finances, but some can be devastating. Most of us learn from our mistakes. Others are lifelong recidivists. While most financial mistakes are made with the able assistance of someone who profits from them, others are entirely homegrown.

Forewarned Is Forearmed

It was the Greek philosopher Socrates who affirmed that a knowledgeable person is distinguished by knowing what he or she doesn't know. In matters financial as well, those words should be your philosophical maxim. It will help you avoid whimsical or impulsive spending or investing. (Never buy on impulse, especially from a stranger. The likelihood of disaster, no matter how safe it seems, is guaranteed to be titanic.)

Look Before You Leap: Four Oversold Financial Products

Any of the four financial products that are discussed below may work well for you. However, too many people buy them in the mistaken belief that these products can accomplish something that they cannot. The mistake lies in not understanding what you're buying. Perhaps we can't blame the salespeople who, in the hallowed tradition of their trade, heavily promote their product and tell people what they want to hear.

1. **High-yield investments.** Whenever interest rates decline, the high-yield investment promoters come out of the woodwork. Are you concerned that your interest-earning investment yields have dropped from 7 percent to 5 percent? No problem. They'll be able to provide you with an investment that yields 7 percent. The question you need to ask is, "if mainstream investments are only paying 5 percent, what kind of investment pays 7 percent?" There's no free lunch. You can receive the 7 percent, but you'll be taking more risk than you are or should be comfortable with unawares. So never believe that an investment that provides a substantially greater yield than mainstream investments are paying is able to do so without subjecting your money to more risk. If you can stand the risk, fine. But don't be led to believe that your money is "just as safe."

2. **Living trusts.** You've probably seen the ads in the newspaper inviting you to a living trust seminar. Living trusts are often touted as the ultimate estate-planning tool. True, living trusts provide some advantages over a will, but they certainly don't replace it. A lot of people who succumb to the living trust pitch have been led to believe that living trusts save income and estate taxes. They don't. While a living trust *may* make sense for you, be sure that you understand what they can—and cannot—accomplish. Then you can decide if a living trust is worth the expense. (For more information on living trusts, see page 240.)

3. **Pension maximization insurance.** This is a type of insurance that is sold to

a married person who's about to retire on a pension. By insuring the soon-to-be pensioner, he or she can waive the usual joint life annuity payment option on the pension plan in favor of a single life annuity. It's called "pension maximization" because a single life annuity (where payments cease upon the death of the annuitant) pays a higher benefit than a joint life annuity which promises lifetime annuity payments to both spouses. The life insurance protects the pensioner's spouse because, if the pensioner dies first (resulting in a termination of the annuity payments), the surviving spouse has the life insurance policy to fall back on. Can pension maximization work? Certainly. But you have to ask yourself a few questions before signing up. Buying a cash value life insurance policy when you're nearing retirement age is expensive. What happens if you fail to keep up with the payments? What happens if the insurance company gets into financial trouble? Is your spouse capable of managing the life insurance benefits if and when the time comes? So, as with any long-term financial commitment, be sure you are comfortable with all eventualities.

4. **Long-term care (LTC) insurance.** LTC insurance is another long-term financial commitment that many seniors are willing to make. Before you acquire an LTC policy, it's important to understand fully what the policy offers and what it does not. For example, if you have to go into a nursing home in, say, 20 years, what percentage of your expected nursing home costs will the policy pay for? Are there any exclusions from the policy that make you uncomfortable? Make sure all of your questions are answered to your satisfaction. If so, then you've done the right thing to purchase the policy. (For more guidance on LTC insurance, see page 56.)

AVOIDING SCAMS

The best scam artists appeal to one of the two emotions that are surefire ways to lure you into mistakes: fear and greed. The real pros will appeal to both, as in: "If you don't send me your money today, you'll never be able to take advantage of this once-in-a-lifetime investment opportunity."

Bear in mind that the charlatans always follow the latest trends. So the Internet has become and will continue to be a fertile ground.

Here are a couple of popular scams that are sure to separate a lot of people from their money in the New Century. Don't you be one of them.

➤ **Retirement-plan rollover scams.** If you're leaving your job, you'll have to decide what to do with the money in your employer's retirement plan. There are plenty of people who want to help you make that decision, and not all of them are reputable. Scamsters are contacting retirees and downsized employees, urging them to roll over their retirement accounts into inappropriate investments that can have disastrous consequences. Too many people have ended up paying stiff withdrawal penalties or, worse, investing in speculative deals that wiped out decades of careful saving. To protect yourself, use common sense. Don't be lured by the prospect of a ground-floor opportunity to earn big profits at no risk. Never invest in anything you don't understand. Never authorize a discretionary brokerage account until you have worked with the adviser for a few years to your satisfaction. And never, *ever* commit to anything over the phone with anyone you don't know, even if the caller claims to represent a well-known firm.

➤ **College scholarship scams.** Unscrupulous scholarship search services are taking advantage of families who are struggling to meet ever-rising college costs. Be wary of any scholarship or financial aid offers that come in the mail or over the Internet. They typically guarantee to find a scholarship or other form of financial aid for a fee that's paid in advance. Don't fall for the bait. Never pay for anything until you receive something in writing—not just a glossy brochure—that satisfies you that the outfit and the offer are legitimate. And remember that college

> ### POND'S LAW OF URGENCY
>
> The faster you have to send in money to take advantage of a once-in-a-lifetime investment opportunity, the faster you will lose all of it.

scholarships don't just appear on your doorstep. You—not the so-called scholarship search service—have to apply.

Avoid Being Taken

Time is the real enemy of unscrupulous salespeople. They know full well that if their offer is not legit, the longer you take to think about it, the more trouble they're in. With any financial decision, time is your ally. No worthwhile financial decision needs to be made quickly, whether it involves an investment or spending money on something. The best thing you can do to avoid being taken is very simple: Get a second opinion from someone—a relative or acquaintance—who you feel could provide an objective opinion of what you're being encouraged to buy. This opinion, free of the hype that you're being subjected to, will be very valuable. By the way, no legitimate salesperson would object to your getting a second opinion.

Borrowing to Invest

Here's a question I'm frequently asked: "Should I take out a home equity loan or refinance my home so that I'll have more money to invest?" When I ask the questioners where they came up with such an idea, most say that their investment advisers had suggested it. (What a surprise!) But a goodly number opine that they came up with the idea themselves. Whatever the source of the idea, it's a pretty bad one. Sure, it certainly sounds appealing at first glance. But the idea of heaping more debt on the house is one that should send up all sorts of red flags. (I even had one fellow tell me that he always borrowed as much as possible on his Chevrolet so that he could "pay for the car and then some with the profits I make by investing the money that I borrow." I guess if this guy is profiting quite nicely on his Chevy loan, he

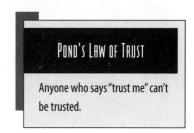

Pond's Law of Trust

Anyone who says "trust me" can't be trusted.

could get filthy rich by buying a Rolls Royce and borrowing against it. I didn't suggest it to him because he'd probably believe it.)

Of course, borrowing to invest from whatever source (including borrowing on margin through your stockbroker) will work so long as you can get a higher return on the investments than you're paying in interest on the loan. When the great bull market of the 1980s and 1990s combined with low interest rates, that seems like a pretty good bet. But what happens if the market turns downward—perhaps like the 1973–1974 bear market and its 40 percent declines. It's great to be enthusiastic about stocks; after all, that's where most of your money should be. Borrowing to buy stocks or stock funds is, I believe, going too far—particularly if you risk losing your house or your retirement nest egg in the process. Just because the market went down doesn't mean your loan will.

How Much Can You Profit from Investing with Borrowed Money?

Even if you're confident that you can make more on stocks than you'll pay in interest on the borrowed money, is the risk really worth the money you'll make? As Chart #19 shows, it depends on how much your invested money makes.

If you're confident that the stock market will produce double-digit growth and you're confident that you'll invest in the right stocks or stock funds to give you year-after-year double-digit returns, then borrowing to invest can work. But you have to decide for yourself if taking on debt to invest is worth the risk. Don't let anybody convince you that it's a good idea. It's your call. While I'm optimistic about the long-term prospects for the stock market, I still think it's too risky to invest that way.

Thinking About Starting Your Own Business?

Being one's own boss has long been the American dream. It's allure will strengthen in the New Century due to job uncertainty, particularly among aging baby boomers, and stories aplenty about entrepreneurs

CHART #19

Is Borrowing to Invest Really Worthwhile?

The chart assumes a $100,000 loan at 8 percent interest invested in securities that provide average returns ranging from 0 percent to 12 percent. The borrower is in the 28 percent tax bracket, but the investment returns are taxed at 24 percent because I've assumed that some of the investments will be taxed at the 20 percent long-term capital gains tax rate. The interest on the loan is assumed to be tax deductible.

Average annual investment return	After-tax investment income	After-tax interest expense	Benefit from investing with borrowed money
0%	$ 0	$5,760	−$5,760
6%	4,560	5,760	−1,200
8%	6,080	5,760	+320
10%	7,600	5,760	+1,840
12%	9,120	5,760	+3,360

who made fortunes. For each success story that makes the news, many other would-be entrepreneurs have fallen by the wayside. If you want to start a business, you must first realize that the odds are against you. Many more people fail than succeed. Most of those who succeed get along okay financially, but they never strike it rich.

While no one starts a business paying much attention to the distinct possibility that it will become a financial mistake, for the majority of entrepreneurs it will be. Starting a business may be risky, but there are ways to manage the financial risk so that you don't jeopardize your financial future.

If at all possible, don't quit your day job until the business is established, and it's clear that you can draw enough salary to support yourself. If this is not possible, you should have two years' worth of living expenses already in the bank, which you won't need to sink into the business.

Figure out how to start your business on a shoestring. High overhead at the outset can kill a business before it has a chance to succeed. Can you work out of your home or a shared office space? If you must have a store or office, negotiate a short-term lease and buy used furniture and equipment.

Don't risk all your personal savings and investments on your new venture. There is nothing so discouraging as seeing a lifetime's worth of savings evaporate, only to be left deeply in debt and having to rejoin the work world.

Try to arrange financing that doesn't require your personal guarantee. This may mean getting someone to provide financing in exchange for stock in your new company, but it is better to own 50 percent of a successful and adequately capitalized business than to own 100 percent of a failing business.

In spite of all these caveats, starting a business is filled with excitement and promise. The satisfaction of launching a successful venture cannot be matched. But if you want to strike out on your own, make sure your personal finances don't strike out in the process. Before taking the plunge, here are some important questions that are culled from the stories of successful entrepreneurs.

1. **Are you prepared for long hours?** Are you prepared to give up your evenings and weekends to launch your business? Most successful entrepreneurs had to spend years devoting almost every waking hour to getting the business up and running.

2. **Do your skills match the business you're starting?** You don't want to have to undergo on-the-job training when your money and livelihood are on the line. For example, don't start a restaurant if your only experience in that line of business is *going* to them.

3. **Are you eager to sell yourself and your product or service?** No matter how good your service or product may be, if you can't effectively sell it to potential customers, your business won't succeed. The technical and managerial skills you bring to your business will all go for naught should you be unable to promote and sell your products and yourself. If you don't have a sales background, you need to take a close and objective look at how comfortable you will be in a sales capacity. You'll probably need to spend a substantial portion of time sell-

ing your product or service and receiving a lot of rejection in the process.

4. **Will you be willing to cut your losses if the business isn't working out?** If you start a business, the odds are regrettably high against your succeeding. There may well come a time when you have to realistically evaluate whether you should continue the business. If you do find yourself facing this difficult decision, you may want to seek the counsel of an accountant or other financial professional. What you don't want to do is throw good money after bad. Far too many entrepreneurs, by nature an optimistic lot, have risked their home, their savings, and almost everything else to support doomed businesses. It is far preferable to cut your losses.

HOT BUSINESSES FOR THE NEW CENTURY

Selecting the right kind of business to enter is always important. The key to finding the right business to start is to first identify your area or areas of experience, then match your expertise to an attractive, growing kind of business. Here are some areas that are likely to experience above-average growth over the early part of the 21st century:

➤ Computer and software products and services
➤ Internet applications
➤ Products and services that make home life easier
➤ Health care
➤ Products and services for senior citizens

You can find additional help for starting and running your own business by clicking on:
http://jonathanpond.com/general.startingabusiness.htm

Chapter 19

■ Spend It All Before You Die (But If You Can't, Plan Your Estate)

E state planning. Ugh! estate-planning is as depressing as life insurance for the simple reason that, with both, you'll never live to see the fruits of your efforts. But that doesn't mean you should ignore either. Once you get it over and done with, you'll feel at least some comfort in knowing that your heirs aren't going to have to go through the considerable hassle of settling an estate that is bereft of a will and other estate-planning documents. Sure, they may not be upset by your demise, but they will surely be upset if they have to suffer the expense and delay of having the court decide how to distribute your estate.

There Are Only Three Places Your Money Can Go After You Go

Have you decided how you want your assets distributed after your demise? (Wouldn't life be great if you had only liabilities to pass on, rather than assets?) There are only three places your money can go after you go:

➤ To your heirs (although they probably don't deserve any of your money)

➤ To charity
➤ To the government (it definitely doesn't deserve your money)

While there's no joy in contemplating our own mortality, if you give forethought and advance planning to the settlement of your estate, you can be reasonably sure it will be distributed the way you want. If you don't, at a minimum, you'll cause your loved ones a lot of grief, and I'm not talking about the kind of grief that people suffer from the loss of a loved one. Instead, I'm talking about the grief that's caused by an improperly planned estate or worse, no estate-planning at all. At best, your heirs will have to go through the hassle of settling a so-called "intestate" estate. The word "intestate" means dying without a will, but the practical effect means that a sizable portion of your assets could go to the government in the form of estate taxes not to mention extra legal fees. And whatever one's attitude about the three places your money can go that I enumerated above, I don't know of anyone who prefers that their money go to the government. So unless you detest your heirs and you want to get back at them from the grave, here are some of the basic matters you need to think about and documents you need to have prepared.

FUNDAMENTALS OF ESTATE PLANNING

The most important goal of estate-planning is retaining control over *your* assets, during your lifetime and even after death. Through careful planning, you can control the distribution of your estate free of interference from the government and the court system. Now, I know this doesn't sound like a laugh riot, but it is essential if you are to make your death as easy on the next generation as possible. Hence, every estate plan should include a will that specifies exactly how the estate is to be divided. Without a will, the probate courts will distribute the

> **POND'S LAW OF "GOOD-BYE AND GOOD RIDDANCE, UNCLE CHARLEY"**
>
> The best way for you to show your family how much you dislike them is to die with no estate-planning documents.

estate with no regard for your wishes. They will follow a set of prescribed formulas and procedures, the result of which is not only higher-than-necessary legal fees but a badly distributed estate as well. If you die without a will when your children are quite young, for example, do you know that in most states your children will inherit half of your estate? While that seems like the generous thing to do, in fact, it makes caring for them quite difficult. If you had a will, you would almost certainly have bequeathed all of your estate to your spouse. The way you own property may also be important in estate-planning. The type of ownership—whether sole tenancy, joint tenancy, or in trust—affects the rights and limitations of those who now own or who will own the property.

A will is only the first step in a sound estate plan. A simple will cannot fulfill the second objective of estate-planning, which, for people who have large estates, is tax savings. To save as much in estate taxes as possible, an estate plan should balance the many options available. While you probably understand the need to have certain basic estate-planning documents, you may not be familiar with the full range of strategies and techniques that can help you in the here and now as well as benefit your heirs in the hereafter. These are discussed in Chapter 20.

THE THREE ESSENTIAL ESTATE-PLANNING DOCUMENTS

Every adult should have three basic estate-planning documents:

➤ a will
➤ a durable power of attorney (or living trust)
➤ a health-care proxy

Don't try to prepare them yourself. Have an attorney do it. There are a lot of mistakes that we make in life that can later be rectified, but if you mess up on your estate-planning documents, even a séance cannot help. A fourth estate-planning document that I highly recommend, a letter of instructions, is discussed on pages 242–245. You don't need an attorney to prepare a letter of instructions.

VALID AND UP-TO-DATE WILL

Everyone knows the importance of preparing a will, but most adults don't yet have one. What's the problem? Do you think you're immortal? Do you really want to turn over the responsibility for distributing your estate and taking care of your family to the government?

IMPORTANT CONSIDERATIONS IN DRAFTING A WILL

Before your death, your will is a private document, the contents of which need not be known to anyone other than you and your attorney. The two signing witnesses must see you—the testator—sign the documents. They must know that you intend the document to be your will, but they do not need to know its contents. In some states, the witnesses do not even have to see you sign as long as you acknowledge to them that the signature is yours.

Upon your death, however, the will becomes a publicly accessible legal document that is under the jurisdiction of the probate court system. Through the probate court, the state assures that your will is valid, that your assets are protected against loss or theft, that your bills and taxes are paid, and that all your remaining assets go directly to the beneficiaries you have designated in your will. I recommend that, despite the privacy afforded by a will, you discuss its contents with your intended heirs. Doing so not only gives you the opportunity to explain or clarify certain will provisions to those directly involved, it also improves the chances that your will's provisions will be carried out as indicated, with a minimum of doubts and animosity.

A common misconception is that a will limits your flexibility, but a will can always be altered to reflect changes in your

POND'S LAW OF INTESTACY

If you die without a will, the state determines how your estate will be settled, and it will distribute a sizable portion of your estate to a family member whom you had intended to disown.

circumstances or desires. In fact, updating the will to reflect such changes is an important part of ongoing estate-planning. Getting married or divorced, starting a family, losing loved ones, and becoming disabled all are changes that, more likely than not, will require revisions in your will. Indeed, in many states, marriage, divorce, or a new baby invalidates any existing will. You can either write a new will that declares any previous wills invalid or append a codicil to an existing will. (Codicils are subject to the same legal stipulations as are wills.) Moving to a new state may invalidate a will drawn up under the laws of your previous state. Earlier wills should be saved for reference. If a current will is declared invalid, the latest dated, legally valid will is considered as your legal will.

DECIDING HOW TO DISTRIBUTE YOUR ESTATE

The vast majority of parents sincerely want to treat each of their adult children the same when planning how their estates are to be distributed. But very often, the children are not the same when it comes to their need for or ability to handle money. This is obviously a very difficult matter to address, and many parents don't want to address it. But imagine how much harm might be done to, say, a spendthrift child who receives an inheritance and a year later has squandered it. Sometimes, the most unfair thing to do is treat each child the same both with respect to how they receive the money and when they receive it.

For some tips on ways to distribute your estate in a manner that will most benefit your heirs, click on:

http://jonathanpond.com/estateplanning.distributions.htm

THE EXECUTOR

When your will is created, you will have to appoint an executor (also referred to as a personal representative) to ensure that the settlement of your estate is properly administered upon your death. Otherwise, the courts will appoint one.

An executor ensures that your will is probated and that the wishes stipulated in it are properly carried out. The executor assembles your assets and arranges for their appraisal, liquidates assets as required, and distributes the estate according to the will. He or she also files income tax, estate tax, and inheritance tax returns and pays the debts and taxes for the estate. All these matters need to be settled in accordance with legal and tax requirements. Failure to do so may result in penalties.

An executor should have financial knowledge, be a reliable record-keeper, and be sensitive to the needs of your beneficiaries. He or she should also be trustworthy, have high ethical standards, and have sufficient time to perform all of the duties of an executor—which can be time-consuming. Family members may or may not be up to the task.

If you choose a family member to be your executor, you may set him or her up for criticism. He or she will probably be blamed for the inevitable problems and delays that occur when an estate is settled. If you want to appoint a family member as an executor but don't want to burden them with all the details, mention in your will that you expect them to hire necessary professionals (lawyers, accountants, and the like) to assist in settling your estate. For a large estate, you might consider appointing a bank trust department, estate-planning attorney, or other professional to serve as the executor. Assigning a professional to this position removes the burden from your family and lowers the possibility that any conflicts might arise. On the other hand, professionals may be rather impersonal for a family that has suffered a traumatic loss. A solution could be to appoint co-executors (for example, a bank trust department and a family member) and thus get both the financial expertise and the personal touch.

You can learn more about the tasks that an executor must perform by clicking on:
http://jonathanpond.com/estateplanning.executor.htm

Where Should You Store Your Will?

Although it is advisable to make photocopies for your files and for family members, there should be only one original copy of a will at any time. Deciding where to keep the original is a vexing problem. Options include a home safe, a business safe, a bank safe-deposit box, your lawyer's office, a trust company (if one has been named as an executor), or the clerk of your local probate court, who will hold it for safekeeping in a sealed envelope. Where you should store your will depends on state and local probate law. For example, many such laws automatically seal the safe-deposit box upon death, making the will inaccessible pending a court order and creating a messy complication. Wherever you decide to store your will, always make certain that its location is known by family members or close friends.

Is Your Will Up-to-Date?

Things change. Family circumstances shift, as does your financial status. People move to different states. Federal and state tax laws change. Therefore, you must periodically review and revise your will to ensure that its contents conform to current laws and regulations and that it still reflects your wishes. Dying with an out-of-date or invalid will can be almost as bad as dying without a will at all.

For more tips on wills and what to do before you consult an attorney about your will, click on:
http://jonathanpond.com/estateplanning.wills.htm

Durable Power of Attorney, or Living Trust

If you ever become incapacitated (through accident, illness, or just plain aging) and are unable to handle your own affairs, a court order may appoint a guardian or conservator to manage your money. The court may not appoint the guardian whom you would have chosen. Even if the court ultimately does approve your choice of guardian, the approval process will be subject to unnecessary red tape and confusion. The simplest way to protect yourself—and to ensure that your property will continue to be managed as you see fit—is to appoint a guardian for yourself through a durable power of attorney.

Preparing a durable power of attorney ensures that if you ever become unable to manage your own financial and personal affairs, someone whom you trust will act on your behalf. A power of attorney may be special—applying to only certain situations—or general—giving the attorney-in-fact virtually limitless control over your affairs. General powers of attorney may be dangerous, are subject to abuse, and are usually unnecessary.

If you use special powers of attorney, you can give different people responsibility for different jobs. For example, you may want one person to make decisions regarding your health care and housing but another to manage your finances. A power of attorney may also be either indefinite (durable) or last for a specific length of time. No matter how it is assigned, it may be canceled at any time, and it terminates immediately upon your death.

LIVING TRUSTS

Living trusts, an alternative to a durable power of attorney, can provide a variety of estate-planning advantages, such as avoiding probate and keeping your financial matters private. Living trusts—not to be confused with living wills—allow you to specify whom you want to take over your financial affairs if you become incapacitated. Living trusts may be preferred by residents of states where the probate process is particularly burdensome.

A *funded living trust* is used to hold your property, naming yourself as the principal beneficiary. Regardless of your age or mental condition, the trustee is legally bound to act in your best interests according to the trust's instructions.

A variation of the funded living trust is the *standby trust,* which can be established under a revocable agreement stating that assets can be transferred into the trust only if you become unable to manage your own finances. As long as the trust remains unfunded, there may not be any administration fees.

Living trusts are a hot product, and many attorneys and financial institutions have been aggressively promoting them, leading many people to believe that living trusts are the answer to every problem. This is not necessarily the case. While some can benefit from living trust arrangements, others will find them to be a waste of time and money.

How do you determine if a living trust makes sense for you? Don't rely solely on an attorney who advertises or gives seminars on living trusts—it's obvious what these people will tell you. Instead, speak with an attorney who is experienced in estate-planning but who doesn't ballyhoo the supposed virtues of living trusts. In other words, consult with an attorney who can give you an objective evaluation of whether a living trust is right for you.

For additional information on durable powers of attorney and living trusts, click on:

http://jonathanpond.com/estateplanning.incapacity.htm

HEALTH-CARE PROXY

Advances in medical technology mean, plain and simple, that people's lives can be sustained even when they are terminally ill and have no hope of leading an active, independent life. A health-care proxy (also called a living will, health-care power of attorney, or advance directive) is a document, signed by you and witnesses, that tells your health-care provider that you do not want life-prolonging medical procedures implemented when recovery from the condition is impossible and there is no chance of you regaining a meaningful life. You also designate someone, typically a family member or close friend, to be responsible for making sure your wishes are adhered to. (My mother refers to that person as "the plug puller.") Laws vary from state to state in specific details, but most permit the person designated in the health-care proxy to direct terminal care and protects the attending physician from liability. It is, however, not always a smooth process.

Specific information on health-care proxies can be found by consulting with an attorney or by contacting Choice in Dying, 1035 30th Street, NW, Washington, DC 20007, 202-338-9790 or click on:
http://www.choices.org/

The legal and religious aspects of health-care proxies are controversial, and despite the document, your wishes maybe ignored. Nevertheless, a health-care proxy in the hands of family, physician, clergy, or attorney may persuade the court to allow the individual his or her right to die. Everyone should consider preparing a health-care proxy; it can provide comfort to family members at a difficult time. Also (forgive me, but this is a financial book), a health-care proxy can save a lot of money. The cost of keeping someone alive by artificial means can drain a family's estate.

It is advisable for anyone who spends significant time (such as winters or summers) in a state away from his or her home state to also have the correct health-care proxy documents for *that* state as well.

Preparing a Letter of Instructions

A letter of instructions is not the most pleasant item to prepare, but you will be doing your heirs a big favor by doing it. It is an informal document that gives your survivors information concerning important financial and personal matters that must be attended to after your demise. Although it doesn't carry the legal weight of a will and is in no way a sub-

Make Sure Your Durable Power of Attorney Works

A durable power of attorney is not always sufficient to give the person designated enough power to take over financially. Some institutions require more documentation.

There was a case I learned of in which a mother had given her son power of attorney. Later, when she became incapacitated, the son needed to tap into her money to pay her expenses. He found to his dismay that the mutual fund company where his mother kept much of her money required that an additional form be signed and witnessed. Fortunately, in this instance, the son was able to obtain his mother's signature.

Make sure that the financial institutions and other organizations that are critical to your financial affairs will in fact accept your power of attorney. Therefore, you may want to send a draft of this document to these third parties to see if changes are needed. At the very least, you should contact the institutions to determine if additional documents are required, and then complete these forms.

You should also make sure your power of attorney is very specific in spelling out what powers you are giving the individual you designate. By taking these extra precautions, with the advice of your attorney, you will help ensure that the person you appoint won't face any obstacles in caring for you.

stitute for a will, a letter of instructions clarifies any special requests to be carried out upon death. It also provides essential financial information, thus relieving family members of needless worry and speculation.

Here are some things that should be put in a letter of instructions:

➤ The location of important papers, including the will, birth and marriage certificates, and military records
➤ The location of documents relating to your personal residence, including an inventory of household contents and warranties and

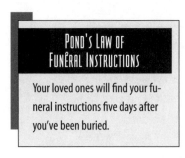

POND'S LAW OF FUNERAL INSTRUCTIONS

Your loved ones will find your funeral instructions five days after you've been buried.

receipts. You may also want to include a list of mementos naming next to each item the person you would like to receive it

➤ Details of the whereabouts of your safe-deposit box and a list of its contents

➤ The locations of previous income tax and gift tax returns

In addition to providing the location of important items, a well-prepared letter of instructions will provide information about:

➤ Checking accounts
➤ Credit cards
➤ Outstanding loans
➤ Debts owed to your estate
➤ Summary of life insurance policies and other expected death benefits
➤ Summary of investment accounts, including location of statements and certificates
➤ An expression of your wishes about your funeral and burial preferences, including any advance arrangements that may have been made
➤ The names and addresses of people and institutions that should be notified

Obviously, your survivors will benefit greatly if you prepare a letter of instructions. But you will also benefit insofar as a well-prepared letter is a great way to organize your personal records. Be sure to keep it up-to-date since the information is likely to change.

DO YOUR LOVED ONES KNOW WHERE YOUR LETTER OF INSTRUCTIONS IS LOCATED?

Finally, put a copy of your letter of instructions in any easy-to-find location and make sure your loved ones know where they can find it. They will appreciate your thoughtfulness. Incidentally, my wife and I have taped our letters of instructions to the refrigerator door, amongst our kids' artwork. Our friends think this is rather maudlin, but at least it's well known where the darn things are located. Why don't you do the same?

You can download a letter of instructions worksheet by clicking on:

http://jonathanpond.com/estateplanning.letterofinstructions.htm

SPECIAL NOTE FOR COUPLES

While I'm on the subject of organizing your records, do both you and your spouse or partner know enough about the family finances to be able to take over when the inevitable happens and one of you dies? Here's a suggestion: The partner who's not up to speed should periodically take over the family financial chores for a month. He or she should also be involved the next time income tax return information needs to be prepared.

> ### POND'S LAW OF FAMILY HEIRLOOMS
>
> The more meaningless a family memento is, the more vehemently your children will argue over who gets it after your demise.

GUARDIANSHIP FOR CHILDREN

Have you appointed a guardian for your child in your will? (If you're a grandparent, you should ask your children if they've appointed a guardian.) Many parents fail to make this important arrangement. A guardian becomes responsible for a minor child's or disabled adult's care and upbringing if the parents die early. Failure to designate a guardian in your will can cause a lot of problems. With the increasing num-

> ### POND'S LAW OF SPOUSAL DEMISE
>
> The spouse who knows the most about the couple's finances will die first.

ber of less traditional family situations, such as divorced parents and step-parents, the possible complications are ever greater.

Your attorney may advise you to divide guardianship duties so that the responsibility for taking care of the child's health and well-being is given to one party, and the responsibility for taking care of the child's financial affairs is given to another. The most important reason to appoint both a personal guardian and a financial guardian is that the particular relative or friend whom you trust completely with the child's upbringing may not have the expertise to deal with money that will be left to the child.

Another important consideration is that if your estate is likely to be considerably greater than the resources of the guardian, you may want to consider empowering the financial guardian to provide additional money to the personal guardian's family. This minimizes the potential for resentment when the family is struggling financially to raise the orphans who may end up rich. I'd much prefer my money be used to help the family raising my kids than to have the kids receive a bucket of it later on. For example, some parents have provided for the payment of college tuition out of their estate for the guardian's children as well as their own.

Finally, regardless of how the guardianship arrangement is made, it is vital that you discuss your wishes with the potential guardians prior to naming them in the will. If the children are old enough, they should be included in the discussion, too. So if you haven't done so already, take action now to appoint guardians for your dependent children.

Chapter 20

HAVING YOUR CAKE AND EATING IT TOO: ESTATE-PLANNING TECHNIQUES TO BENEFIT YOU IN THE HERE AND NOW, NOT JUST THE HEREAFTER

> A millionaire is a man who gathers a fortune he doesn't need to leave to people who don't deserve it.
>
> *Anonymous*

While virtually every adult needs the basic estate-planning documents described in Chapter 19, some may also benefit from one or more advanced estate-planning techniques that meet your own estate-planning objectives:

ESTATE-PLANNING OBJECTIVES

Keep the following in mind when planning your estate:

1. **Minimize the problems and expenses of probate, and avoid potential family conflicts.** The more tangled an estate plan you weave, the greater the expense—and the greater the possibility of family conflict—you bequeath. Detail your intentions about your estate so that confusion over your intentions doesn't lead to your inheritors squabbling over and squandering your estate.

2. **Provide your surviving spouse with as much responsibility and flexibility in estate management as desired, consistent with potential tax savings.** If he or she is up to the challenge, you should give your spouse or partner the nec-

essary understanding and power to steer your estate during its most crucial passage through tax-infested waters. When you sit down to chart this out, don't forget about testamentary trusts (trusts that are included in your will). See page 255 for a description of the most common testamentary trusts for married couples. Such trusts, while removing your spouse from direct control of certain aspects of your estate, could in fact end up being in the best interest of your beneficiaries, your spouse included.

3. **Provide for the conservation of your estate and its effective management.** If you have a spouse, partner, children, and/or grandchildren, don't leave home without making sure your estate plans are in order. Your estate plan should include contingency plans to provide for your survivors in the event of your death.

4. **Minimize death taxes as well as income taxes after death.** If your estate is large enough to incur state death taxes and federal estate taxes, there may be actions you can take now to minimize them. The sooner you undertake estate-tax-saving strategies, the better.

5. **Avoid leaving your children "too much too soon."** Many people become so concerned about providing generously for their children that they overlook matters that should influence how their estate should be distributed. Don't make this mistake. For example, consider the varying degrees of need that each child has, and don't turn a blind eye to tell-tale signs of financially inept children.

6. **Provide for adequate liquidity to cover taxes and other expenses at death without the necessity of forced sale of assets.** Given the variety of investments that can be easily "cashed in," it is surprising how many people forget to factor them into their estate-planning. Lack of adequate liquidity at the time of your death could burden your heirs with the stressful task of forced sale of your estate assets in order to provide immediate capital. At-death and after-death expenses are numerous and must be accounted for:

➤ Expenses of final illness and funeral
➤ Federal estate taxes and state death taxes

➤ Federal and state income taxes

➤ Probate and administration expenses

➤ Payment of maturing debts

➤ Maintenance and welfare of the family

➤ Payment of specific cash bequests

➤ Funds to continue running a family business

These needs must be estimated so you can devise an estate plan that will provide your survivors with ready access to sufficient resources.

7. **Provide for estate management in the event of serious disability of you or your spouse.** Plan for the possibility of serious disability. Provide for someone to look after your finances in the event you are unable to do so.

8. **Assemble copies of all important documents affecting your estate plan in a documents portfolio. Make certain all appropriate family members know where to find them.** A thorough letter of instructions (see page 242–245) accompanied by supporting documentation will go a long way toward easing the burden on your survivors of settling your estate. Also, make it a point to review and update your document portfolio at least annually.

9. **Inform all family members about your overall estate plan.** Make a point of periodically discussing the specifics of your estate plan with your spouse and children or other family members.

ADVANCED ESTATE-PLANNING TECHNIQUES DESCRIBED IN PLAIN EVERYDAY ENGLISH

Good estate-planning attends to a couple of important matters which, unfortunately, you will never live to see. There is a qualitative benefit for everyone and a quantitative benefit for affluent individuals and families. The qualitative benefit is quite simple. By giving some thought to how you want your estate settled and how you want to be cared for in your later years, you are providing your loved ones with the comfort of know-

POND'S LAW OF CARING CHILDREN

The larger the estate you have to pass on to your children, the more kindly they will treat you in your old age.

ing that important emotional matters will be settled as smoothly as possible. The quantitative benefit is a lot more complicated. Suffice it to say that proper estate-planning can result in much more money going to your heirs and charity. Make no mistake about it, the estate tax laws are confiscatory. You could end up giving up half or more of your estate to the taxing authorities.

SAY WHAT?

It's a shame how arcane estate-planning is. Of course, the lawyers like it that way. They have honed their speaking skills to a point where they might as well be speaking Swahili when they describe various estate-planning techniques that you might find appropriate. Let's listen in on some conversations that lawyers are probably having with their clients at this very moment:

> "Given the recent turn of events in your family, don't you think you should consider taking advantage of the deceased child exception to the generation-skipping transfer tax exemption?"

> "Congress has really put a damper on GRITs, but there's still some opportunity left with GRATs, GRUTs, and, obviously, QPRTs."

> "I'm sure you and Mr. Jones will agree that the most suitable arrangement is an income only charitable remainder unitrust with pickup provisions."

Huh?!? At the risk of oversimplifying some complicated techniques, I'd like to explain in plain English some estate-planning strategies that you may want to consider if your estate is either up there or, as you and I hope, likely to get up there. But first, let me respond to a couple of questions that you may have at this point: First, what do I mean by "estate"? Your taxable estate consists of just about everything you own, including retirement plans. It may also include life insurance. Second, how high is "up there" when it comes to needing more estate-planning than the basics that were described in Chapter 19? It depends, of course. All of our situations are unique. But if you're single, and your estate is approaching or more than $1 million, then you might benefit from some of these techniques. If you're married and your estate is near or more than $1,500,000, you might benefit as well. Further, if your estate is likely to grow to such lofty levels in the future, it's not too early to at least begin to learn about these estate-planning strategies.

Before you take any action on these, you need to meet with an *experienced* estate-planning attorney. When your estate-planning needs grow beyond the usual will and durable power of attorney, the complexity of the analysis and documents grows exponentially. Seek out an attorney who devotes all or most of his or her time to estate-planning matters.

In order to find out which estate-planning strategies may make sense for you, you first need to take an inventory of your estate. To help you do that, click on
http://jonathanpond.com/estateplanning.estateinventory.htm

ANNUAL GIFTS

Annual gifts are arguably the best and most painless way to whittle down an estate that would otherwise be subject to estate taxes. Anyone can make as many $10,000 annual gifts as they want, so long as the gifts go to separate human beings. (The annual gift exclusion is scheduled to rise with the cost of living in the future, but it will only rise in $1,000 increments, which means that the cost of living will have to rise by 10 percent before the annual gift limit is raised to $11,000.) For families who can afford to make annual gifts, the potential reduction in the size of an estate can be sizable.

Consider the following example. A couple has two adult children, both of whom are married, and both of whom themselves have two children. If each spouse gives $10,000 annual gifts to the two children, the two children-in-

EXEMPTION FOR GIFT AND ESTATE TAXES WILL RISE TO $1 MILLION BY 2006

Before a new round of tax rules were enacted in the late 1990s, the estates of everyone who died were entitled to a $600,000 exemption from estate taxes and gift taxes. In other words, the first $600,000 of value of the decedent's estate was not subject to federal estate taxes. But anything above $600,000 was subject to federal estate tax, beginning at a rate of 37 percent. The $600,000 exemption had not been adjusted since 1986. The new rules gradually increase this estate tax exemption according to the following timetable:

Year of Death or Gift	Exemption from Estate and Gift Taxes
1999	$650,000
2000 and 2001	$675,000
2002 and 2003	$700,000
2004	$850,000
2005	$950,000
2006 and thereafter	$1 million

Thus, people will be able to pass on greater amounts to their heirs free of either estate or gift taxes. It's important that you review your estate plan to take this provision into account. Otherwise, your current will may result in your estate having to pay more taxes than necessary. Also, if you're married, you may not have sufficient assets in the name of each spouse to qualify for the maximum exclusion. You should address these items with your attorney to ensure that you take full advantage of the new more generous estate tax regulations.

law, and the four grandchildren, they can give a total of $160,000 per year. If they do this for 15 years, they will have reduced their estate by almost $2,500,000. But not only have they reduced their estate by the amount of the gifts, but any appreciation in value of the money gifted to children and grandchildren will also be removed from the estate.

Like so many desirable financial and estate-planning strategies, annual gifts are a "use it or lose it" proposition. Every year you neglect to make an annual gift can never be made up in the future. People postpone making annual gifts for so many years that they end up leaving an estate that was far larger than it had to be. Remember, the estate tax starts at 37 percent, rises rapidly to 45 percent, and goes as high as 55 percent.

> **POND'S LAW OF ABSOLUTE CERTAINTY**
>
> If you ask your children whether it's appropriate for you to make annual cash gifts to them, you can be absolutely certain of an affirmative response.

If your estate is subject to a 50 percent estate tax rate, the math is very simple when it comes to annual gifts. Give a $10,000 gift and the recipient receives $10,000. Die with that money, and the government will take $5,000, leaving your heirs with $5,000.

So the annual gift exclusion is compelling if your estate is large enough. By the way, don't ask your children if they think it makes sense for you to make annual gifts. You can probably pretty much guess what the answer will be. I certainly wouldn't recommend starting a major annual gifting program if your estate is under $1 million. You may need that money to pay for health care and nursing home costs late in life. Never give money to your children or other relatives with the expectation of getting the money back later if you need it. You won't.

DISCLAIMERS

A disclaimer is merely a refusal to accept all or part of an inheritance. A lot of families who could benefit from disclaimers either don't take advantage of them or don't realize what they can accomplish. If you're already pretty well off and are likely to face your own estate tax problems, any inheritance may represent money you don't need and, frankly, don't want. By disclaiming all or part of the inheritance, the disclaimed portion will move to the next generation without incurring a further round of estate taxes unless the amount involved is very large.

If you think a disclaimer may make sense, be sure to mention that to your parents or whoever else might have named you in their wills. They

GIFTING MONEY TO ADULT CHILDREN AND PROVIDING VALUABLE MONEY LESSONS AT THE SAME TIME

As the saying goes, the only worthwhile money that comes our way is money we've worked to earn. That's why a lot of affluent parents are concerned about giving annual cash gifts to their adult children and grandchildren. Will this money be put to good use or will it sap their initiative?

Some parents who realize that annual gifts make a lot of sense, but who are concerned about what this money could do to their kids and grandkids, attach strings to their largesse. For example, one chap I spoke with makes requirements such as these to the money he gives to the younger generation:

- Putting at least 10 percent of job income into the company retirement savings plan
- Putting $2,000 into an IRA
- Making extra payments against the mortgage
- Contributing a certain percentage of income to charity

The father gives the child $2,500 for completing each of the above tasks. The same goes for his children-in-law. If all four are accomplished which, according to the father, is usually the case, the gift totals $10,000 per year, the current limit for annual gifts.

Now I realize that a lot of people in the psychology business say you shouldn't tie money gifts (including allowances) to the performance of specific tasks, but I find the process that this fellow uses to be a breath of fresh air. After all, it's his money that he's giving away. Why shouldn't he attach some strings to it? And his children are getting some valuable lessons in the process. What a great financial legacy he's going to impart to his children!

should in turn make sure that their wills provide the opportunity for you to disclaim. Generally, the will must indicate your right to disclaim and also must name the people who will receive the disclaimed inheritance, typically grandchildren. While most wills contain these provisions, it's important to double-check that they do.

UNIFIED CREDIT TRUST FOR MARRIED COUPLES

Unified credit trusts (a.k.a. testamentary trusts), like disclaimers, are over-looked by far too many people. Unified credit trusts can be set up to hold that portion of the estate that is exempt from taxes upon the death of the first spouse by reason of the unified credit (the amount that each of us is entitled to pass on without estate taxes). The trust, which is incorporated in the will of each spouse, is designed to exempt the assets placed in it from estate taxation upon the death of the second spouse.

These arrangements go under a variety of monikers, in addition to "unified credit trusts," including "bypass trusts," "marital-deduction trusts," "A-B trusts," "credit shelter trusts," "power-of-appointment trusts," and "qualified terminable interest property (QTIP) trusts."

There are a variety of ways in which the trust can be established de-pending, for example, upon how much you want to tie up the trust assets after your death. Without these trusts incorporated in each spouse's will, the surviving spouse will likely receive all of the deceased spouse's assets. Although those assets will not be subject to federal estate tax (since all as-sets transferred to a surviving spouse from a deceased spouse are exempt from estate taxes), these assets build up in the surviving spouse's estate. In essence, the first spouse to die has passed up his or her opportunity to use his or her exemption against estate taxes. At the death of the surviv-ing spouse, only the surviving spouse's own exemption may be applied against estate taxes.

How do you know whether you should have a unified credit trust put in your will? First, it is available only for married couples. It's difficult to generalize, but if your combined estate is more than $1,500,000, you should ask your attorney about it. Part of the decision will depend upon the type of assets you have. If you have a lot of assets in retirement accounts, then you may not need a unified credit trust. But it really requires an attorney who understands estate-planning to determine whether a unified credit trust makes sense for you. If so, don't be surprised if the attorney asks you to change the way you and your spouse have designated the ownership of some of your investments and real estate. The attorney will probably recommend that you change ownership from joint name to single name so that they can go smoothly into the trust at the death of the first spouse.

This gets to the issue of the best way to designate ownership of assets. Every family's situation is different. Suffice it to say, however, that for larger estates, many attorneys are of the opinion that owning property jointly with a spouse is a bad idea.

For more information on the pros and cons of the various property ownership designations, click on:

http://jonathanpond.com/estateplanning.ownershipdesignations.htm

LIFE INSURANCE TRUST

While life insurance benefits paid to a beneficiary are not subject to income taxes, they may sooner or later be subject to estate taxes. But if you place your life insurance policies into an irrevocable life insurance trust, you can avoid incurring estate taxes on life insurance benefits. On the other hand, when you set up a life insurance trust, you must give up all ownership rights to the policy. This includes the ability to borrow against the policy and generally to change the beneficiaries. You can place both term and cash-value insurance policies into the trust, but as with many worthwhile estate-planning strategies, you need to check with an estate-planning attorney about both the advantages and drawbacks of life insurance trusts.

A lot of people buy—or rather they are sold—life insurance to help pay estate taxes. For couples, "second-to-die" life insurance policies, which pay benefits only upon the death of the last spouse to die, are the rage. But before you are sold a life insurance policy for purposes of pay-

A SIMPLE WILL CAN BE AN EXPENSIVE MISTAKE

The garden-variety will for married people, which in essence says, "all to my spouse," could end up costing your children or other heirs a lot of money. Assume the husband has an estate of more than $1 million (which, by the way, is by no means an unusually large estate for older persons), and he dies leaving all of it to his wife. No federal estate taxes are owed because the transfer is from a deceased spouse to the surviving spouse.

But what if the wife dies right after the husband? She's got more than $1 million to bequeath plus whatever assets are in her name. Her total estate is in excess of the tax-free exemption. This results in estate taxes that could have been reduced or avoided altogether with some modest estate-planning.

The husband's will should have provided that, at his death, an amount equivalent to his estate tax exemption be put into a unified credit trust for the benefit of his spouse. The trust could allow her the full use of all of the property to meet her needs. But by placing a part of his estate in a trust for her, it will not be subject to estate tax at her death.

Of course, the wife might have died first, but her will could also have been structured to avoid some or all estate taxes no matter who died first. In the above example, the husband and wife should have put assets in each spouse's name sufficient to allow the first to die to take advantage of his or her estate tax exemption. (By willing all of his estate to his wife, he squandered the opportunity to use his estate tax exemption.)

You won't be around to enjoy the estate tax savings from establishing a unified credit trust, but your heirs will certainly appreciate your foresight, which could save $250,000 or more in estate taxes.

ing estate taxes, make sure that you can't find cheaper ways to reduce your estate than buying expensive cash-value life insurance. Annual gifts and, in the case of married couples, unified credit trusts can reduce even fairly sizable estates to the level where estate taxes are either nominal or are eliminated altogether.

Family Limited Partnership

Patriarchs and matriarchs often object to transferring large amounts of estate assets to their children or other heirs because Mom and Dad then have to give up control over those assets. This makes many parents understandably uncomfortable. The family limited partnership is a mechanism that can allow parents to make transfers into the partnership, removing assets from their taxable estates, while retaining control over partnership assets. Family limited partnerships usually work best when real estate and/or a family business is involved, but they can also be used for old-fashioned investments such as stocks and bonds. With family limited partnerships, it may be possible to transfer more than $10,000 worth of assets to a younger generation family member while still staying within the $10,000 annual gift exclusion limit. Family limited partnerships, like most of these other estate-planning strategies, are complicated and require considerable legal expertise.

Qualified Personal Residence Trust

A qualified personal residence trust (QPRT) can be used to transfer a first or second home to your heirs during your lifetime and remove it from your taxable estate. In so doing, you give up ownership of your residence, and one would hope you would transfer it to a trustworthy child who won't evict you from your home during your dotage. Since the beneficiaries of your trust—typically your children—will pick up your tax cost basis in the residence, it's better to transfer a home that has a relatively high tax cost basis compared with its current cost rather than one that you purchased for a song decades ago. Otherwise, you could be saddling them with a big capital gain when they eventually sell the home.

Using up Your Estate Tax Exemption During Your Lifetime

Most people think they need to die before their estate can take advantage of the estate tax exemption, but the rules allow you to use the exemption at any time. If you can afford to part with the money permanently, you should consider doing so during your lifetime. Doing this transfers a sizable chunk of your estate (in addition to the unlimited $10,000 annual gifts you can make) without having to pay either gift or estate taxes, and also removes all future appreciation from estate taxes. For example, if you transfer $500,000 from your estate now and by the time you die the money has tripled in value, you have in essence removed $1,500,000 from your estate. If you use up all or part of your estate tax exemption during your lifetime, that portion will not be available at your death, but as I've just shown, that may not be such a bad deal for your heirs.

Making Taxable Gifts

Those few who are blessed with very large estates, who have already used up their estate tax exemption and are making maximum use of the $10,000 annual gift exclusion, may still want to make taxable gifts during their lifetimes. It seems pretty silly to make a gift now and pay a gift tax on it rather than waiting until death, I know. Because of the different way gifts and estates are taxed, however, lifetime taxable gifts may result in much lower taxes than transfers made after death. Here's an example.

> You have an unbelievably rich aunt whose estate-planning attorneys are urging her to make a $10 million taxable gift to her heirs. (I hope you have such an aunt, and I wish I did.) If she makes the $10 million gift, she would pay about a 50 percent gift tax, or $5 million. So she has spent $15 million to get $10 million down to her heirs. The reason her attorneys suggested that she do so is that if she dies with the $15 million, it will be subject to about a 50 percent estate tax that would amount to $7,500,000. So, of the $15 million she left at death, the heirs would have received only $7,500,000, whereas they could receive $10 million had she transferred the money be-

fore death. The reason for this is that while the estate tax is imposed on the entirety of the estate, the gift tax is imposed only on the amount of the gift.

There's one hook to the use of lifetime taxable gifts. The person who makes the gift has to survive three years from the time the gift is made in order to incur the lower gift tax. If the person who makes the transfer doesn't survive the three years, however, the estate is no worse off than it would have been had he or she died with the money.

Generation-Skipping Gifts

The government loves to collect estate taxes. So it has imposed stiff penalties on people who transfer gifts to distant generations, for example, a transfer from parent to grandchild. The so-called generation-skipping transfer tax is so high that it effectively makes no sense to make such transfers. However, each individual has a $1 million exemption from generation-skipping transfer taxes. (This $1 million exemption is due to be increased for inflation in the future.) Thus the generation-skipping tax exemption allows *very* affluent individuals to move as much as $1 million over their lifetimes to grandchildren without incurring the generation-skipping tax. While you may well incur gift taxes for making such a transfer, transfers to distant generations within the $1 million generation-skipping transfer tax exemption can make sense for those with whopping big estates. Incidentally, the generation-skipping transfer tax does not affect annual gifts discussed on page 251. You can make as many of them to grandchildren, great-grandchildren, whomever, without running afoul of the generation-skipping transfer tax rules.

Spend It All Before You Die

This is my favorite estate-planning strategy, and it's the one I'm determined to make maximum use of! You can eliminate most of your estate-planning problems by simply striving to die destitute.

IS THERE AN OPTIMAL AMOUNT OF WEALTH TO PASS ON?

A lot of families have been fortunate enough to accumulate sizable estates. Over the years, many parents have expressed to me their concern about the effect passing on a lot of money will have on their children. They wonder, "What is a proper amount to pass on to the children?" That got me thinking, and I came up with an amount of $500,000. What will an inheritance of $500,000 do for (and to) your children? Will it make them quit their jobs? No. Will it destroy their initiative? Probably not. Will it make them the object of the affections of a gold digger? No, it's not enough money. On the other hand, will an inheritance of $500,000 help your kids get through the tough cards that life might deal them, like unemployment or disability? Yes, it will. One opportunity that the expectation of an inheritance of that size offers, if it's important to your family, is that your children can pursue careers that aren't very remunerative such as education, public service, and the arts.

The extra income an inheritance of that size will provide will allow them to work in such occupations and yet have enough income to enjoy a pretty high standard of living.

Incidentally, my $500,000 amount is based upon current dollars. If you agree with this approach, you should increase the amount you intend eventually to pass on to account for inflation in living expenses. For example (how do I put this delicately?), if you expect to pass on your estate in 20 or 25 years, you'll probably want to double the $500,000 to $1 million, because by then the cost of living may well have doubled.

For more details and up-to-date information on the various estate-planning techniques described above, click on:

http://jonathanpond.com/estateplanning.techniques.htm

ESTATE-PLANNING ADVANTAGES OF THE ROTH IRA

The Roth IRA is one of the best income tax breaks for retirement savers and retirees to come along in years. In addition to the great income-tax saving features of the Roth IRA, it also provides some estate tax breaks for those who may be in a position to pass on their IRA money to heirs.

With a traditional IRA, once you reach age 70½, you must begin making annual withdrawals in certain minimum amounts, but with a Roth IRA, you don't have to withdraw any money at any time after 70½. This allows for more tax-free growth while you're alive. It also allows you to pass on more to heirs than a traditional IRA.

A Roth IRA can also lower the tax bite on your estate because it's a better asset than a traditional IRA for passing on to heirs. The income taxes imposed on traditional IRAs at death—"income in respect of a decedent" (IRD)—will reduce the amount actually going to heirs. IRD is not due on Roth IRAs. This means that a traditional IRA could be subject to as much as a 40 percent income tax as well as possible estate taxes. Together, income and estate taxes could easily eat up 70 percent or more of a traditional IRA. If you die with a Roth IRA, on the other hand, while your estate may have to pay estate taxes on it, no income taxes will be due. This will result in your heirs receiving much more from an inherited Roth IRA than from an inherited traditional IRA.

Finally, if you leave the Roth IRA to a younger heir, it should be possible to stretch out the withdrawals over a longer period of time than a traditional IRA. Such a stretch-out allows for astronomical growth. For example, if you left a Roth IRA with just $30,000 to a six-year-old grandchild, the tax-free distributions from it could total more than $4 million. These advantages can make the Roth IRA extremely valuable, even for seniors. Some tax experts are calling the Roth IRA the ultimate tax shelter.

TAXWISE CHARITABLE GIVING

There aren't many things in your financial life that are better than making *charitable* contributions. Why? Because not only do you feel good by giving money to help support your favorite charity, but you also save taxes. As good as simply writing out a check is for your soul and your tax return, there are a number of charitable giving techniques that will allow you even greater benefits that can save on income taxes now and estate taxes later.

DONATE APPRECIATED SECURITIES

It doesn't make any difference to the charity whether you make your donation with a check or securities. But if you've got some stock that has appreciated in value, you're better off donating the stock rather than cash. When you donate appreciated securities, you generally get a tax deduction for the total amount that the securities are worth when you turn them over to the charity. Therefore, you don't have to pay a capital gains tax on the appreciation as you would had you sold the securities. The following example will show you the benefit of donating appreciated securities.

> You want to make a $5,000 donation to your favorite charity and are undecided as to whether you should simply write out a check or donate $5,000 worth of some stock you've had for years and that you paid $2,000 to acquire. If you donate the cash, it doesn't take a genius to realize that you're out of pocket $5,000. Of course, if you donate $5,000 worth of stock, it also would appear that you're out $5,000. But the stock is actually worth somewhat less than $5,000 since, it order to convert it into cash, you'd have to sell it and pay tax on the capital gain—in this instance, about $600 in tax ($3,000 capital gain times 20 percent capital gains tax). If you've got the choice, donate appreciated securities rather than cash. In this example, if you donate the cash rather than the stock, you're left with stock worth $4,400, but if you donate the stock rather than cash, you're left with $5,000.

By the way, as much as you might like to unload them, don't give to a charity securities that have declined in value since you bought them. It's better to sell the dogs and take the loss on your income taxes. You can't take the loss if you donate them.

CHARITABLE GIFT ANNUITIES, POOLED INCOME FUNDS, AND CHARITABLE REMAINDER TRUSTS

These are known as "deferred gifts" since the securities or cash you give now don't end up in the charity's coffers until later, usually at your demise. Despite that depressing note, these strategies may seem too good to be true during your lifetime, but they aren't. Here's what they accomplish in addition to helping a worthy charity:

➤ A partial charitable deduction from income taxes
➤ A lower estate tax bill
➤ Avoidance of capital gains taxes if you donate appreciated securities
➤ A lifetime income

It's the lifetime income that makes deferred giving arrangements so alluring, particularly for retirees who want to convert some investments that provide little or no income into solid income producers.

All of the above deferred giving techniques can accomplish the benefits that I just described. Which one you choose depends mainly on how much money you want to contribute and how much control you want over the future income you'll receive. Charitable gift annuities and pooled income funds are the easiest to set up and maintain. All you do is give your money—or, better, appreciated securities—to the charity and they will combine them with other donations into a fund that will provide you with a fixed income for a specific period of time or for the rest of your life. They do all the complicated calculations and paperwork.

Charitable remainder trusts, on the other hand, involve putting the money or securities into a separate trust that can allow you more control over such matters as the timing and amount of the money paid out from the trust. A charitable remainder trust allows you to tailor the donation to your specific circumstances as opposed to the "cookie cutter" charitable gift annuity and pooled income fund. There are usually costs of setting up and maintaining a charitable remainder trust, and a gift of at least $50,000 is necessary to justify the cost. On the other hand, charitable organizations are happy to accept gifts for a charitable gift annuity or pooled income fund at a minimum level of $10,000—even $5,000 in some instances.

As I mentioned earlier, you are entitled to a partial tax deduction for your deferred gift. The amount of the tax deduction is based in large part upon your age when you make the contribution. The older you are, the higher the percentage deduction. The amount of the income you will receive from any of these deferred gifts varies according to a variety of factors, including the current level of interest rates. The following example illustrates how a deferred gift works.

> Madeleine Magdalen, who is well into her retirement years, wants to recognize one of her favorite charities with a sizable gift of $100,000. But she's not in a position to give the money away outright. Instead, she wants to make a deferred gift of some stock that she bought many years ago and which pays her a dividend of only 1 percent. Madeleine also wants to avoid the time and expense of setting up a charitable remainder trust. The charitable organization informs her that it has a charitable gift annuity available that will pay her 6 percent of the value of the securities—$6,000 per year for the rest of her life. Also, based primarily on her age, she will receive a charitable deduction of $55,000 for her $100,000 gift. Since the amount she can deduct for charitable contributions is restricted, any amount that is not available for deduction in the current tax year may be carried forward to future years. After checking with her tax and estate planning advisers, she goes ahead with the contribution. Here is what Madeleine has accomplished:
>
> - Increases her income from the stock that was donated from $1,000 to $6,000 per year
> - Avoids paying capital gains tax on the stock
> - Receives a $55,000 charitable income tax deduction
> - Removes $100,000 in assets from her taxable estate

And, of course, Madeleine has also made a wonderful gift to the charity.

Charitable Lead Trusts

Charitable lead trusts are, in many respects, the opposite of charitable remainder trusts and the other deferred giving programs I just described. Deferred gifts involve the charity paying you income for the rest of your life in exchange for your giving them the property after your death. A charitable lead trust, on the other hand, involves your giving up the income you receive from the securities you donate for a period of time. Then, your heirs can usually receive the investments in the charitable lead trust without your estate having to pay any taxes on them. So charitable lead trusts are a great estate tax saving technique for people who can afford to part with the income they receive from their investments but who want their heirs to eventually get the investments back. Charitable lead trusts can be established during your lifetime or at death.

Good Advice

While I've provided the skinny on these wonderful charitable giving programs, you may be able to surmise that they are pretty complicated. So where should you turn for guidance? The charities themselves will be happy to help you. After all, you're contemplating a very nice gift so they're eager to make it easy on you. You may need some legal and tax advice as well. If you don't think your attorney is up to the task of dealing with these strategies, your charity can direct you to attorneys who are. Finally, if you're thinking about making a large gift, but you would like to have the money go to more than one charity, some large charities are now geared up to manage a donation for multiple charitable beneficiaries, so long as it receives the lion's share of the money.

You can obtain more details on charitable giving strategies and up-to-date information on the regulations that govern them by clicking on:

http://jonathanpond.com/charitablegivingstrategies.htm

■ Control Your Financial Destiny by Taking Advantage of the Unprecedented Financial Opportunities of the 21st Century

> Oh money, money, money! I often stop to wonder how thou canst go out so fast when thou comest in so slowly.
>
> *Ogden Nash*

Looking into the Crystal Ball—What's Going to Happen in the New Century

The 21st century will provide unprecedented economic and investment opportunities. It will be up to you to take advantage of these opportunities. The days of the employer providing for your long-term financial well-being through steady employment and generous retirement plans are over. In that respect, we are retreating a century to the early 1900s, a time when financial survival and financial success were primarily the responsibility of the individual, not the employer or the government.

YOUR NEW CENTURY ACTION PLAN: THE TOP 21 FINANCIAL IDEAS FOR THE 21ST CENTURY

A lot is going to be happening over the first part of the New Century that could affect your financial future. Here are my top 21 financial opportunities and challenges for the 21st century.

1. Investors should pay close attention to **tax-efficient investing.** By including tax-friendly investments in taxable accounts and tax-unfriendly investments in retirement accounts, investors will enjoy greater after-tax returns and higher investment accumulations.

2. The 21st century Technological Revolution will replace the Industrial Revolution of the 19th and 20th centuries as the place where investment fortunes are won and lost. Successful investors will include in their portfolios a healthy portion of **technology stocks or technology funds** and stocks of companies that will benefit from the Technological Revolution. A whole new generation of blue chip stocks will emerge in the early 21st century, dominated by technology stocks, some of which probably weren't even in existence a decade earlier.

3. In spite of some declarations of its demise, **investment allocation** is not dead. While large company U.S. growth stocks were dominant in the late 20th century, their dominance will not continue indefinitely. Wise investors will allocate their investments among all major investment categories.

4. The stock market will not continue to advance at the levels it advanced in the 1990s. Nevertheless, **stocks will continue to reward long-term investors** with average returns well in excess of the rate of inflation. Don't be unrealistic when estimating future stock market returns.

5. The **investment markets will become more volatile** in the New Century due to historically high stock and real estate markets. Investors will have

to learn to cope with this volatility and protect their portfolios through diversification both within and among investment categories.

6. Low inflation in the early 21st century will require investors to alter somewhat their approaches to investing by emphasizing investment categories and industries that stand to benefit from low inflation. Both bonds and stocks should benefit from subdued inflation. While investor attention was focused on the high-flying stock market at the end of the 20th century, bonds were paying interest that was well above the rate of inflation. Since companies will have difficulty raising prices in a low-inflation environment, stock winners will be companies that can increase profitability by reducing costs through technology, acquisitions, or other means.

7. **Foreign economies will rebound** from their late-20th century malaise and become engines for worldwide economic progress. They will provide attractive investment opportunities in both U.S. multinational companies and foreign companies.

8. Investors will benefit from considering alternatives to traditional actively managed mutual funds, including **index funds and individual stocks.**

9. **Competition within and between the stock brokerage and mutual fund industries** will provide low-cost investment alternatives and greater access to timely information. Individual investors who exploit these products and services judiciously will benefit.

10. The **family home** will become a better investment for many individuals because of the increased capital gains exclusion available to home sellers. Homeowners who will benefit most include those who occupy homes and renovate for resale and those who plan to sell their home and buy a less expensive one.

11. For families having to meet the challenges of paying for college, **Qualified State Tuition Programs** (QSTPs), also known as "Section 529" programs, will become a popular and effective tax-advantaged college savings program.

12. The insurance industry will provide more opportunities to **buy insurance directly** from companies rather than through an agent. Specialists in providing low-cost insurance will proliferate.

13. Changes in the tax rules that Congress is likely to enact early in this century will provide **additional tax incentives** in areas that received breaks in the late 1990s, including retirement savers, college savers, homeowners, and retirees. A flat tax system and privatization of Social Security are not likely to be enacted.

14. New attitudes toward retirement will alter the retirement landscape. **Gradual retirement,** which involves a reduction in work schedule rather than outright retirement, will become increasingly prevalent. Many semi-retired individuals will continue working part-time indefinitely either out of financial necessity or by choice. Employers will be eager to accommodate this new generation of dedicated, experienced, and lower-cost workers.

15. Retirees in the New Century should expect that **Social Security will provide a smaller portion of total retirement income needs** than has been enjoyed by earlier generations. This will be due to a combination of additional means-based limitations on benefits as well as advancing the age for Social Security eligibility.

16. Most employers will further **curtail, if not eliminate, employer-funded retirement plans** and substitute voluntary employee-funded plans. Many government and educational institutions and nonprofit organizations will reduce their retirement plan funding as well. The retirement funding burden will unmistakably and permanently be shifted to the employee.

17. The **Roth IRA** should become a focal point of retirement planning. In addition to its estate-planning advantages, the ability to withdraw Roth IRA money tax-free during retirement can provide retirees with considerably higher after-tax income.

18. Debt won't be the important wealth building strategy that is was last century. Limited tax deductibility of loan interest and lower tax rates have made **debt much less attractive.** Being debt free will become as

fashionable in the 21st century as being debt laden was fashionable in the 1970s and 1980s.

19. **Longer life expectancies** will challenge both senior citizens and their children. The 21st century retiree will have to plan on living 35 or more years in retirement. Many will spend more years retired than they did working. This poses enormous financial challenges to retirees and lifestyle (if not financial) challenges to their children. It will be common during the New Century for middle-aged individuals to have both parents and grandparents who are in some measure dependent on them.

20. More **generous estate transfer rules,** combined with simple estate tax reduction techniques such as annual gifts, will allow families to transfer, tax free, considerable wealth to younger generation family members. The sooner families start to plan their estates, the better.

21. The **computer and the Internet** will become a dominant means of obtaining personal financial guidance in the 21st century. They will also ease the chore of record keeping and provide immediate access to personal portfolio information. The Internet is a double-edged sword. Depending on the way it's used, it can be either a blessing or a curse.

A FEW WORDS TO THE WISE

The above opportunities don't just jump onto your lap and the challenges aren't solved on their own. You have to take control of them. But if you do, you'll be able to control your financial destiny in ways that are exciting and filled with promise.

BE HAPPY WITH WHAT YOU'VE GOT

There is far too much preoccupation with money these days—and not enough with personal financial planning. Instead of obsessing over more money, people should be thinking of ways to do better with what they

"LIFE IS UPSIDE DOWN"

One of my earliest financial lessons came from a family friend—a very amiable fellow who could identify with children as well as he could with adults. I grew up in a suburb of Washington, D.C., and he used to enjoy teaching youngsters about life as much as he enjoyed debating with adults about political affairs. One Friday evening he came to the door to take my sister, along with his young daughter, to a party. I answered the door, but my sister wasn't quite ready. While he was standing at the door, he said (I can remember it as if it happened last night, although I must have been seven or eight at the time): "Jonathan, life is upside down. I'm busy with my career, but I have no money and have to spend Friday night driving my kids to parties. When I'm older I'm going to have more money, and I'll even have a chauffeur to drive me around. But you know what? I won't need the money or the chauffeur then. I could sure use them now, though. Life is upside down. When you're young and could use some money, you're poor. When you're older and don't need as much money, that's when you've got it." You won't be surprised that I have remembered that wonderful message when I tell you who the messenger was. He was Hubert Humphrey, then a young member of Congress, later called "the Happy Warrior." He did what he said he was going to do: earn more money and have a chauffeur. And he also spent a lifetime in public service dispensing his wisdom to young and old alike. His remarks to me more than 40 years ago are just as accurate today as they were then. Our financial lives are, in many ways, upside down. There's not a lot we can do about it, but it doesn't prevent us from being able to achieve our financial goals. It just makes them a bit tougher.

have. We all want financial security, of course. Earlier in the book, I discussed some basic and what should be obvious ways to become financially secure. Let me work backwards. In order to become financially secure, you have to accumulate an investment portfolio. You can't do this unless you save regularly. In order to save regularly, you have to spend less than you earn. Now let me get down to an even more basic requirement than that. In order to spend less than you earn, you have to learn to *be happy with what you've got.*

No matter how obvious this sounds, many of us have difficulty practicing it. But, I repeat, the best way to spend less than you earn is to be happy with what you've got. A lot of people don't like to hear this. They want a fancier car or an imported kitchen or an exotic vacation or a larger house. After all, the advertisers tell us that we have to have these things to be happy. By golly, our neighbors have some of these things, and they sure seem happy. What a crock! The neighbors probably feel the same way about you as you feel about them. If you can be happy with what you've got, you'll find it a lot easier to save the money to make the investments that give you financial security. It's as simple as that. Don't get me wrong. I'm not saying that you should be resigned to your current financial situation. You should strive to advance in your career, earn more money, and invest better. You should have high financial aspirations, but at the same time you should realize that you've probably already got a lot of material things. Life is a series of choices, and as long as you think you're deprived of things, you're going to want to acquire more things. More things won't make you any happier, but more things could put a dent in your financial future.

GET RICH SLOWLY

Getting rich quickly is a one-in-a-million long shot. But if you work hard, do what's needed to advance in your career, save regularly, invest those savings wisely, and periodically address the other important personal financial matters, getting rich slowly is a pretty sure bet in the New Century. Best of luck.

■ Epilogue

Take the Pledge

If you would indulge me for just a moment, I'd like to ask you to take a pledge that will, I hope, spur you on to a wonderful and successful financial future. Please read these words out loud:

I (state your name)
Do hereby pledge
To retire rich.
And once I'm retired,
I will arrange my spending
So that I may—
Die destitute.

■ INDEX

Page numbers in *italics* refer to charts.